PRESS CONCENTRATION AND MONOPOLY:
NEW PERSPECTIVES ON NEWSPAPER OWNERSHIP AND OPERATION

COMMUNICATION AND INFORMATION SCIENCE

Edited by
BRENDA DERVIN
The Ohio State University

Recent Titles

Susanna Barber • News Cameras in Courtrooms
Jorg Becker, Goran Hedebro & Leena Paldan • Communication and Domination
Lee Becker, Jeffrey Fruit, & Susan Caudill • The Training and Hiring of Journalists
Herbert Dordick, Helen Bradley, & Burt Nanus • The Emerging Network Marketplace Revised
  Edition
Sara Douglas • Labor's New Voice: Unions and the Mass Media
William Dutton & Kenneth Kraemer • Modeling as Negotiating
Fred Fejes • Imperialism, Media, and the Good Neighbor
Glen Fisher • American Communication in a Global Society Revised Edition
Howard Frederick • Cuban-American Radio Wars
Gladys Ganley & Oswald Ganley • Global Political Fallout: The VCRs First Decade 1976–1985
Gerald Goldhaber & George Barnett • The Handbook of Organizational Communication
W. J. Howell, Jr. • World Broadcasting in the Age of the Satellite
Heather Hudson • When Telephones Reach the Village
Meheroo Jussawalla, Donald L. Lamberton & Neil D. Karunaratne • The Cost of Thinking:
  Information Economics in the Asian Pacific
James Larson • Television's Window on the World
John Lawrence • The Electronic Scholar
Thomas Lindlof • Natural Audiences
Kenneth Mackenzie • Organizational Design
Armand Mattelart and Hector Schmucler • Communication and Information Technologies
Kaarle Nordenstreng • The Mass Media Declaration of UNESCO
David Paletz • Political Communication Research
Everett Rogers & Francis Balle • The Media Revolution in America and in Western Europe
Jorge Reina Schement & Leah Lievrouw • Competing Visions, Social Realities: Social Aspects
  of the Information Society
Herbert Schiller • Information and the Crisis Economy
Jorge Schnitman • Film Industries in Latin America
Jennifer Daryl Slack • Communication Technologies and Society
Jennifer Daryl Slack & Fred Fejes • The Ideology of the Information Age
Keith Stamm • Newspaper Use and Community Ties
Charles H. Tardy • A Handbook for the Study of Human Communication
Robert Taylor • Value-Added Processes in Information Systems
Sari Thomas • Studies in Mass Media and Technology, Volumes 1–3
Lea Stewart & Stella Ting-Toomey • Communication, Gender, and Sex Roles in Diverse
  Interaction Contexts
Tran Van Dinh • Communication and Diplomacy
Tran Van Dinh • Independence, Liberation, Revolution
Barry Truax • Acoustic Communication
Georgette Wang and Wimal Dissanayake • Continuity and Change in Communication Systems
Frank Webster & Kevin Robins • Information Technology: A Luddite Analysis
Carol Weinhaus & Anthony G. Oettinger • Behind the Telephone Debates

PRESS CONCENTRATION AND MONOPOLY: NEW PERSPECTIVES ON NEWSPAPER OWNERSHIP AND OPERATION

Edited by

**Robert G. Picard, James P. Winter,
Maxwell E. McCombs, and Stephen Lacy**

ABLEX PUBLISHING CORPORATION
NORWOOD, NEW JERSEY

LIBRARY OF CONGRESS
Library of Congress Cataloging-in-Publication Data

Press concentration and monopoly: new perspectives on newspaper ownership and operation / edited by Robert G. Picard . . . [et al.].
        p.   cm.
    Bibliography: p.
    Includes index.
    ISBN 0-89391-464-9
    1. American newspapers—Ownership.   2. Canadian newspapers—
Ownership.   3. Press monopolies—United States—History.   4. Press monopolies—
Canada—History.   5. Journalism—Economic aspects—United
States.   6. Journalism—Economic aspects—Canada.
I. Picard, Robert G.
PN4888.O85P74   1988
071'.3—dc19   87-33328

Ablex Publishing Corporation
355 Chestnut Street
Norwood, New Jersey 07648

Contents

Preface   vii

PART I: ECONOMIC AND COMPETITION FACTORS
CHAPTER 1: Microeconomic Foundations   3
           Barry Litman
CHAPTER 2: Concentration and the Industrial Organization
           Model   35
           John C. Busterna
CHAPTER 3: Pricing Behavior of Newspapers   55
           Robert G. Picard
CHAPTER 4: Limits of Competition   71
           Diana Stover Tillinghast

PART II: INFLUENCES ON MANAGEMENT AND THE PUBLIC
CHAPTER 5: Editors and Their Roles   91
           *Patrick Parsons, John Finnegan, Jr.,
           and William Benham*
CHAPTER 6: Interlocking Directorships and Economic Power   105
           James P. Winter
CHAPTER 7: Monopoly and Socialization   117
           Carlos Ruotolo

PART III: INFLUENCES ON CONTENT
CHAPTER 8: Concentration, Monopoly, and Content   129
           Maxwell E. McCombs
CHAPTER 9: Monopoly and Content in Winnepeg   139
           Doris Candussi and James P. Winter
CHAPTER 10: Content of Joint Operation Newspapers   147
            Stephen Lacy
CHAPTER 11: Editorial Diversity and Concentration   161
            F. Dennis Hale

PART IV: ISSUES FOR POLICY CONSIDERATION
CHAPTER 12: Antitrust Law and Newspapers   179
            David C. Coulson

CHAPTER 13:   Policy Implications   197

BIBLIOGRAPHY   208
AUTHOR INDEX   223
SUBJECT INDEX   227

Preface

If one steps aside from the arguments about group ownership of media, joint operating agreements, and monopoly newspaper markets, it is clear that both regulatory and laissez-faire perspectives are grounded in proud philosophical traditions, that are mutually exclusive.

Under Thomas Jefferson's view of the role of the press in society, monopolies and the growth of groups in the mass-media business need to be regulated if they limit the diversity of ideas. The potential decline in pluralism suggested by such developments in media merits governmental regulation (such as forced divestiture of corporate holdings) to restore a competitive balance and maintain social equilibrium.

Under James Madison's view, regulatory limits of economic activities in media are unwise, because such actions undermine the financial ability of news organizations to pursue controversial stories. The press' primary social responsibility is to avoid governmental controls, particularly when regulation might result in an emasculated press that is impeded from pursuing information that society does not want to know.

Both Madison's and Jefferson's perspectives are well reasoned, integral to more than two centuries of thinking about the press' role in society, and motivated by humanitarian concerns. Madison was fearful that societies were rationalizing and would try to protect themselves from annoying publications, while Jefferson thought persons were rational and would make sound decisions only if they were exposed to a diversity of ideas. Each perspective serves as the underpinning for much of the current opinion about economic developments in media, yet each side reaches opposite conclusions regarding the phenomena and leaves little room for compromise between them.

Greek scholars termed the condition where reasoned arguments reached mutually exclusive conclusions a state of *antinome*. States of *antinome* are particularly difficult because each perspective presents opposite options for public policy and claims either choice is irreversible once initiated. In the case of media expansion, for example, can society risk the regulation of ownership if it has a chilling effect on investigative reporting or takes away the financial resources to pursue controversial stories? Alternately, can a free society permit the potential homogenization, standardization of its best sources of news, information, and opinion?

Given the importance of these issues, the most surprising aspect of media economics debate is the dearth of evidence about the actual impact of chains and monopolies on journalists and the communities they serve. Most of the research about such issues, to date, has been done on an ad hoc basis or has reflected philosophical argumentation without extensive data to substantiate the authors' claims. None of the available literature really provides pragmatic, reliable, independent information about the results of concentration and monopoly.

Although some empirical evidence about the consequences of chain ownership, joint operating agreements, and newspaper monopolies exists, it is rarely comprehensive or considers the actual impact in light of concrete issues, such as news diversity, employee relations, advertising rates, or concern for public service.

In 1983, members of the Mass Communications and Society Division of the Association for Education in Journalism and Mass Communication (AEJMC) began a coordinated study of the impact of concentration and monopoly on news organizations, journalists, and communities. The effort was organized to provide a new and wide-ranging spectrum of evidence about the effects of various market conditions. The motivation was to provide empirical evidence for mass media professionals and scholars to consider in continuing arguments over the wisdom of current developments.

The Mass Communications and Society Division of AEJMC has about 550 members worldwide who are interested in the news media's social responsibilities and freedoms. Since its inception more than two decades ago, the division has committed itself to encouraging independent, scholarly examination of media and society topics. In pursuit of that goal, the division has financed *Mass Comm Review*, a leading academic journal, for the past 16 years.

In this case, the division decided to examine a single topic of social importance, where scholarly contribution seemed greatly needed. Our objective was to demonstrate that scholars can assist in examination of real-world media issues and provide important evidence for public policy debates. More immediately, we hope readers find this book useful and will continue to investigate the research questions that are raised here.

These pages reflect 3 years of collaborative effort by more than 30 researchers in the U.S. and Canada. Although division members volunteered to take part in these studies, the backgrounds, motivations, and training of the authors are quite diverse and reflect conflicting perspectives about the role of news media in society. That diversity was one of the great strengths of the research processes in this project.

Elements of the research printed here were first presented and critiqued at AEJMC national conventions in 1984, 1985, and 1986. Experts with different views about concentration and monopoly were invited to bring quantitative, historical, philosophical, and critical perspectives to discussions of the research in all stages of preparation.

The Mass Communications and Society Division is particularly indebted to Robert Picard of Emerson College, who originally organized the project and is one of the editors of this volume, and to Jim Winter of the University of Windsor, who worked as co-project director and also helped edit this book. The division also thanks the many other contributors to this book and hopes to hear from its readers in future meetings and conventions.

Robert Logan
University of Missouri
Mass Communications and Society Division Head, 1985–1986

PART I

Economic and Competition Factors

CHAPTER 1

Microeconomic Foundations

Barry Litman

Department of Telecommunications
Michigan State University

The foundation of any applied economic analysis of the newspaper industry, or for that matter any media industry, lies with the basic principles of microeconomic theory, also popularly known as the "theory of the firm." The industrial organization model explained in Chapter 2 takes these abstract theoretic concepts and adds body and institutional substance to them in an effort to formulate rules of thumb by which the concepts can be measured, categorized, and later assessed. The industrial organizational model also sorts out, reconfigures, and reassembles the disparate economic concepts into a more unified whole, which is appropriate for the media industry under examination.

The starting point for any economic primer is the four standard theoretical models of market organization commonly mentioned in the economics literature. These include perfect competition, monopoly, monopolistic competition, and oligopoly. Each of these abstract models represents a different and distinct combination of assumptions concerning the nature of demand, cost efficiencies, conditions of entry, and, perhaps most importantly, the distribution of power among the firms and their relationship to the marketplace through which the products are transacted.

These four market structures can best be viewed as a continuum with perfect competition and monopoly at the extremes and monopolistic competition and oligopoly at interior positions (see Figure 1). Positions along the continuum reflect assumptions concerning the degree of market power possessed by an individual firm relative to the power embedded within the market. The degree of

(A) Continuum of Market Power

| Perfect
competition | Monopolistic
competition | Oligopoly | Monopoly |

(B) Daily Newspaper Industry Continuum

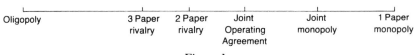

| Oligopoly | 3 Paper
rivalry | 2 Paper
rivalry | Joint
Operating
Agreement | Joint
monopoly | 1 Paper
monopoly |

Figure 1.

market power and control is smallest with perfect competition, and highest with the pure monopoly case.[1]

Perfect Competition

The perfectly competitive firm is one of a large number of identical firms that has such an insignificant share of the market that its presence or absence is scarcely noticed. In this context, the firm is virtually powerless and totally subservient to the forces of the market. The market determines the appropriate price through the intersection of industry supply and demand. The firm then takes the price as a given and responds with the appropriate profit maximizing output level.

Each firm acts as a "price taker," since it faces a horizontal demand curve which indicates that it can supply as much product as it wants at the prevailing market price without affecting that price. The horizontal demand curve is said to be perfectly elastic, indicating that all firms produce identical products that are

---

[1] For more in-depth coverage of this section on market structures, see Milton H. Spencer, *Contemporary Microeconomies,* Fourth Edition (New York: Worth, 1980), chapters 8–10. Also, Edwin Mansfield, *Principles of Microeconomies,* Fourth Edition (Toronto: W. W. Norton, 1983), chapters 24–25.

perfect substitutes for one another. Any firm which raises its price, by even the smallest amount, faces the loss of its entire product supply, since it will be abandoned by the all-knowing consumer in favor of the identical product from another firm at a lower relative price.

As market supply and demand conditions change, the firm experiences shifts in its financial position. However, the theory of perfect competition permits no long-term fortunes to accrue to the individual firm or the industry, since entry is assumed to be very easy. Hence, short-term excess profits are dissipated as new firms enter the industry, increase the supply of product and drive down the price until normal profits (zero excess profits) are restored. Actual entry becomes the disciplinary force which establishes the familiar condition of long-run equilibrium—a stable state of affairs that corresponds to economists' conception of utopia and that often is used as the benchmark to contrast "imperfect" market structures. These equilibrium standards include:

(1) *Optimal allocation of society's resources.* Since price is equated to marginal cost at the long-run equilibrium point, the proper amount of product is being produced in this industry. Price represents the valuation to consumers of the marginal unit of output, while marginal cost represents the opportunity cost to society of allocating scarce economic resources to the marginal unit of this product as opposed to some other product. At equilibrium, marginal benefits equal marginal costs.

(2) *Optimal plant size.* At the point of long-run equilibrium, the long-run average cost of production is at its minimum. Hence, society is not only producing the socially optimum quantity of product, but is producing it in the socially optimal, minimum-cost plant.

(3) *X efficiency and technological progressivity.* Due to the extreme degree of competition between firms, each firm must stand ready to take advantage of every available opportunity to minimize costs and stay on the frontier of technological progress. Firms slow to innovate will soon discover they have higher costs and face severe financial repercussions. Ultimately, they cannot survive in this industry. Furthermore, since the consumer is blessed with perfect information, it will be unnecessary to advertise or spend excessive amounts of money on other product differentiation devices.

(4) *Normal profits.* Normal profits prevail at the long-run equilibrium position of stability. Normal profits mean that prices just cover the average costs of production whereby average costs include payments to the factors of production, plus a fair rate of return to entrepreneurs for their time and invested capital. Normal profits, when combined with the aforementioned cost efficiencies, imply that consumers need pay only the *minimum* price necessary to bring forward production. This "reasonable" price will not distort the distribution of income in society, but, rather, will be neutral.

(5) *Automatically functioning market.* The market mechanism works automat-

ically and effortlessly, triggered by the selfish desires of producers to maximize their profits and the sovereignty enjoyed by consumers in the valua-
tions they place on different products. As consumer wants, needs, and tastes
change and as technology makes the production/distribution process more
efficient, the market automatically adjusts to a new long-run equilibrium
and transfers scarce resources to their most valued uses.

Besides the fact that the assumptions underlying this perfectly competitive
model are unrealistic, other shortcomings also should be mentioned. First, the
market mechanism tends to ignore certain goods which are not easily priced in a
market economy ("public goods") and fails to account for harmful externalities
such as pollution, which are not internalized as private marginal costs by firms.

Second, there may not be enough excess profits in this industry to permit the
research and development which brings forth the technological progress that
benefits the consumers. Such industries may be reliant on their input suppliers
or government-sponsored research projects to achieve the desired level of
innovation.

Finally, life under perfect competition may be very dull, since no variety
exists among the standardized products and there is no incentive created within
the system for product differentiation of any kind.

Monopoly

The monopoly firm encompasses the entire market for a specific product; the
industry demand curve is its demand curve, and all the power of the marketplace
is embedded within its corporate headquarters. Since it is generally assumed that
no close substitute for the product exists and hence the demand curve is relatively
inelastic,[2] the consumer must either deal with the monopolist on its terms or
abstain from consumption of the product. Whereas the perfectly competitive
firm was pictured as a slave to the market price, the monopolist is the price maker
and supplies product according to its own profit-maximizing dictates.

Figuratively speaking, the monopolist "stands at the gateway of commerce
and can extract a toll from all who pass" (*Munn v. Illinois*, 1877). In this process
of collecting tolls, the monopolist (compared to the perfectly competitive firm) is
said to restrict output, charge higher prices, and earn excess profits.

---

[2] In more formal terms, price elasticity refers to the percentage change in quantity demanded in
response to a percentage change in price ($\%\Delta Q_D \div \%\Delta P$). If the absolute value of this fraction is less
that 1, this is referred to as an inelastic portion of the demand curve; if the absolute value equals 1, it
is unitary elastic; and if the absolute value is greater than 1, it is elastic. The more inelastic a demand
curve, the fewer close substitutes exist for the product; conversely, the more elastic it is, the greater
the number and closer the substitutes will be.

In the perfect competition model, freedom of entry dissipates any excess profits in the long-run. In monopoly, these excess short-run profits are perpetuated in the long run through various barriers to entry. The barriers to entry may take the form of pervasive economies of scale, control over strategic resources and patents, absolute cost barriers,[3] and various predatory practices designed to discourage entry. In sum, short-run positions of power can be transformed into long-term control if the barriers to entry are sufficiently high.

Furthermore, if this possessor of market power also tends to be a corporate giant, it can further parlay its power into "immunity from the discipline of exogenous control mechanisms (Galbraith, Adams, & Mueller, 1975). According to Adams,

> Through separation of ownership from management it has emancipated itself from the control of stockholders. By reinvestment of profits (internal financing), it has eliminated the influence of the financier and the capital market. By brainwashing its clientele, it has insulated itself from consumer sovereignty. By possession of market power, it has come to dominate both suppliers and customers. By judicious identification with, and manipulation of the state, it has achieved autonomy from government control. Whatever it cannot do for itself to assure survival and growth, a compliant government does on its behalf—assuring the maintenance of full employment; eliminating the risk of, and subsidizing the investment in, research and development; and assuring the supply of scientific and technical skills required by the modern technostructure. (Galbraith et al., 1975, pp. 87–88)

However, barriers to entry and strategic control are never impregnable. Schumpeter (1950) talked about a different form of long-term competition which threatened the possessors of monopoly power. He called this competitive force "the gale of creative destruction."

> The competition from the new commodity, the new technology, the new source of supply, the new type of organization—competition which commands a decisive cost or quality advantage and which strikes not at the margins of the profits and outputs of the existing firms but at their very foundations and their very lives. . . . The competition we now have in mind acts not only when in being but also when it is merely an ever present threat. It disciplines before it attacks. The businessman feels himself to be in a competitive situation even if he is alone in his field. (Schumpeter, 1950, pp. 84–85)

Examining the monopoly market structure according to the same performance standards used in the competitive model, we see that, at the long-run equilibrium point, the monopolist:

---

[3] For greater detail on the concept of barriers to entry, see Richard Caves, *American Industry: Structure, Conduct, Performance,* Sixth Edition (Englewood Cliffs, NJ: Prentice-Hall, 1987), Chapter 2.

(1) misallocates society's resources by producing at the output level where price exceeds marginal cost. Hence, consumers value additional product more than the cost to society of producing that marginal product, yet it is not produced because it would diminish monopoly profits;

(2) produces in a suboptimal - sized plant at a unit cost exceeding the minimum point of the long-run average cost curve, thereby wasting scarce economic resources;

(3) has no incentive to be cost efficient or technologically progressive. Whereas the monopolist clearly has the financial resources to invest in research and development and could be vigilant in minimizing its costs, it lacks the compelling pressure to spur it on in these endeavors. Monopoly power acts as a narcotic rather than a stimulant toward such goals unless the Schumpeterian "gale" must be confronted head on;

(4) earns excess profits which have been perpetuated by high barriers to entry. Such excess profits reflect excessive prices greater than the minimum necessary to bring forth production. Depending on the importance of monopoly products relative to consumer disposable income, this may adversely affect the distribution of income in society in favor of monopoly stockholders;

(5) controls the market and determines how it functions and its timing. Power vests in the monopolist, not in the market. As noted above, the monopolist may obtain such control that there are no external checks and balances on its behavior. In the extreme, it could perform society's planning function according to its own self interests.

Monopolistic Competition

The hybrid model of monopolistic competition has elements of both monopoly and competition and, for that reason, often is pictured as more closely corresponding to real world industries than the market structures at either end of the continuum.

Like its perfectly competitive counterpart, the monopolistically competitive firm is one of many such firms in the industry and individually accounts for a very small share of the total industry product. Unlike its counterparts, this firm has some control over its economic fortunes, some ability to act independently by virtue of a downward-sloping demand curve. The significance of the downward-sloping demand curve (as contrasted to the horizontal one) is that small increases in price do not drive away all consumers to the outstretched arms of rivals; the firm retains a loyal following of customers.

The shape of the demand curve is related to the nature of the product. Firms in monopolistic competition produce similar but not identical products (as in perfect competition). To coexist in the industry, the firm must utilize some means of product differentiation to create a market niche—to distinguish itself in the minds of consumers as providing some unique product or attribute. Common techniques available include quality differentials, service and location differentials, and, most prominently, advertising.

As long as consumers believe some difference exists between two firms providing essentially the same product, this is sufficient for the firm to establish a loyal following of customers. The impression should not be created that the monopolistically competitive firm can act with impunity and exploit its position in the same way as the monopolist. Rather, the demand curve for the firm will be relatively elastic due to the large number of close substitute products within the industry, and this will constrain its behavior to only marginal changes in price and product attributes.

Within its range of discretionary action, the firm believes it is independent and seeks to establish profit-maximizing levels of prices, output, quality, and advertising expenditures. Since the monopolistically competitive firm is representative of a large number of similarly situated rivals, each facing similar industry conditions, all firms tend to react the same way to the same economic stimuli, and thus the individual firm's assumption of independence from its rivals is never achieved. The industry slowly gropes toward a short-run equilibrium with the rival firms having similar prices, product-quality levels, and advertising expenditures.

Should excess profits exist at the short-run equilibrium position, these profits will be dissipated in the long run due to the relative ease of new firms in entering the industry—the same assumption used in the perfectly competitive model. The entrance of new firms is visualized as reducing the share of the market of existing firms (a leftward movement in their demand curves) until long-run equilibrium is achieved, all excess profits are squeezed from the industry, and no further incentive remains for additional firms to enter or existing firms to expand their level of operations.

Since the monopolistic competition model is a hybrid, we therefore discover that its performance standards are not as desirable as those of perfect competition, yet not as obnoxious as monopoly; rather, they are somewhere in the middle. In this regard, prices are above what would occur in a perfectly competitive industry, and a resulting misallocation of society's resources occurs since prices exceed marginal costs. The resulting "shortage" of product is produced in a suboptimal-sized plant (as with monopoly). In addition, there may be excessive expenditures on persuasive advertising or other non-utility-generating means of product differentiation.

While it is true that, in the long run, the favorable standard of normal profits occurs, this is achieved by falling prices (due to entry and loss of market share) in conjunction with the rising level of costs associated with product differentiation. As a result of excessive costs, many economists believe that excess capacity exists and that the industry is populated by too many firms inefficiently producing and distributing their product.

Oligopoly

As with monopolistic competition, the oligopoly market structure is a hybrid form but generally pictured as lying closer to monopoly that to the competitive ideal. The salient feature of oligopoly is that there are relatively few firms which collectively comprise the entire industry. Within this grouping of relatively large firms, the distribution of market shares may be balanced or else dominated by one or two industry giants. The product may be relatively homogeneous or highly differentiated.

Each firm and the industry as a whole face a relatively inelastic demand curve, indicating that there are no close substitute products. Like its monopolistically competitive counterparts, the individual oligopoly firm seeks to distinguish itself by carving out a market niche and obtaining a loyal following of customers. This can be achieved through advertising, branding, or the other forms of product differentiation mentioned above; furthermore, the small number of sellers within the industry, and hence the lack of viable alternatives, creates a naturally inelastic demand curve for the firm.

It is usually assumed that some barriers to entry exist within the industry which help perpetuate excess profits in the long run. The barriers, whether in the form of economies of scale, absolute cost advantages, or whatever, may not be as formidable as those discovered under monopoly, and hence the oligopoly structure may not be as impregnable.

Because of the small number of sellers, a mutual interdependence exists among the oligopoly rivals. Each oligopolist is so powerful that its pricing, product differentiation, or research activities cannot go unnoticed; such actions directly affect the market as a whole and threaten market shares of rival firms. Since rivals desire to maintain their relative standing, they must react (usually in kind) to any precipitous action of their brethren. Because all rival firms face similar industry conditions and economic stimuli, each oligopolist contemplating changes must assess how its rivals will respond to any action it may initiate.

This process is what is referred to as mutual interdependence, and, depending on the assumptions a firm makes concerning the rivals' reactions, different models of oligopoly behavior may result. The range of reaction assumptions and the corresponding behavior of rival firms can cause oligopoly performance to move closer to the results discovered under monopolistic competition or, alternatively, nearer the monopoly end of the spectrum. Let us discuss a few of the possible scenarios.

First, assume that rivals choose to totally disregard each other's reactions to changes in prices and advertising. As one firm lowers price and initiates an advertising campaign, the other firms protect their market shares through corresponding actions, and thus trigger a second and succeeding series of price cuts and advertising expenditures until full-fledged warfare breaks out. This warfare continues until all excess profits are squeezed from the industry through compression of the profit margin from above and below. The result of such a nonlearning scenario will be approximately the same market shares as initially existed with performance standards similar to those associated with monopolistic competition.

Under a second scenario, assume the rival firms closely scrutinize each other's reactions but totally mistrust each other's motives, believing their rivals are out to inflict the worst possible economic damage upon them. This is operationalized in the following way.

Given an initial market price, the representative oligopolist assumes that, if it initiates a price increase, its rivals will not follow suit; hence, it will lose a significant share of business because its prices for a similar product are now relatively more expensive. At the same time, if it lowers prices, its rivals will exactly match such price cuts to avoid having market shares siphoned off by this relatively lower-price competitor. Perfectly matched price cuts gain some minor additional sales (less than proportionate) for all firms at the expense of interindustry producers. A kinked demand curve therefore exists for each representative oligopoly firm. It is damned if it raises prices and damned if it lowers prices, and hence does neither. A kind of price rigidity becomes built into this industry until wide variations in demand or costs shift the industry toward a new rigid equilibrium price.

This scenario of the kinked demand curve formerly was considered the general theory of oligopoly but was found not to correspond to a variety of industry situations; it now seems relegated to new industries and industries where different companies enter de nouveau or via acquisition and are unfamiliar with existing industry competitors or practices.

A more likely scenario occurs through a modification of the first two scenarios. Under this hybrid approach, firms are assumed to be capable of learning from past actions and willing to trust each other to the extent of recognizing the right of mutual existence.

The firms may begin under the independence assumption (as in the first scenario) and initiate a price or advertising war, but, after a few of these self-defeating skirmishes, which only benefit consumers, it becomes clear to all competitors that it is a wiser policy to cooperate with each other than to fight it out in the trenches. If everyone "agrees" to maintain high product prices, low input prices, or limited advertising expenditures, then the industry as a whole can maximize profits, and each firm's share of these higher profits will be "greater" than if it acts independently and engages in a cycle of rivalrous behavior. Of course, direct consultation with competitors over prices, output, territorial exclusivity, or the like is illegal under Section I of the Sherman Antitrust Act. Nevertheless, as the oligopoly matures and the firms come to know and trust each other, a "meeting of minds" can occur. Through experience, each competitor acquires the ability to predict with near certainty the behavior of its rivals under differing economic conditions.

Certain common cooperative practices become routine and regular in the industry, and no open consultation need occur for the oligopolists to communicate to each other the beneficial policy for the entire industry. Price leadership and standardized markup procedures are two common devices for such "signaling" in an industry. If this type of tacit cooperation operates smoothly, the result may be a "shared" monopoly indistinguishable from the performance of a single monopolist making all the decisions itself. Under this scenario, the spirit of mutual cooperation replaces mistrust, and the "live and let live" philosophy accrues financial dividends to all who participate.

If it is indeed true that the formation of a spirit of cooperation among oligopoly firms yields maximum profits, then every oligopoly should move in this direction as the industry matures and the firms come to know and trust each other. Yet some industries will find the process of reaching a common understanding much easier than others. Certain barriers will impede their efforts and make the resulting cartel unstable.[4]

Barriers to Oligopoly Consensus

For a cartel to become operational, common agreement must be reached between the rival firms over what the standardized price should be. To the extent that physical quality differentials exist between products, no single price would be optimal for all firms; firms producing higher-quality merchandise will seek higher prices than those selling lower-quality product, and agreement may be impossible. It is, of course, possible and more realistic to move away from the concept of a single standardized price and have multiple grades of product quality, each with different prices and with fixed price differentials between the grades. Such a complex pricing scheme is more difficult to obtain than price agreement with a single homogeneous product.

In a similar manner, if the firms have different cost structures because of different levels of efficiency, this may complicate the achievement of price consensus even if the product is homogenous. The high cost producers will seek higher prices to cover their excessive costs, while the efficient firms will discover their profit-maximizing point at a lower price. The greater the difference in average cost between the efficient and inefficient firms, the harder it will be to achieve a price consensus. It may be true that the high-cost producers should not be protected (via a high price) and eventually will be eliminated from the industry, but, if the high-cost producers also produce the higher-quality products mentioned above, then the same misunderstandings may occur.

This whole process may be further complicated by wide variations in market

---

4 For more detail on this subject, see F. M. Scherer, *Industrial Market Structure and Economic Performance*, Second Edition (Chicago: Rand McNally, 1980), Chapter 7.

shares among the oligopoly firms. High-volume producers may be better able to take advantage of scale economies than smaller firms, and this could explain their superior cost structure. Yet, to the extent that they have demand curves (market shares) which lie further out than their smaller rivals, their profit-maximizing equilibrium may require a higher price, everything else being the same. In summary, the greater the market share difference between the major firms, the greater the difficulty of achieving an oligopoly consensus on price.

Another impediment to forming a spirit of cooperation lies with the number of significant firms in the industry. Since true consensus requires participation of all major firms in the industry, the larger this critical mass, the harder it will be to obtain an agreement. While a half dozen firms should pose no major hurdle, once the critical mass grows above a dozen, the probability of achieving a consensus diminishes more than proportionately.

Assume for the moment that all of the above problems are somehow solved and the initial consensus is reached; the question then is how stable the agreement will be. A practical rule of thumb is that the greater the difficulty in achieving consensus, the harder it will be to sustain it, because those factors which impede its development create the incentive for price "cheating" to emerge.

For example, if a disagreement exists over the standardized price, those firms desiring lower prices may grant secret price concessions on a marginal (additional) part of their sales. This incentive to shade prices (and perhaps simultaneously to achieve scale economies) will be more prevalent during times of economic distress or when excess capacity exists in the industry. Furthermore, the greater the *number* of rivals, the greater the probability that one or more firms will actually engage in this kind of price cheating, thereby threatening the fragile consensus.

As these instances demonstrate, industry members must somehow be monitored and cheaters disciplined so that the consensus is restored. Cheating will be most easily detected the greater the number of market transactions. Firms that enter the market *frequently* and with relatively small-size orders expose themselves to discovery more readily than those that enter occasionally and with large and/or custom-made orders.

The process of detection can be facilitated if an industry trade association becomes involved in circulating information about past transactions of industry members. Although trade associations have been severely limited in recent antitrust decisions from linking specific transactions to individual companies, their summary reports can pinpoint general industry trends of price deviations from commonly agreed-upon standards.

The ability to detect price cheaters is only as effective as the measures of enforcement and, especially, punishment handed out. It generally becomes the responsibility of the dominant firms to discipline recalcitrant rivals by some temporary or permanent form of predatory conduct. On the other hand, if enforcement/punishment is ineffective, this will further destabilize the tacit cartel.

Finally, the question often arises of how perfect the consensus can be. Will the industry truly operate as a shared monopoly? The answer is that, even if all of the above factors are favorable toward achievement and perpetuation of a consensus, the agreement can never run as smoothly as, or operate with the precision of, a single monopolist making a single set of operating decisions.

It is generally agreed that the urge to compete against rivals cannot totally be suppressed and will surface in one or more areas of interaction between the firms, often in the advertising or product development dimension. These non-price areas are likely to spawn competition because it is very difficult to respond immediately to an effective advertising campaign or product improvement, whereas price cheating can elicit an instantaneous reaction in kind. Of course, if this form of rivalry gets out of control and jeopardizes firm and industry profits, emergency adjustments or limits may have to be enacted. The real danger is that an advertising war could trigger a price war, thereby totally destroying an industry consensus.

In conclusion, while no oligopolistic consensus is likely to be complete in all possible dimensions, the smart firms will *cooperate* in the most important revenue generating areas and *compete* in minor areas which do not jeopardize industry profits significantly. In essence, this cooperation/competition strategy places a floor below which profits cannot fall. The closer the oligopoly firms move toward the position of shared monopoly, the closer their performance standards will be to those of the monopoly firm mentioned above.

Newspaper Industry Classifications

In seeking to place the daily newspaper industry within one of the four theoretical market structures outlined above, one is immediately struck by both the outward simplicity of the task and its hidden complexity. One seldom witnesses an industry (other than utilities or quasi-utilities like cable television) in which the relevant market is local and the number of competitive firms is generally two or fewer.

For the 1400 or so cities with a single daily newspaper, the task is easy; they are clearly monopoly newspaper towns. In a number of other cities, a single company owns two separately titled dailies (usually the result of a prior merger) or else a morning and afternoon edition with the same name. These situations will be referred to as *joint monopolies*, since one company still makes decisions governing this multiple-product line. This is analogous to General Motors, which still operates Buick, Chevrolet, and its other divisions even though they have separate names and retain some individual autonomy.

There are two variations of the duopoly situation as well. In some 26 cities, two or more companies independently own and operate dailies in rivalrous competition with one another, while, in 21 other cities, the papers are separately owned but function under some sort of joint operating agreement that removes their business practices from direct competition. These agreements really constitute a formal, legally sanctioned price-fixing cartel.

Most of the previous research[5] has looked upon this entire group of duopoly situations (and a few triopolies) and labeled these markets as "competitive," since they are in such stark contrast to the monopoly markets. The impression has been falsely created that the monopoly and nonmonopoly situations span the entire continuum presented in Figure 1 (a) when in reality they cluster near the monopoly extreme in Figure 1 (b).

Two distinct patterns of behavior are likely to emerge within the oligopoly sector of the daily newspaper industry. First, if the rivals seek to eliminate one another and reap the rewards of a monopoly position, then full-scale economic warfare may ensue in every dimension of the product and every area of interfirm contact, including pricing, product differentiation, newspaper "quality," and distribution patterns. This may even be carried to the extreme of predatory practices, with the unfavorable consequences that follow for the bottom line. The winner in such a life-and-death struggle would be that newspaper organization with the greatest staying power and deepest corporate pockets. The losing paper would be either forced into bankruptcy or else acquired by the successful firm.

In the second oligopoly pattern, firms generally will recognize each other's right to exist in the market and forge a spirit of cooperation in many important areas of contact. As explained above, it is likely that dailies will cooperate in those areas which are most visible, and in which it is easy to detect someone "cheating" on an agreed-upon standard and easy to retaliate in kind. Such areas as subscription and newsstand prices, and advertising prices per thousand readers (or milline rates), would be easiest to control; on the other hand, the competitive instinct should surface in such content differentiation areas as distinctness of format, depth of coverage, and reporting style. These latter areas defy standardization, and, furthermore, successful retaliation cannot be assured as in the pricing dimension. Of course, rivals operating under joint operating agreements automatically control the revenue side of this equation.

Neither pattern of rivalrous behavior is permanent. Oligopoly firms may change strategies, depending on short-term alterations in market shares, local business conditions, new technological developments, and pressures from corpo-

---

[5] For typical examples see Raymond Nixon and Robert L. Jones, "The Content of Non-Competitive vs. Competitive Newspapers," *Journalism Quarterly* 33 (Summer 1956), pp. 299–314; David H. Weaver and L. E. Mullins, "Content and Format Characteristics of Competing Daily Newspapers," *Journalism Quarterly* 52 (Summer 1975), pp. 257–264; Lee B. Becker, Randy Beam and John Russial, "Correlates of Daily Newspaper Performance in New England," *Journalism Quarterly* 55 (Spring 1978), pp. 100–108.

rate parents. The only factor common to both patterns (in different degrees) is the presence of significant (and costly) product competition.

Product competition is intricately related to the special nature of the newspaper product. As explained in Chapter 2, newspapers simultaneously produce both information and advertising. This creates interdependent advertising and circulation demand functions, and the incentive for the newspaper to expand circulation so that advertising rates (per line or column inch) and/or advertising space can be increased. Oftentimes, the added readers are uneconomic when viewed from the circulation market alone, because the marginal costs of attracting and serving them are greater than the marginal revenues. However, losses on the circulation side are counterbalanced by excess profits from the advertising sector, thus creating a form of internal subsidization. Circulation expansion will continue until excess profits from advertising just match circulation losses, and the firm as a whole has no further incentive to grow. Product competition is the vehicle for achieving this added circulation.

This drive for circulation is bolstered by two other factors unique to the newspaper industry—the first being that widespread scale economies exist for the daily newspaper within its proximate delivery zone, the second that a "circulation spiral" (Gustafsson, 1978) enhances the prestige and financial success of the leading newspaper.

The "circulation spiral" occurs because the newspaper with the highest circulation tends to attract a disproportionate percentage of advertising linage. For example, a newspaper with 60% of the market circulation will attract, say, 70% of the advertising linage in the market. Because people buy newspapers for advertising as well as news, this makes the newspaper even more appealing to readers and causes successive rounds of increased circulation and advertising space. The "circulation spiral" robs the training newspaper of advertising and also combines with economies of scale to help eliminate the trailing paper as a viable competitor. As the profit margin for the leading newspaper increases, it can concentrate more money on maintaining or increasing its quality and promoting its product through advertising in other media. The trailing newspaper finds itself squeezed more and more by declining profit margins and an increasing need to improve and promote its product; the result of this process is usually its demise.

Therefore, newspaper markets with two or three dailies do not fit easily into any of the four models. The characteristics of market power and cooperation in some areas of interaction suggest oligopoly, but the life-and-death product competition suggests the product differentiation and advertising competition generally associated with the theory of monopolistic competition.

Given the advent of new satellite transmission technologies and emergence of national newspapers like *USA Today*, and to a great extent the *New York Times*, *Wall Street Journal*, and others, the focus on the local market is gradually being replaced or at least supplemented by a concern for chain ownership. While others have adequately documented the growing importance of chains and their modus operandi of merging rather than starting from scratch, national concentration of ownership has not yet reached the point of alarm where public policy should advocate restricted growth.

As a group, the chains constitute a monopolistically competitive industry; however, most of the action and abuse (mentioned in Chapter 2) still seems to occur at the local level, where the chains methodically avoid contact with one another. Hence, depending on whether one focuses on the local or national level, the market structure for daily newspapers takes a different form.

If one looks at another sector of the news industry, the wire services, one discovers only a handful of major companies. *Associated Press* and *United Press International* dominate while the *New York Times, Washington Post–Los Angeles Times* and a few in-house chain services split up the rest of the market for national and international news. This strong oligopoly is perpetuated by high barriers to entry associated with the widespread scale economies inherent in establishing and staffing national and international news bureaus, while simultaneously gaining access to a sufficient base of daily newspapers throughout the country. Acting in a manner similar to the television networks, these major news services dominate the national news pages of the vast majority of small dailies who act as non-exclusive affiliates or members of a news cooperative.

If one lets the mind wander further, there even exists a special situation of monopolistic competition in the local daily newspaper industry—the Chinese daily press in New York, Los Angeles, and San Francisco. Some 19 dailies are circulated in these major communities of Chinese descent. These dailies contain local news and advertising, plus international news from mainland China, Taiwan, and Hong Kong. Many of these papers are actually overseas editions of dailies originating in the three home countries.

Recent evidence shows that tremendous competition exists between these Chinese dailies for the loyalty of their readers (Lau, 1985). Product is differentiated by political slant and country of origin. Of course, this may also be seen as an atypical situation, since the newspapers receive subsidies from the home countries and, therefore, are little more than propaganda organs for the struggle of international Chinese politics. While it may be true that this special situation is more an illustration of *noneconomic* or *irrational competition* than monopolistic competition, the economic theoretic models refined by the industrial organization rules of thumb are nevertheless clearly applicable to a wide variety of print industries.

Economies of Scale

The most important economic factor which affects the structure of the various print industries and impinges directly on public policy discussions is the presence (or absence) of *economies of scale*. By economies of scale, we will reference those technical and financial factors affecting the *long-run average costs* (LRAC) of production (and distribution).

The long-run average cost curve is quite different from its short-run counterpart, often called the *average total cost curve* (ATC). The short run is that period of time during which the plant and equipment are fixed, and entry cannot occur. A firm will combine its fixed and variable inputs in the optimal proportions to produce its profit-maximizing product. The total costs of the fixed and variable inputs (fixed costs and variable costs, respectively), divided by the total product, yields average total costs. The ATC curve has the familiar "U" shape, illustrating that unit costs initially decline until overcome by the law of diminishing marginal returns.

In contrast to this short-run situation, there are no fixed inputs in the long run; all inputs are variable, including plant size. The firm must now choose, not only its profit-maximizing output level, but also the most efficient-sized plant to produce it in. It has at its disposal a whole series of hypothetical ATC curves, each associated with a different-sized plant (different possible short-run situations). If one assumes an infinity of different plant sizes (most easily conceptualized in varying square footages), there will be one unique minimum-cost plant associated with each possible output level in the long run. The long-run average cost curve is pictured in Figure 2 as an envelope of this infinite number of ATC curves, uniquely connected at the points of tangency. Movements along the LRAC in the region of declining unit costs are called economies of scale, while regions of increasing unit costs are labelled *diseconomies of scale;* the point of minimum LRAC is known as the *minimum efficient scale* (M.E.S.).

There are two basic kinds of factors which cause the LRAC curve to decline; they can be grouped in the categories of technical factors and pecuniary (financial) factors. *Technical factors* refer to the underlying technical process of production. Production can be visualized as a functional relationship with output, depending on the combination of labor, land, capital, raw materials, and en-

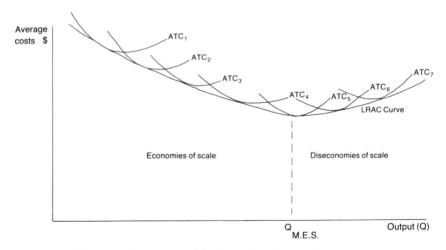

Figure 2.   Derivation of the Long-Run Average Cost Curve

trepreneurship—the so-called factors of production. In mathematical form, this would be represented as $Q = f(X_1, X_2 ..... X_n)$ where Q = output and X_i = the factors of production.

Assume an initial level (and price) for each factor and a process for combining them to yield a value for Q. If one now hypothesizes a 100% increase in all factors of production (*ceteris paribus*) and permits them to be combined in whatever manner is most efficient, then three possible outcomes can occur: (a) a more than proportionate increase in output, (b) an exactly proportionate increase in output, or (c) a less than proportionate increase in output.

The first case is referred to as *increasing returns to scale* and suggests a greater productivity for the factor inputs, and, given constant factor prices, this translates naturally into lower average costs per unit of output. In the second case, which is known as *constant returns to scale*, one finds the same productivity of the factor inputs at the initial and doubled level and, hence, a constant average cost per unit of output. The third case is known as *decreasing returns to scale* and demonstrates lower productivity of the factor inputs when they are doubled and, hence, higher average costs per unit of output.

These, then, are the technical factors underlying the presence or absence of scale economies. Rising productivity associated with larger scale can be explained by the fact that larger units can be more efficiently organized through greater specialization of tasks and division of labor, more effective use of by-products, and more effective matching of optimal equipment to the size of the task. For example, larger-capacity equipment that does not cost proportionately more can be substituted once a plant gets beyond a minimum threshold capacity.

There also are a couple of other technical efficiencies that are related to economies of scale and may entail significant cost savings for the firm. The first is known as *economies of scope* and refers to the situation when one firm simultaneously produces more than one product and discovers cost complimentariness between the products, yielding lower unit costs for each product than if they were separately produced. The second is called *economies of density* and refers to the distribution side rather than the production process. The denser the area of distribution, the lower the unit costs of distribution and, hence, the lower the average cost for the entire firm's operation. Distribution cost savings become more important the higher the proportion of these costs are to the total costs of operation. They are especially important in the daily newspaper industry.

When the LRAC curve turns upward into the diseconomy range, this is often attributed to managerial inefficiencies associated with running very large enterprises—the requirement of additional layers of bureaucracy and loss of effective control by top management.

Pecuniary efficiencies are financial economies attributed to being large within one's own industry or a major employer within a local area. Big firms are able to contract for large quantities of raw materials or other intermediate product from various suppliers. Such large orders reduce transaction and transportation costs to the supplier, who can pass some of these savings along to the large purchasers.

Furthermore, to the extent that these supplies are specialized or tailor-made and oligopsony buying power resides in the hands of a few major purchasers, they may be able to secure other discounts and concessions as well. An excellent example of quantity discounts is found in the purchase of advertising time and space in all the media; large purchasers can achieve significant savings on a cost per unit of time and space basis.

If firms are very large employers within a local community or region, they may have enough political and economic clout to secure important favors or concessions from local or state governments. This will be especially true if they threaten to locate new plants or move their entire operation to another area. These concessions come in several familiar forms, ranging from tax abatements or exemptions, to government subsidized access roads, utility connections, site renovation, or even government-sponsored employee training programs. One need only recall the mad scramble to obtain General Motor's new Saturn facility to understand how significant such cost savings can be.

Shapes of LRAC Curves

The shape of the LRAC curve is crucial in determining the number of significant competitors in an industry and the prospects for future deconcentration of an existing industry. Looking at panel (A) in Figure 3, one sees that efficient-sized firms will produce at or near Q_1, the minimum efficient scale, with an average cost of AC_1. Firms producing at approximately one-third of M.E.S., at Q_2, will have significantly higher average costs AC_2 and compressed profit margins; otherwise, they will have to compete in a specialty component of the market and hence not be full-fledged competitors.

If the M.E.S. output level is large relative to the total industry output, then this industry will have a high likelihood of being an oligopoly and a propensity for remaining one in the long run. Potential entrants will find it difficult to obtain the heavy capital financing and then capturing the requisite share of the market to compete on an equal footing with existing firms. This is the way widespread scale economies fortify market concentration and function as a barrier to entry. It helps to explain the duopoly situation existing in competitive newspaper cities. In the extreme situation of a continuously declining LRAC curve (without limit), the result is a natural monopoly or utility. The central policy question regarding the death of competitive dailies and the inevitability of monopoly centers precisely on the shape of the long-run-average cost curve.

If the LRAC appears as in Figure 3 (B), this would indicate an industry wherein minimum efficient scale is easily achieved from both the financial standpoint as well as through capturing a sufficient market share to justify production at M.E.S. Such industries would correspond to the monopolistic competition model, and entry would be relatively easy in the long run.

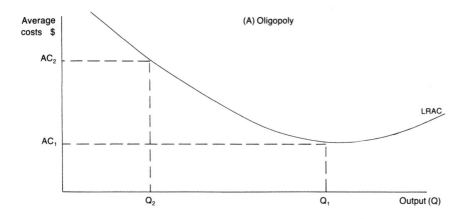

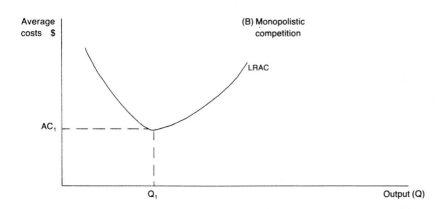

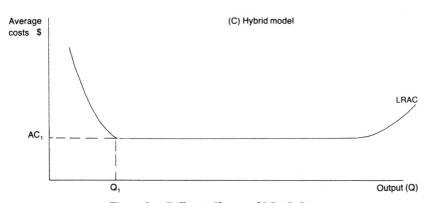

Figure 3.   Different Shapes of LRAC Curves

Finally, if the LRAC curve appears as in 3 Figure (C), this would indicate that minimum efficient scale is reached at a fairly low level and remains constant over a broad range of output. In such an industry, no advantage accrues to being a large or small producer—each is equally efficient, and entry is relatively easy in the long run. One would then expect a market structure composed of large and small-sized firms, each able to coexist with one another. Depending on other factors, this cost structure could be consistent with either monopolistic competition or a weak oligopoly situation.

Movements of LRAC Curves

Also it is interesting to discuss movements of the long-run-average cost curve. Three factors can cause shifts in the LRAC curve. The first is a change in technology, which is usually envisioned as favorably reducing costs through greater efficiency of factor inputs, that is, requiring fewer factor inputs to produce the same level of output. This improvement in technology shifts the LRAC curve downward and may also affect the proportions of factor inputs used, depending on whether it is labor saving, capital saving, or neutral (no change in factor proportions).

The second factor shifting the LRAC curve is known as *external diseconomies*. These are diseconomies beyond the scope of an individual firm, diseconomies which occur as the industry itself gets very large and places demand pressure on specialized resources or skilled labor, thereby causing factor prices to rise. These diseconomies raise costs rather than affecting productivity, and shift the LRAC curve upward.

The third factor reflects the fact that new firms may have higher costs of production than existing firms, for some period of time. Reasons for such cost disadvantages are: (a) it may take time to learn how to produce efficiently and to learn trade secrets which come only through experience; (b) extra initial costs may be involved in differentiating product from existing firms, luring away their customers, establishing an identity and feeling of trust with the consumer; and (c) extra interest surcharges or underwriting fees may be levied by banks and security dealers to reflect the extra risk associated with new ventures as opposed to older ones.

Measurement of LRAC Curves

While the economic concept of the long-run-average cost curve is very rich in theoretical terms, its actual measurement is not so easily accomplished in real world media industries; often it can be estimated only through indirect means.

To bridge this theory gap, it is first necessary to determine whether output should be measured at the plant level, firm level, or both. Microeconomic theory discusses scale economies and the derivation of the LRAC curve in terms of an optimal-sized plant—as if a single plant can always be expanded to whatever size is necessary to exhaust all technical cost savings. In real industries, most firms have a portfolio of optimal- (and even some suboptimal) - sized plants, and the discussion changes to determining where multiplant and firm-size economies lie.

The optimal-sized plant and optimal-sized firm are related, but certainly are not identical concepts. In the context of the newspapers industry, this might translate into measurements of the minimum efficient scale (in circulation) necessary to sustain a competitive daily newspaper and, likewise, the minimum number of such dailies needed to attain all economies associated with group ownership. All too frequently in the past, these issues of competition and chain ownership have been artificially separated, rather than seen as different components of an unified whole.

Several techniques are available for measuring the shape of the LRAC curve.[6] Most have been applied to the single plant or multiplant level rather than to the firm as a whole, since economists have generally been interested in separating out technical efficiencies involving real resource savings from pecuniary efficiencies involving redistribution of income. Such a distinction is not made in this discussion.

The first technique is called *engineering estimates* and involves obtaining information through interviews and written questionnaires from professional engineers and managers about various costs associated with different-sized plants. Since these people are intimately involved in designing, constructing, and operating new plants within the industry under examination, they will be most knowledgeable and familiar with where all cost efficiencies lie at both the single and multiplant levels. In conjunction with data given in specialized trade journals, one can then estimate the cost curves for the newest facilities currently in use or on the drawing boards.

In the context of the newspaper industry, this would require discussions with the principals involved in new and refurbished operations of various sizes. It would presume a wide variation of different plant sizes in the planning or construction stages throughout the industry. If such information could be systematically obtained, it would also permit measurement of the gradient (slope) of the LRAC curve—the cost disadvantage faced by firms producing at one-third or one-half the minimum efficient scale.

A second approach is called the *historical cost* technique and involves obtaining cross-sectional data on plant size and average costs from a wide variety of different firms within an industry. A statistical regression equation would then fit together these different data points into an average cost curve. The higher the statistical fit, the closer this estimated cost curve would reflect historical cost associations in the industry.

---

[6] For more detail on this area, see F. M. Scherer, *op. cit.*, chapter 4. Also, William G. Shepherd, *The Economics of Industrial Organization* (Englewood Cliffs, NJ: Prentice-Hall, 1979), Chapter 12.

Besides the obvious difficulty in obtaining such confidential data, it is unlikely that the sample will contain plants of the same vintage or capacity utilization. It is possible to make adjustments and allowances and thereby standardize such a data set, but the results will not be as reliable, because of different variations in accounting practices (such as depreciation allowances) and internal pricing discrepancies across firms. Also, this technique suffers from the fact that the observed cost of producing various output levels is different from the minimum cost of production. Nevertheless, with all its shortcomings, if the data are available across enough firms and can be adjusted as described above, the technique can provide a reasonably good estimate of "current practice" cost relationships.

The first two methods primarily involve measurements at the plant or multiplant level and require detailed cost information. The third method looks more broadly at the profitability and survivability of different-sized firms in the marketplace and *indirectly* links such performance to the attainment of plant and firm efficiencies of all kinds. This *survival* technique asks the basic question of whether firms can withstand all the pressures of the marketplace and continue operations and thrive in the long run. Such "survivors" must then be efficient firms. The fact that such durability may reflect market power rather than efficiencies is one of the technique's shortcomings, and why it is referred to as an indirect measure of scale economies. At best, it can only give broad ranges of optimal size; it cannot pinpoint the gradient of the LRAC curve.

To conduct a survivor estimate of minimum efficient scale, one needs data, from a large cross section sample of firms in an industry for a considerable period of time, intended to capture the long run. This time period should be a minimum of 5 years and perferably 10 years. The data should be broken down (at the firm level) according to sales, market shares, assets, profitability before taxes, number and size distribution of plants, and similar type measures. A series of associations can then be made to relate firm size (assets, sales) with survivability (profitability, market shares, etc.). These can be best illustrated in a series of questions.

(1) Have firms of certain sizes exited from the industry or been acquired in merger deals during the time span under examination? What was the minimum size of new entrants to the industry which have remained as viable concerns for a period of time after entry?

(2) Are firms of certain sizes more profitable than other firms? Is there an optimal range of firm sizes for which profitability (as measured on sales or invested capital) is stable, yet above or below which profitability declines?

(3) Are firms of certain sizes (as measured by assets) increasing their market shares at the expense of smaller or, perhaps, larger firms?

It also would be desirable to derive measures of mean/median firm size along with the standard deviation. This could be measured alternatively by the amount of assets, value added, number of plants or employees. Here it would be assumed that firms which constitute "outlying cases" will not be as efficient as those closer to the averages.

Once again, it should be stressed that these associations only provide a raw, indirect measurement of the scale economy concept and cannot be separated into technical or pecuniary efficiencies; nevertheless, the usefulness of the survivability technique becomes immediately apparent in the newspaper industry. It would facilitate measurements concerning such issues as: (a) what size competitive newspapers are disappearing and surviving? (b) what is the minimum efficient scale to launch a new daily in a formerly unserved city? and (c) what is the optimal size for a chain organization?

Economies of Scale in Daily Newspapers

Perhaps the single most important issue and trend in the newspaper industry during the last half century has been the decline in the number of competitive daily newspaper cities in the United States. About two dozen cities remain where two or more independently owned and operated papers fight for circulation and advertising dollars. This trend has been explained by Rosse and others (Rosse & Dertouzos, 1979, pp. 429–471; Compaine, 1982a, ch. 2) as a direct and inevitable result of pervasive economies of scale present in the newspaper business. Since the previous discussion has highlighted the derivation of economies of scale in general, it is now possible to apply these principles to this unique case.

Because of his preeminence in this area, we will follow the lead of Rosse and Dertouzos (1979, pp. 437–448, 459–466) in the initial exposition of this matter. Rosse notes that the daily newspaper industry has several unique properties which complicate the nature of the long-run-average cost curve. These complications include: a product with fairly heavy "first copy" fixed costs, the fact that quantity is multidimensional in terms of number of pages per issue and number of copies printed, and, finally, the fact that all stages of production are integrated together, with distribution playing an unusually heavy role in the total value added of the final price of the product. Like other media, newspapers simultaneously sell circulation to the consuming sector and space to the advertising sector, with interrelated demand curves across both sectors; one difference is that advertising in newspapers is generally considered to be more informational than in other media and is desired by readers, at least in moderation. In this sense, advertising is a "good" rather than an unwanted "bad."

To handle these complications in deriving the LRAC curve in the confines of two dimensional space, Rosse follows conventional practice by assuming one or another factor is fixed and then examines the relationships between the remaining ones. He first holds quantity of pages per issue and relative newshole fixed and explains that the long-run marginal cost (LRMC) of producing additional copies ("reproduction costs") is roughly constant across a broad expanse of output. This occurs because the variable costs in the press room are mainly labor, equipment, newsprint, and paper handling, and each of these factors is finely divisible; hence, such costs rise exactly proportional to increases in circulation.

Using the same assumptions, he then examines the "first copy" costs, which include all costs associated with creating the news and advertising content of the newspaper. These would be the costs of reporting, editing, page makeup, etc. Given the fixed issue size and percentage newshole, these first copy costs do not vary with the length of the press run (the number of copies printed) and, hence, steadily decline as circulation increases, giving the LRAC curve the shape of a rectangular hyperbola.

If one now holds the number of copies fixed (the other quantity dimension) and varies the size of the issue, one encounters the same relationships as before. The reproduction costs of increasing the number of pages and changing the relative newshole involve the same finely divisible variable costs mentioned above, with the same result—a constant LRMC across a wide number of different-sized issues. Distribution costs are handled in the same way as first copy costs. Once one has established a distribution system, it can handle any increase in the bulk of the newspaper. Since it has this fixed-cost aspect to it, the long-run average costs associated with distribution decline asymptotically, as did first copy costs.

When the sharply falling average costs associated with the first copy and transportation dimensions are then added to the constant LRMC of reproduction, the overall effect is a sharply declining long-run average cost curve across all these stages of production of daily newspapers. It is this telltale shape which fortells the demise of the competitive newspapers and inevitability of the monopoly market structure. Rosse does note that such economies of scale are not continuous ad infinitum; eventually, marginal transportation costs increase as delivery problems occur the farther one moves from the newspaper's densest area of natural advantage. These rising transportation costs stop newspaper expansion at some natural boundary point.

One cannot disagree with the theoretical arguments of Rosse, but his translation of these concepts into the graphical analysis only holds true for the short-run situation. *The basic flaw in his graphical depictions is that they purport to represent the long-run situation, yet he fixes certain inputs such as first copy costs and transportation costs by implicitly assuming that one such level of expenditures on these crucial inputs is satisfactory for all possible expansions of output.* This is equivalent to assuming, in the underlying production equation, that output can double or triple with no corresponding increase in the factor inputs.

Let's examine this dilemma in greater detail for the transportation sector, which, surprisingly, is only mentioned for the second quantity dimension, the number of pages per copy, although it clearly is critical in the number of copies as well.

In the long run, if we wish to double or triple the number of copies (number of pages fixed), this clearly means hiring more loaders, putting more truck capacity on the roads, hiring more drivers, helpers, establishing more distribution centers, and recruiting more paper-delivery people. Similarly, if number of copies is fixed and number of pages is permitted to increase, this adds extra bulk per newspaper and requires the same additional truck capacity and personnel mentioned in the first case. If both quantity factors change simultaneously (as is usually hypothesized for the long run), then delivery costs must undeniably increase.

If we recall that average costs equal total costs divided by output, then the crucial question is whether distribution costs increase more than proportionate, exactly proportionate, or less than proportionate with expansions in both quantity dimensions. If the latter situation holds, average costs decline, and one encounters economies of scale in distribution.

This is probably the situation which exists for the proximate delivery zone of daily newspapers, since many of the extra costs will rise at a slower rate than expansion in circulation or newspaper size. For instance, it is relatively cheaper to buy a larger truck than two smaller trucks and to build larger neighborhood distribution facilities than smaller ones. Furthermore, since an increase in circulation within the proximate delivery zone implies greater density, it will be more efficient and faster to deliver and unload 5,000 newspapers at, say, five stops than 2,500 newspapers at 10 stops.

In summary, in the long run it is necessary to hypothesize a whole series of different transportation cost curves, each associated with a different combination of circulation and bulk. No single transportation cost can adequately represent all quantity situations.

The same analysis holds for first copy costs and, to some extent, for the relative newshole dimension. If a newspaper contemplates doubling or tripling its circulation, it undoubtedly will have to make changes in the content of the paper by some upgrading of its quality and/or appearance. This would not be limited only to the case where it is trying to take away readers from its competitors. It also applies to the nonnewspaper reader whom it wants to include in this expanded circulation base. It must offer something new or different, which usually means something more costly, whether this comes in the form of an all-day format, more color photographs, zoned editions, or more fast-breaking, in-depth coverage which accompanies having more reporters on the street.[7]

In short, there is no unique first copy cost associated with every possible circulation level; rather, there exists a series of such costs (as in the transportation

---

[7] Confirmation of this fact is given by Lacy who discovered that newspapers in non-monopoly markets tend to give a higher percentage of their news sections to news copy and a higher percentage of their total newspaper to news and editorial material than do newspapers without competition. Competitive newspapers also have more wire services and reporters per given amount of space than do monopoly newspapers. This implies higher long-run average cost curves should competition prevail over time. For greater detail, see Stephen Lacy, "The Effects of Ownership and Competition on Daily Newspaper Content," (Doctoral Dissertation, University of Texas, 1986).

case). As the circulation increases, it becomes more expensive for the newspaper to make the quality adjustments needed to wrest the marginal potential reader from his or her more valued activity and, if necessary, to get this elusive reader to switch loyalties from a competing daily.

The same analysis applies if the quantity dimension is additional pages per issue. The extra content cannot be assumed to cost nothing. This would only be true if additional space were filled with leftover copy from reporters or wire services. More likely would be the situation where the newspaper doubles issue size by hiring more reporters, editors, photographers, and other personnel as well as subscribing to additional news and feature services. In each of these first copy situations, the critical question once again is whether first-copy costs increase more than proportionate, exactly proportionate, or less than proportionate with the increase in circulation and issue size. It is presumed that, across a wide expanse of output ranges, the latter situation will occur, thereby resulting in a declining long-run-average cost curve.

In the reproduction cost dimensions, Rosse is generally accurate. Certain variable inputs are fairly divisible, and one experiences constant returns to scale, a condition where the LRMC = LRAC. However, his focus on the short run may unnaturally limit his analysis. Firms contemplating doubling or tripling their circulation or number of pages are unlikely to purchase identical machinery in multiples or build a second expansioniary plant of equal dimensions as the first. Rather, they will seek out larger-scale printing presses and associated equipment which are more heavy duty and durable and capable of printing and assembling papers at a faster rate. While such presses are more costly on an absolute basis, they will be more efficient on a per unit basis in handling the extra output.

To be more specific, if one wished to move from a circulation of 50,000 to 250,000 or from 16 pages per issue to 64 or beyond, one would design an optimal-sized facility employing the most cost-efficient equipment rather than just adding on multiples of existing equipment. One would also hope to take advantages of economies of specialization and division of labor. While offset printing has narrowed the cost gap and made smaller newspapers more competitive with larger ones, that gap has not totally disappeared, and, furthermore, there is no single optimal offset printing press but rather different models suitable to different press runs. Certain quantity discounts may also accompany such a planned expansion. These savings would most likely surface in the purchase of raw materials, such as newsprint. What all this means is that, at least at the lower to intermediate levels of circulation and issue size, there is likely to be some advantage associated with being large in the reproduction-cost category. After this threshold is reached, the constant-cost nature may then appear; this would signify an L-shaped LRAC curve.

The long-run average cost curves in each stage of production are now given in Figures 4 (A) and (B) for the two separate quantity dimensions. Each of these

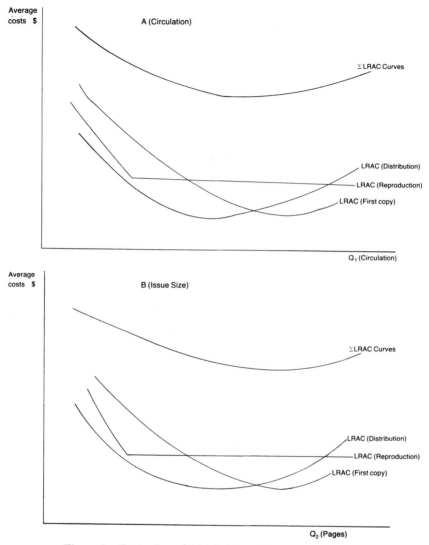

Figure 4.   Derivation of LRAC Curves for Daily Newspapers

curves represents an envelope of the family of short-run average total cost curves described above. Notice that first copy costs are almost continuously declining, while transportation costs decline at first and then rise the farther away one proceeds from the newspaper's area of natural advantage. Reproduction costs show only modest economies of scale. The summation of each of these curves in each diagram clearly illustrates the widespread nature of the scale economy factor explaining increasing concentration of the daily newspaper industry. Finally, it is possible to combine Figures 4 (A) and (B) to yield a LRAC surface in three-dimensional space which simultaneously illustrates the declining cost nature of daily newspapers across both quantity dimensions (see Figure 5). Additional economies may also appear for the multiple newspaper firm. These are discussed in later chapters of this book.

Overcoming Scale Economies

Given the proposition that scale economies in daily newspapers have been so overbearing during the last half century, what then explains the persistence of the remaining duopoly situations and the emergence of new forms of umbrella competition outside the major metro areas? Is their survival traceable to the dogged determination of well-heeled pioneering newspaper families, the deep pockets of chain owners and media conglomerates, or is it merely irrational competition? An alternative set of possible explanations would be that scale economies can be overcome by new technologies and product differentiation.[8] We now examine these in turn.

The newspaper industry has made great technological progress during the last decade or so by combining new developments originating in the printing sector, with breakthroughs coming from the computer, telecommunication, and photography industries. Some of the most prominent of these new technological developments are:

(1) computerization of the message creation stage
(2) cold type photocomposition and paste-up
(3) offset presses
(4) satellite delivery of facsimile pages

These developments have led to significant improvements in speed and efficiency throughout the production process, with dramatic reductions in the composing room workforce and a shift from skilled to semi-skilled personnel (Malone, 1979, pp. 536–538; Compaine, 1980, ch. 6). These improvements have been both labor and capital saving and, therefore, have shifted the long-run average cost curve downward for daily newspapers of all sizes. The first three of these improvements can also be considered as deconcentrating in the sense that they *have reduced the gradient of the LRAC curve—making it more L-shaped*

---

[8] Of course, the population of the city and the proximate delivery zone may be large enough so that two daily newspapers can each exhaust all scale economies. This would be true of only the half dozen largest cities in the United States. Another exception would be where large chain owners sought to perpetuate historic newspapers for reasons of prestige and simply "averaged in" their losses with profits arising from other newspapers in the chain. Economic theory predicts that such cross subsidization cannot occur indefinitely.

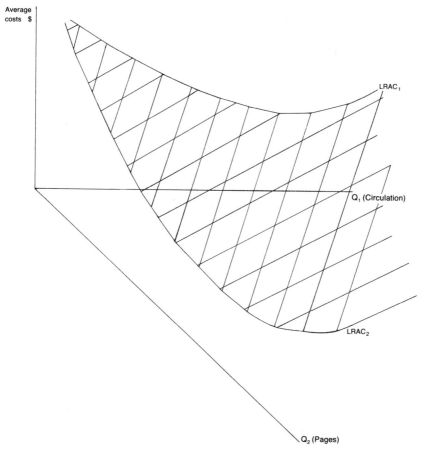

Figure 5.   Derivation of the LRAC Surface

and flatter across a wide expanse of different circulation and issue sizes.[9] This lowers the barrier to entry associated with scale economies and permits small- and medium-sized papers to become more cost competitive with their larger brethren. These favorable circumstances should at least slow down the trend of disappearing competitive metro dailies and engender new competition across the different strata.

The advance in satellite and microwave transmission of facsimile news pages has meant that metro papers can now have viable satellite printing facilities

---

[9] These technological developments have also helped to vertically disintegrate the daily news-paper industry, thereby reducing barriers to entry. Dailies can now share presses and microwave or satellite links with other businesses, which obviously reduce the unit costs for all users of such technology.

which reduce the extra time and costs associated with distribution beyond the proximate delivery area. *This flattens out the LRAC curve at the tail end*, since it was precisely these higher distribution costs which counterbalanced the pervasive economies of scale in the other stages of newspaper production.

This should be most helpful to the biggest metro dailies as they seek to expand their influence into more distant statewide locations. It probably will not adversely affect suburban dailies, as long as they reside within the magic radius of miles where such an investment in decentralized printing and microwave transmissions is unjustified. On the other hand, this technology bridges the distance gap and introduces a new element of rivalry into medium-sized cities which formerly had a protected monopoly status. This new statewide rivalry will not destroy the out-of-town dailies just as zoned editions did not bankrupt the suburban press; nevertheless, there may be some slippage of readership if the statewide papers become substitute rather than complementary products.

This same technology, when aided by satellites, has permitted the distribution of national newspapers like *USA Today* and the *New York Times*. While such newspapers have solved the distance problem (and remain somewhat price competitive), it still remains problematical whether they can deliver appropriate content to replace or complement the local orientation of daily newspapers. They face the same problem that mass circulation magazines experienced with the dawn of the television age and the extreme specialization of content which sprang up in the magazine industry.

Product Differentiation Strategies

According to Rosse and Dertouzos (1979, pp. 448, 461–466), product differentiation is the other way to overcome the domineering forces of scale efficiencies and to perpetuate competitive daily newspapers. Through product differentiation, a newspaper firm can build an inelastic demand which gives it some flexibility to raise prices without losing an appreciable segment of its loyal readers. This degree of pricing power thereby permits the firm to maintain a satisfactory profit margin by counterbalancing the effects of higher average costs (attributable to suboptimal size) with higher prices.

There is an ever-present tension and conflict between the centrifugal forces (associated with scale economies) pushing the firm towards higher circulation and the centripetal forces of product differentiation pushing the firm to accept a somewhat smaller yet segmented audience. Rosse and Dertouzos (1979, pp. 481–486) argue that it is the weakening of the centripetal forces, primarily due to the advent of television and population movement to the suburbs, which has permitted scale economies to win this struggle and has sounded the death knell for competitive dailies in some of the largest markets in the country.

In addition to its function as a counterbalancing force, product differentiation plays several other important roles in oligopoly market situations. In the discussion above in connection with print industry classification, it was mentioned that such spirits of cooperation seldom were complete across all areas of interface; rivalry would likely surface in nonprice areas, such as product differentiation. This situation is indeed likely in the duopoly newspaper markets; the firms compete for readership while simultaneously building their market niche through product differentiation (also known as "audience segmentation" in media industries).

The areas available for differentiation are familiar and include, among others:

(a) time of issue —   morning vs. afternoon or all day
(b) editorial orientation — Democrat vs. Republican; Conservative vs. Liberal
(c) appearance —   tabloid vs. standard format; differences in headlines, photographs, paper, print, etc.
(d) quality —   differences in accuracy, depth of coverage, reporting/writing styles; number of special features; percentage of advertising

While the first three categories can generally be measured objectively, the "quality" differences in newspapers require a subjective assessment and have been the focus of several research studies (cited throughout this book) seeking to compare monopoly and nonmonopoly newspaper performance. One interesting new approach around this subjectivity problem is to substitute the "financial commitment" of newspapers in their news and editorial functions for the elusive concept of "quality."[10]

While all of these broad areas are available for product differentiation, there is a limit to such a strategy. The joint product nature of newspapers and the "circulation spiral" mean that newspapers compete for readership by differentiating themselves, but at the same time they must remain substitutes in order to compete for the general circulation market. This "paradox" of product differentiation means competition is limited to certain areas. As a result, some components and practices are not truly within the discretionary areas for daily newspapers; they are standard for everyone and collectively form the bundle of news and information known as newspapers.

Therefore, while major city dailies compete over the way that they cover local and national sports, politics, weather, and fast-breaking news, they nevertheless must include such information to be considered a newspaper, attract a mass audience, and remain a viable substitute product. The "paradox" is that a newspaper must do a certain amount of product differentiation to create a market

---

[10] Recent research demonstrates that such a financial commitment does occur in non-monopoly as contrasted with monopoly markets. See Barry Litman and Janet Bridges, "An Economic Analysis of Daily Newspaper Performance," *Newspaper Research Journal* 7 (Spring 1986), pp. 9–26 and Stephen Lacy, *op. cit.*

niche and frustrate scale economies, yet this cannot be carried to the extreme or else it loses its identity and ceases to be a full-fledged newspaper. It could, of course, coexist in a specialized part of the information market, as does the *Wall Street Journal*. Evidently, consumers consider the entire bundle of stories as a kind of least common denominator (minimum level of satisfaction) without which they would stop reading; they then prefer one newspaper product over another according to how much satisfaction they receive in a few specialized areas (e.g., sports, fashion, or whatever is of personal interest).

In summary, markets in the newspaper industry group at the monopoly end of the market structure continuum. Single newspapers within a city can exercise a great deal of monopoly power in setting advertising and subscription rates. Markets that have two or three daily newspapers exhibit characteristics of oligopoly in market power and pricing behavior, and characteristics of monopolistic competition in product and promotion competition. Economies of scale and the joint product nature of newspapers are responsible mostly for the predominance of local monopolies in the industry. Only the arrival of new deconcentrating technologies and successful audience segmentation can frustrate these forces in the long run.

Theories and concepts discussed in this chapter will be used in Chapter 2 to develop an industrial organization model of the newspaper industry, with the purpose of better understanding behavior within particular markets.

CHAPTER 2

Concentration and the Industrial Organization Model

John C. Busterna

School of Journalism and Mass Communication
University of Minnesota

Many studies in the area of press concentration describe the level or nature of press concentration, attempt to draw links between concentration levels and various behavior measures (such as advertising prices or local news hole size), or suggest ways in which policy changes (such as antitrust activity) may affect how newspapers behave. These studies use, either implicitly or explicitly, a model taken from a subfield of economics called industrial organization. The model argues that the *structure* of economic markets affects the *conduct* of participants in those markets, which, in turn, affects the *performance* of those markets.

The industrial organization perspective, as represented by this structure–conduct–performance paradigm, provides several important benefits for the media economics scholar. First, the model provides a systematic means of dissecting the various components of a market under study—in this case, we are concerned with the newspaper market. Second, the model gives us a framework for studying how various market forces interact to affect activities in a market. Third, the model can give us some understanding of why market processes may break down. Finally, the model gives us a tool to make market performance more nearly achieve the ideal through means other than direct governmental control of market performance.

This last point is of particular concern to industrial organization economists. Society wants good performance from the producers of goods and services. However, the predominant economic/political philosophy in the United States and, to a lesser degree, in Canada disapproves of direct government intervention to control performance through such means as nationalizing production and profits. The industrial organization model argues that certain forms of market structure and market conduct lead to undesirable market performance. By government intervention, particularly in the area of market conduct, good performance can be achieved in a relatively free market environment. Thus, we see the government breaking up some monopolies (one type of market structure) and preventing some price collusion (one form of market conduct) while still maintaining the essential nature of a free market economy.

This chapter presents the industrial organization model and suggests some adaptations of the model for studying mass media markets. Some problems are raised concerning how the particular issue of press concentration fits into the model. Finally, a general outline of a research program in the area of press concentration based on an industrial organization perspective is presented.

As sociology studies the behavior of social groups and psychology studies the behavior of individuals, industrial organization studies the behavior of economic markets. The familiar industrial organization terms of *structure, conduct,* and *performance* are each usually preceded by the word *market*, since it is market level variables that are studied.

A *market* is here defined as a closely interrelated group of buyers and sellers. Markets have two components which together suggest how the buyers and sellers are to be interrelated: the product market and the geographic market. A common product market consists of sellers providing the same product, or close substitute products, to a common group of buyers. The geographical dimension is an important consideration when a product market is essentially local or regional in nature. Soft drink bottlers in San Francisco and Atlanta are clearly in the same product market, but they do not sell to a common group of buyers since they only compete with bottlers in their respective regions. Of course, not all cases have such easily defined product and geographic boundaries. Both legal definitions and economic analysis have tried to lend assistance in drawing the proper boundaries.

The legal definition of a relevant market is set forth by the Supreme Court in *United States v. E. I. duPont de Nemours & Co.* (1956). The Court stated: "That (relevant) market is composed of products that have reasonable interchangeability for the purposes for which they are produced—price, use and qualities considered" (at 404).

In another Supreme Court case, more specific economic criteria were set forth to define the relevant market. In *Brown Shoe Co. v. United States* (1962) the Court stated: "The outer boundaries of a product market are determined by the reasonable interchangeability of use or the cross-elasticity of demand between the product itself and substitutes for it" (at 325). For cross-elasticity of demand to exist between two products, both of the following conditions must be present: A decrease in price for one product must lead to a decrease in the quantity demanded for the other product, and an increase in price for one product must lead to an increase in the quantity demanded for the other product.

Though the Supreme Court in these two cases was concerned about defining the relevant market for cellophane and shoes, precisely the same test must be made in defining the relevant product and geographic market for newspapers. This definition contains enough slipperiness to provide some controversy when trying to define what constitutes the market within which newspapers compete for the purposes of economic analysis. This issue will be taken up later.

The Industrial Organization Model

The dynamics of the industrial organization model have already been alluded to: Market structure affects market conduct which affects market performance. However, this rough paradigm requires a considerable amount of explanation. There are a number of texts that provide considerable detail regarding the industrial organization field.[1] A far less ambitious description will be provided here beginning with a diagram (Figure 1) of a traditional industrial organization model, followed by brief definitions of the terms in the diagram.

Market Structure

Market structure refers to how a given market is organized. There are a few key dimensions to market structure that are of particular interest for the study of newspaper concentration. The degree of seller *concentration* refers to the number and relative size of sellers in a given market. It is, of course, the key structural variable for studies of newspaper concentration. Concentration is commonly defined in two ways. Concentration may be measured as the percentage of sales controlled by the largest four (or 8 or 16) firms in a market. It may also be measured by way of different formulas that note the dissimilarity of market share among all competitors in a market. No matter which way we may choose to measure concentration, newspapers operate in very highly concentrated seller's markets.

There is a related term—*buyer concentration*—that refers to the number and relative size of buyers in a market. In some markets, manufacturers face a limited number of suppliers of goods needed in the manufacturing process. This situation may have some impact on the manufacturers' activities.

Product differentiation, the third market structure factor, refers to the extent to which buyers perceive real or imagined differences among the products of the various sellers. Perceiving the products of competing sellers to be fairly different may have the effect of reducing the level of competition between sellers, since

---

[1] Two "classics" are Joe S. Bain, *Industrial Organization* (New York: John Wiley & Sons, 1968) and F. M. Scherer, *Industrial Market Structure and Economic Performance*, Second Edition (Chicago: Rand McNally, 1980).

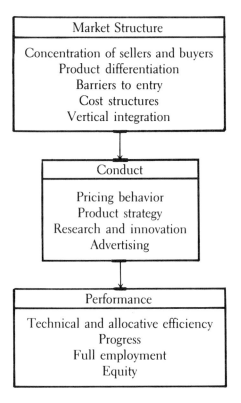

SOURCE: F. M. Scherer, *Industrial Market Structure and Economic Performance*, 2nd ed (Chicago: Rand McNally, 1980).

Figure 1.   Traditional Industrial Organizational Model

many buyers may see the sellers as operating in different markets rather than being competitors.

The fourth market structure characteristic to be looked at here is the *condition of entry* to a market. This is defined as the ease or difficulty that exists for potential new sellers who may wish to enter the market. If the barriers to new entrants is low, this should have the effect of forcing current sellers to behave as if they were in a less-concentrated market. This is because an attempt to earn higher-than-normal profits would simply invite a rash of new competitors who would drive prices and profit margins down.

Cost structure refers to the relationship between fixed production costs and total production costs in a market. When fixed costs are quite high, there is a substantial reward for large producers due to economies of scale. These economies of scale can be of such magnitude that they become a substantial cause for highly concentrated markets. Public utilities are a typical example of markets with such high fixed costs that public policy makers have usually abandoned the market and allow only government-regulated monopolies to exist.

Vertical integration refers to the degree that producers have ownership control of the various markets which comprise the production and distribution stages from raw materials procurement to the final retail sale. The best-known case of vertical integration in the media field is *United States v. Paramount Pictures, Inc.* (1948) where the Supreme Court allowed the motion picture companies to own only two of the three stages of motion picture production: production, distribution, and exhibition. Most companies chose to give up ownership of their theatres.

Market Conduct

Market conduct refers to the behavior that sellers and buyers use in the market. Special concern is given here to the extent to which sellers coordinate, or seem to coordinate, their activities.

Pricing behavior is the most common type of market conduct to be analyzed. It refers to the procedures used by sellers (or buyers) to determine price levels, such as price fixing, price leadership, price discrimination, and discounts. Here we are concerned with whether there might be price collusion in a market, or if a seller discriminates among various buyers by charging them different prices that are not justified by different costs.

Product strategy refers to decisions made about the design and quality of the product. Another element of product strategy consists of practices used to distribute a product in the market. This might include an agreement among sellers to divide buyers geographically and agree not to compete for the same buyers.

Research and innovation are related ideas that refer to the effort made to change the product or differentiate it from competitors' products over time. Market conduct characterized by relatively frequent improvements in the real quality of a product is good. However, a product market where poor quality is offered, little or no improvements are made, or where only nonsubstantive or "style" changes are made would be considered poor market conduct. The industrial organization perspective is concerned with investigating how various market structure elements may affect product policy and innovation, and how performance is altered by different product and innovation strategies.

Advertising really refers to the whole gamut of promotional activities in which firms may engage. Promotion policy includes how sellers compete with each other on "nonsubstantive" grounds via advertising and sales promotion. Economists traditionally see these activities as ranging from useless to harmful, since they are often attempts by sellers to market the product in some way other than by simply providing price and product attribute information that would otherwise not be known to potential purchasers. To repeat, the industrial organization analyst is interested in how these policies are determined, particularly in the extent to which the policies of different sellers or buyers may be interdependent—and, thus, anticompetitive.

Market Performance

There is a long list of various market performance goals. A few of the more common goals are discussed here. Two common market performance measures used by economists are technical and allocative efficiency. *Technical efficiency* refers to producing a given level of output with the least amount of productive input. To borrow an example from the television industry, we might ask if three commercial networks providing fairly similar entertainment content might not be the most efficient use of scarce spectrum space.

Through a fairly complex set of arguments, *allocative efficiency* comes to mean whether a particular market earns normal or excessive economic profit. Excessive profit is seen as allocative inefficiency, since it indicates that resources in the market are underutilized; i.e., there ought to be more competitors in the market, which would increase competition and drive profits down to normal levels.

Progress refers to the extent that the firms in a market increase output per unit of input over time. *Full employment* refers to the ability of a market to maintain stable full employment of resources. *Equity* usually means that producers do not get excessive rewards for their efforts and that there is relative price stability. These last few performance goals do not appear to be particularly relevant to what society might normally expect from newspapers, so some effort is made to argue for some new performance criterion later in this chapter.

The Newspaper Market

Any analysis of the nature or effects of newspaper concentration must begin with a definition of the newspaper market. This is because newspaper concentration can be measured only after the product and geographic limits of the newspaper market have been set. How these limits are defined can radically affect the level of concentration that is found in a given newspaper market. If the product and geographic limits are defined quite broadly, then the measured level of concentration will be relatively low. On the other hand, if very narrow product and geographic markets are defined, then newspaper concentration will be relatively high. We can turn to antitrust cases to see how the courts have defined the newspaper market, and we can also investigate directly the reasonable interchangeability of daily newspapers with other media.

Antitrust case law has generally seen daily newspapers as operating in their own product market separate from other media. This generalization is stronger in excluding broadcast stations from the daily newspaper market (*United States v.*

Citizen Publishing Co., 1968, 1969; *United States v. Times Mirror Co.*, 1967, 1968) than it is from excluding other print media from the daily newspaper market (*Huron Valley Publishing Co. v. Booth Newspapers*, 1972; *Greenville Publishing Co. v. Daily Reflector, Inc.*, 1974). Case law has typically defined the geographic market for daily newspapers to be the Retail Trading Zone (RTZ) (Oppenheim & Shields, 1981, p. 15). The RTZ, which consists of one or more counties, is that area where a daily obtains most of its retail advertising linage and the majority of its circulation.

These definitions of the product and geographic market for daily newspapers seem to be reasonable interpretations of the theoretical economic criteria for defining markets. In order for two products to compete in the same market, they must be reasonable substitutes for each other. Daily newspapers perform two functions that are, in part, duplicated by other media. Dailies provide editorial and advertising material to audiences.

Broadcast stations also provide these same two functions, but it seems that the two media types serve complementary material—rather than competitive material—to their audiences. Certainly, very little of the material provided by daily newspapers is found in broadcast station material. Broadcast stations devote a considerably higher proportion of their content to entertainment, and cover the news in far less depth than dailies. To some degree, broadcast stations also compete with daily newspapers for advertising dollars. In practice, however, most advertisers do not see the different media types as good substitutes for each other. Advertisers and advertising agencies will usually select the media types within which an advertising campaign will run prior to the negotiation process to purchase time and space. This is because it is believed that there are other more important factors in determining advertising effectiveness than the cost efficiencies between various media outlets. Thus, there is only a small cross-elasticity of demand between daily newspapers and broadcast stations for advertising revenue. Television stations get most of their advertising revenue from national advertisers, while daily newspapers get the vast majority of their ad revenue from local retail and classified advertising. The classified, department store, and supermarket advertisers, which are the bread and butter of any daily newspaper's revenue, cannot substitute television or radio for those messages in any significant way.

Shoppers and weekly newspapers may serve as the closest thing to meaningful intermedia competition that a daily faces. Both these media alternatives provide advertising in roughly the same format. Weeklies provide information content similar to dailies, although usually for a more narrowly defined geographic area. However, there are significant ways in which these media do not compete with dailies. For example, larger advertisers must usually stick with the daily newspaper, since it is the most efficient way to reach the area from which these advertisers draw their customers. Audiences will find these other media lacking in news coverage beyond the limited geographical areas they serve—if they contain any news at all. For these audiences, shoppers and weeklies may be viewed more as complementary products rather than competing products. This level of mixed competitiveness between dailies and these other print media is reflected in inconsistent antitrust case law. However, in order to focus the analysis for the remainder of this chapter, it seems sensible to restrict the discussion to the daily newspaper market.

The use of the RTZ to define the geographic limits of a daily newspaper's market seems logical, since the majority of advertising and circulation revenue comes from this area. Certainly, daily newspapers which share the same RTZ compete in the same market. What is the case where one daily's RTZ is a subset of another's? James Rosse (1975) has referred to this situation as the umbrella model of newspaper competition. In this model, larger metropolitan newspapers cast an umbrella over a second layer of more geographically limited dailies which, in turn, cast umbrellas over still more limited weeklies and shoppers. The lower-level media may not compete with each other, but do compete in their own service area with larger print media which hold umbrellas over them. It is in this sense that a federal district court ruled that *The Los Angeles Times* and *The San Bernadino Sun* competed in the same geographic area even though the *Times* was distributed over a far larger area. The relevant geographic market in this merger antitrust case was San Bernadino County, the RTZ of the *Sun* (*United States v. Times Mirror Co.*, 1967).

From this discussion it seems that the product market is the daily newspaper and the geographic market is the Retail Trading Zone. This definition is consistent with antitrust case law and with the application of economic analysis to the daily newspaper business. This market definition will undoubtedly not find universal agreement among scholars and practitioners who discuss the issue of newspaper concentration, but an important point needs to be made. Any analysis of newspaper concentration must include a specific definition of the product and geographic market, along with a justification for the definition. Without such a prerequisite, analysts in this field may simply be talking past each other with no common ground for a meaningful discussion. With a definition of the product and geographic market, it becomes possible to analyze various propositions.

The Chain Ownership Case

One of the most discussed topics in the newspaper concentration area is chain ownership, the ownership of two or more daily newspapers in separate cities by the same firm or individual. Scholars and practitioners who express concern over what they see as a move toward greater chain ownership of daily newspapers are implicitly defining the product market as the daily newspaper, and the geographic market as the entire United States. It has been shown here that this definition of the newspaper market clearly does not square with the definition found in antitrust case law, nor is it in harmony with the requirement for products to be reasonably interchangeable in order to be in the same market. The daily newspapers that comprise a given chain are certainly in the same product market, but are not in the same geographic market, in most cases. They do not draw from the same audience or advertising pool. So it seems that the chain acquisition of a daily newspaper does not contribute to newspaper concentration (unless there is a geographic overlap with another newspaper in the chain), and the analysis of the effects of chain ownership is not properly a subset under the general topic of newspaper concentration studies. Instead, chain ownership studies seem more concerned with studying the effects of a certain type of ownership (local vs. nonlocal), rather than studying the effects of concentration, per se, since whether a particular daily newspaper is chain owned or not has no bearing on the level of concentration the newspaper faces in its market.

For those who insist that chain ownership is a newspaper concentration issue, they must argue, for example, that *The Detroit Free Press* and *The St. Paul Pioneer Press and Dispatch* compete with each other in the same market. Both newspapers are owned by the Knight-Ridder chain. This market could be either the information market, where newspapers attract audiences with advertising and nonadvertising content, or the advertising market where newspapers sell the attention of their audiences to advertisers. There certainly seems to be no way that one could argue that the two newspapers compete with each other for any type of advertising revenue. Most of each newspaper's advertising is local, and national advertisers would not consider transferring their ad dollars from one newspaper to the other because they can get a more efficient advertising rate. There is virtually a zero cross-elasticity of demand from advertisers. It also seems that there is no competition between the two newspapers for the information used to attract audiences. Much of this information is of a local nature, so that people living in Detroit would not consider switching their newspaper subscription to the St. Paul paper should the *Free Press* raise its subscription price. The national and international information in the two newspapers is roughly equivalent, and comes from the same sources in any case. So, again, there appears to be no cross-elasticity of demand—no reasonable interchangeability—between two daily newspapers that operate in separate geographic markets.

Structure of the Daily Newspaper Market

With a definition of what constitutes the product and geographic boundaries of the daily newspaper market, it is possible to apply the structure–conduct–performance framework of the industrial organization model specifically to newspapers. The level of seller concentration is extremely high. In 1981, only 2% (or 30 out of 1,534) of cities with daily newspapers had two or more competing papers published in the same city (Compaine, Sterling, Guback, & Noble, 1982, p. 37). Of course, according to the umbrella theory some smaller dailies face competition from metro or regional dailies that does not show up in the 2%

figure. However, it seems clear that most dailies do not face effective competition from other, separately owned, dailies in their RTZs.

Even those markets that have two or three competitive dailies are still considered extremely concentrated by conventional economic definitions. The most common measure of concentration is the percentage of sales belonging to the four largest separately owned firms in a market. While it would be burdensome to verify, there must be few, if any, RTZs that have more than four independent dailies available, and, even if such a case existed, the largest four would take almost all of the circulation and advertising sales revenue. Judge Learned Hand, in the landmark Alcoa case, stated that 90% "is enough to constitute a monopoly" (he really meant oligopoly) for the purpose of possibly finding a violation of the antitrust laws (*United States v. Aluminum Company of America*, 1945, p. 434). There must be no daily newspaper market in the United States that has a four-firm concentration ration of less than 90%, and nearly all must be at 100%.

However, the highly concentrated nature of daily newspaper markets does not necessarily mean that these newspapers violate antitrust law. Dicta from *United States v. United States Steel Corp.* (1920) have developed into what is called the "rule of reason" for determining whether the firm or firms in a monopoly or oligopoly market are in violation of the antitrust laws. It states, ". . . the law does not make mere size an offense or the existence of unexerted power an offense. It . . . requires overt acts" (at 451). The industrial organization model suggests a reason that would make the high concentration levels in daily newspaper markets innocent of wrongdoing and beyond the corrective arm of the antitrust laws. Another element of market structure, the cost structure of newspaper markets, seems to provide the explanation. Fixed costs, or what Owen (1975, pp. 16–20) calls "first copy" costs, are quite high for newspapers, while the marginal cost of producing additional copies of a newspaper is very low. This allows the largest newspaper in a market to operate most efficiently, which "innocently" helps to drive out all, or at least most, competition. This cost structure feature seems fairly impervious to manipulation by antitrust action because of the *U.S. Steel* "rule of reason" noted above. After all, there is no economic basis for wanting to punish the most cost-efficient firm in a market.

Another market structure component, product differentiation, serves to hide the fact that daily newspaper markets may be even more concentrated than they already appear to be. Probably most readers of the *New York Times* would not consider the *New York Post* as an acceptable substitute, because of the level of real and imagined product differentiation between the two newspapers. Thus, the number of different "reasonably interchangeable" daily newspapers is less than the total number of daily newspapers in New York. For a similar reason, we should not even consider *The Wall Street Journal* and *USA Today* to be operating in the same market as "regular" dailies. These papers do not provide local news or advertising, which are the two most important elements of the typical daily newspaper.

Because of the enormous first copy costs mentioned above, the daily newspaper market is also characterized by high barriers to the entry of new competition. Potential entrants are discouraged because of the need to garner such a large market share in order to reach acceptable levels of cost efficiency. Loren Ghiglione (1984) suggests that a daily needs a 40% market share to survive. This is unrealistic for virtually any potential entrant into a market that already has a daily. Again, this market structure component has the effect of making newspaper markets even more concentrated than they appear to be, since existing dailies need to have little concern that high advertising or circulation prices may cause a new daily to enter the market.

The last market structure component to be investigated is vertical integration. Every product, including newspapers, has various stages of production and distribution from raw material through final sale to the end user. Each of these stages can be seen as a separate market, with some degree of interdependence between the various stages. This degree of interdependence is what is meant by vertical integration. If there is a high degree of interdependence (e.g., ownership of all stages by the same set of firms), then the product is said to be highly vertically integrated.

The daily newspaper market is characterized by a high degree of vertical integration, with the owners of the final stage of production (the printing press) also controlling the intermediate editing stage and a good part of the information-gathering raw materials stage. The cost structure of the printing and distribution stage, with its very high fixed costs, is the main cause of the high concentration in daily newspaper markets. Vertical integration allows the monopolist or oligopolist owners of printing presses to extend their economic control to the earlier stages of production (reporters, news services, editors), causing greater concentration at these stages than would otherwise occur without the vertical integration. If daily newspaper markets were not vertically integrated, then printing presses and delivery services would act as common carriers by renting out their services to groups of reporters and editors, much as a local cable operation could rent out channels on its system. Since only about 16% of the cost of producing a newspaper goes into the creation of the nonadvertising content, it is conceivable that concentration in the daily newspaper field could be reduced if the newspapers were vertically disintegrated. With several news-gathering and editing entities sharing the same printing press and delivery system, the heavy fixed-costs barrier could be significantly reduced (Owen, 1975, p. 58).

Conduct of the Daily Newspaper Market

According to the industrial organization paradigm, various components of market structure should have some effect on the nature of market conduct. The previous section describes a market structured by a high degree of seller concentration caused by very high fixed costs of printing and distribution. This has monopolized (or oligopolized) the earlier stages of production and set up virtually insurmountable barriers to new entry. Those few markets that appear to have some degree of oligopolisitic competition through two or more separately owned daily newspapers may actually experience less competition than appearances suggest, due to real or imagined product differentiation that exists among the so-called competing dailies.

The four areas of the market conduct of daily newspapers are pricing conduct, product strategy, research, and advertising (promotion). Given the monopoly market structure in which most daily newspapers operate, there is little chance for the more common types of pricing misconduct such as price collusion and predatory pricing to occur. However, the possibility of collusion and predatory pricing can occur in markets that have more than one daily newspaper, particularly when two newspapers are owned by the same company (*Times-Picayune Publishing Co. v. United States*, 1953; *Syracuse Broadcasting Corp. v. Newhouse*, 1956; *Kansas City Star v. United States*, 1957). When two newspapers are commonly owned, forced combination advertising rates will probably be viewed as violating antitrust laws, whereas voluntary combination rates would not. In either case, common ownership certainly provides the opportunity for collusion as well as predatory prices, should a competitor loom on the horizon.

One other very severe form of price collusion that does exist in some daily newspaper markets is the mutual setting of advertising rates between two newspapers operating under what is called a joint operating agreement. These agreements, made legal by the Newspaper Preservation Act of 1970 (Public Law 91-353, 84 Stat. 466, 15 U.S.C. Sections 1801–1804), allow two separately owned daily newspapers operating in the same geographic market to carry out what would otherwise be viewed as blatantly illegal behavior. The Newspaper Preservation Act allows separately owned newspapers to collude on the setting of advertising and circulation rates, to agree upon the division of submarkets between the two papers (e.g., morning edition for one newspaper and evening for the other), to share equipment, and to pool profits and distribute them in some predetermined manner. All these types of market conduct would normally be prohibited by the antitrust laws. Except for editorial departments, which are supposed to remain independent, the Newspaper Preservation Act effectively allows two separately owned newspapers to act as if they were under common ownership.

One type of pricing behavior that is not protected by the Newspaper Preservation Act is possible price discrimination through advertising volume discounts. Price discrimination consists of the sale of units of a product or service at price differentials that are not justified by differences in supply cost. Many daily newspapers offer volume discounts to large advertisers so that these advertisers pay less per unit of space than smaller-volume advertisers. Price discrimination exists if the volume discounts do not represent passing on to the large advertiser costs savings due to handling a larger piece of business. Certainly a daily newspaper incurs less costs in soliciting and servicing a department store that purchases a large number of large space ads than in soliciting and servicing a large number of advertisers that purchase small space ads only infrequently. Weighing the actual costs of soliciting and servicing different size advertisers is clearly a complicated matter. In fact, it is conceivable that small advertisers actually benefit from price discrimination, since the cost of soliciting and servicing these clients may not be reflected properly in the volume discounts. Another area of possible price discrimination by daily newspapers may be the price differential many dailies charge for retail versus national advertising.

The more important issue regarding price discrimination in an industrial organization model concerns what structural element gives rise to the possibility of price discrimination, and what impact this price discrimination might have on market performance. Certainly the monopoly, or near-monopoly, structure of daily newspaper markets is the most important factor that facilitates price discrimination (if price discrimination does exist). Most buyers of advertising space face only poor alternatives to the newspaper. The seller monopoly precludes bidding competition that would force advertising prices more into line with costs. Price discrimination can have a significant ill effect on market performance. Price discrimination will redistribute income in the direction of the discriminating newspaper and away from some advertisers. It also seems to have a feedback effect on market structure by increasing the barriers to entry by other newspapers, since the existing monopolist controls bulk contracts with large advertisers. Price discrimination by newspapers can also effect competition in the advertiser's own product and service markets, if certain competitors are given lower advertising rates.

Given the monopoly, or strong oligopoly, market structure enjoyed by daily newspapers, one would expect little effort or money devoted to product improvements, research, or promotion costs. This is because the lack of product rivalry or competition eliminates the need to gain, at the expense of rivals, through these various marketing strategies. This seems to be an appropriate characterization of daily newspaper markets.

While there have been some cost-reduction improvements made in newspaper production over the past two decades, newspapers have traditionally been slow to innovate. Furthermore, many of these changes were not the result of research and development expenditures by newspapers themselves. In fact, most newspapers seem to spend little, if any, money trying to lower costs or improve quality of the product itself. Some changes in product design have questionable utility for consumers—graphics changes, for example, to make some dailies look more like USA Today. Promotional expenditures by newspapers are also relatively low. Newspapers advertise themselves considerably less intensively than magazines, books, radio stations, television stations, motion picture producers, or motion picture theatres. Cable system operators have about the same advertising intensity as newspapers—and they are government licensed monopolists

("Schonfeld Tracks Ad Spending," 1985, p. 34). Certainly, it may appear from the point of view of the newspapers that they are besieged by competition from local broadcast stations for advertising revenue, and newspapers may believe that they are carrying out all sorts of promotional efforts to get those dollars. However, the evidence indicates differently.

Market conduct of this type yields both an advantage and a disadvantage for market performance. The good effect is that newspapers do not waste too much money on superficial style changes or image-oriented advertising campaigns that would add to the cost of producing the newspaper but provide no real benefit for consumers. This added cost would likely be passed on to the public in the form of higher subscription and single copy costs and to advertisers in the form of higher advertising rates. On the downside, with little incentive to innovate, few real improvements are made.

Some newspapers seem to practice predatory and exclusionary tactics in the areas of market sharing and zoned editions (or weeklies or shoppers produced by the daily). Zoned editions, or weeklies or shoppers developed by a daily, can be predatory if their purpose or effect is to drive other smaller dailies, weeklies, or shoppers out of the market, and if the advertising prices charged are "predatory." The key here is what constitutes a predatory price. In theory, if the daily sets predatory prices for its zoned editions, shopper, or weekly, it will set them below marginal costs so that it is actually losing money. The idea is temporarily to "cross-subsidize" this loss by profits from the daily until the rival daily, weekly, or shopper goes out of business. Then prices can be raised to make up for the earlier losses. Of course, this is a textbook case of predatory pricing, and it would be much more difficult to identify it in practice. However, the potential for this predatory practice is present, and it is augmented by the strong market position of the daily.

Performance of the Daily Newspaper Market

From the industrial organization model presented earlier, two performance criteria were said to be of particular importance for newspapers: technical and allocative efficiency. The price we pay for goods and services can be said to comprise two parts. One component is the costs incurred in producing and marketing the product. The other is the profit that goes to the seller. Technical efficiency is the extent to which the production and marketing costs component is minimized per unit of output. Technical inefficiency harms the economic performance of the market since resources are wasted that could be better utilized for other purposes. In addition, buyers are harmed by having to pay a higter price for the good or service in question. Allocative efficiency is the extent to which the profit level is just sufficient to maintain an efficient level of production in the market. An excessive profit rate is allocatively inefficient because it indicates that an insufficient level of output is being achieved in the market. A larger output would be required in order to lower price and return profit levels to normal.

In regard to the level of technical efficiency of daily newspapers, probably the most important issue is the extent to which "plant facilities" (e.g., printing presses and circulation trucks) are used efficiently. From the analysis of the structure of daily newspaper markets, the high fixed costs that are incurred by each daily in a market owning its own production and distribution facilities appears to make monopoly the most cost-efficient level of concentration. A market comprised of several dailies would result in a far higher input cost per unit of output than a market with one daily, one printing press, and one fleet of delivery trucks that takes advantage of spreading these high fixed costs over the greatest number of copies. One may conclude from this that the high concentration levels that exist in newspaper markets (structure) lead to a strategy of providing a general-purpose, mass-appeal product (conduct) with the highest possible degree of technical efficiency.

However, technical efficiency may not be maximized under the current form of monopoly, or near monopoly, structure. One printing press in a geographical market will certainly have less excess capacity than three separately owned printing presses in the same market. But even that one printing press appears to have excess capacity that, if used, will improve the level of technical efficiency in such markets. This could occur with the proposal to vertically disintegrate the daily newspaper (Owen, 1975, p. 185). With this proposal, printing presses and delivery equipment would be separated from the information-gathering and editing units they now own, and would be required to serve several such units as a common carrier. The conceivable results would be that technical efficiency could be maximized, advertising and subscription prices should fall, and the public should benefit from more diverse content with the freedom to select information from more than one newspaper.

One would expect that highly concentrated markets, such as daily newspaper markets, would have a significant amount of allocative inefficiency. In a highly concentrated market, the monopolist or oligopolist has a great deal of power over the pricing conduct in the market. A single or dominant seller can exert a significant control over prices by manipulating output. By restricting output, the market-clearing price will rise as buyers must bid up the price of the reduced output. The result will be "excess" profits earned by the firms that exert this market power. Therefore, by looking for the existence of excess profits in a market, one can find evidence of allocative inefficiency.

It is difficult to obtain profit data for newspapers, since many are privately held. Compaine et al. (1982, p. 33) compiled a list of 13 publicly held companies that derived a substantial portion of their revenue from newspaper operations in 1980. The median return on sales for this group was 8.5% compared to a median return of 4.8% for the Fortune 500. While measuring profit rate as the return on sales is not as good a measure as the return on equity, the figures still seem to indicate that newspapers are a fairly profitable business. The general interest level in buying and owning newspapers also seems to be indicative of the strong profitability of the business. The high profit rate suggests a lack of allocative efficiency which is consistent with the high concentration/high barriers to entry that daily newspapers enjoy.

By considering only the technical and allocative efficiency of daily newspaper performance, one misses the quality aspect of performance. Bain (1968, pp. 421–425) presents the term *product performance*, which attempts to measure this quality of performance dimension. Product performance is the extent to which the market attains the optimal balance between buyer satisfaction and the cost of production. This measure of market performance is generally downplayed by economists because it is difficult to measure, and efficiency concerns seem more relevant in the soft drink or laundry detergent market in any case. However, this performance criterion seems to be of particular importance to the evaluation of the economic performance of daily newspaper markets. Newspapers do more than capture peoples' attention and sell that attention to advertisers. They provide information on many subjects crucial in a democracy. Various quality elements of that information content take on importance far beyond their attention-getting value.

Many people believe that diverse content from the various media in a market is a measure of quality product performance. Some types of content are seen as intrinsically good (e.g., the amount of space devoted to local news), so, as more quantity is produced, quality is said to increase. Other people claim that some newspapers are "better" than others, for a host of reasons. These are all examples of ways that quality of performance may be measured. We can relate various market structure and conduct conditions to some measure of quality (that measures buyer satisfaction in some way) in order to see which factors seem to enhance or detract from product performance. In fact, this is what many researchers have done, as seen in several chapters in this book. This is, perhaps, the one area where the study of newspaper economics is most different from the economic analysis of nonmedia industries. A greater emphasis is placed on the quality of product performance, since newspaper content is seen as having much greater importance to our society than the quality of widgets.

Research Suggestions Using the I.O. Model

Using the industrial organization model in studying newspaper economics has a number of benefits. The model helps to identify various elements within a market. This can be accomplished by studies which describe one or more structure, conduct, or performance elements in the newspaper market. The industrial organization model also suggest causal links that may exist between different market elements. Here, studies can be performed that attempt to measure the relationships among and between structure, conduct, and performance elements. Finally, the model suggests how alterations in structure and conduct may improve market performance. The work in each of these three areas (descriptive, causal, policy oriented) can be done with either a theoretical or an empirical emphasis. Some examples of research ideas which fit into the industrial organization framework follow.

Descriptive Studies

Descriptive studies are of two basic types: measurement and definition. The most basic work in this area would involve measuring various components of structure, conduct, and performance in newspaper markets. At the market structure level, measurement is needed for concentration levels, ratios of fixed to variable costs, cross-elasticities of demand between various media, and the size of entry barriers. Some market conduct variables that need measurement are advertising price levels, promotional activities, and efforts made to improve the product. Performance measures include determining profit levels of newspapers and profit rates based on equity rather than sales, as well as developing measures of product quality such as news staff size, the amount of space devoted to local news, assessments of overall quality made by blue ribbon panels, a content analysis of the level of diversity of views expressed in newspapers, or the level of diversity that exists in the public on issues of importance that may have been affected by newspapers. The measurement of many of these elements can be very difficult and controversial.

There could also be studies of a more theoretical nature that might attempt to define or redefine some important component of the daily newspaper market. At the market structure level, for example, the definition of what constitutes the product and geographic dimensions of the daily newspaper market is of crucial importance. One could use legal analysis and formulate the boundaries based on antitrust statutes and case law. It is also possible to approach this issue by using economic theory and the concept of cross-elasticity of demand. The results of a purely descriptive study to measure the cross-elasticity of demand for advertising between television stations and daily newspapers could then be used to determine whether the elasticities actually found are high enough to warrant including television stations in the same product market as daily newspapers.

Price discrimination in advertising volume discount rates is another component in newspaper markets that needs to be properly defined and measured. What conditions are necessary for price discrimination to occur? What are the costs that should be included in soliciting and servicing local retail advertisers? Is the small, infrequent advertiser subsidizing the big advertisers, or might it be the other way around? Many newspapers charge higher rates on national advertising than on local advertising. Is this due to a more inelastic demand curve for national advertisers, or does it reflect legitimate additional expense by the newspapers to handle national accounts?

Besides the task of measuring quality components of newspaper markets as was mentioned before, it is also necessary to carry out the more difficult task of trying to define what quality performance is. The economist's measures of performance are characterized by being fairly noncontroversial and quantitative in nature. Unfortunately, many of the possible measures of newspaper quality do not possess both these attributes.

Causal Studies

The next step up from the important descriptive studies are causal studies which attempt to measure linkages within and between market structure, conduct, and performance. The interrelationships of some market structure variables are important. One such area is the effect of high fixed costs and strong vertical integration on newspaper concentration levels. The work of Owen in this area was mentioned earlier.

Another interesting area involves the interplay of seller and buyer concentration. Newspaper markets are characterized by very high seller concentration. What happens to other market structure components when this monopolist or oligopolist encounters a large oligopsonist, such as the big department store or supermarket in town? There may be the effect of raising barriers to entry, since the advertiser prefers a media vehicle that has the greatest household coverage in the market and shies away from smaller dailies. There may also be an impact on market conduct and performance from such a clash.

Two of the common complaints voiced about the impact of the large advertiser are the effect on advertising price structure (the price discrimination issue) and what has been called product performance in this chapter. The performance issue surrounds the possibility of a large advertiser forcing a newspaper to print favorable (and avoid unfavorable) information about the advertiser in the editorial material of the newspaper. This conflict of interest certainly is a measure of poor product performance.

Other causal studies that look at effects between different stages of the industrial organization might include the relationship between concentration levels (monopoly newspapers versus newspapers facing competition) and price levels. Many industrial organization studies avoid the intermediate step of market conduct and attempt to draw linkages directly from market structure to performance. Here we might see studies that compare concentration levels with profit levels or some measure of newspaper quality. There are several examples of the last approach in other chapters of this book.

Policy Studies

This last area of study within the industrial organization framework often takes what is learned from causal studies about the interrelationships of market components and suggests ways that these components can be manipulated in order to improve market performance. Since causal studies generally show that monopoly newspapers should not (and generally do not) perform as well as newspapers that face competition, some policy studies are concerned with how newspaper concentration might be lessened. If causal studies were to show that joint operating newspapers demonstrate better (or worse) performance than monopoly newspapers, then there would be some implications for policy change in this area.

There is some concern over what is perceived as a move toward chain ownership of newspapers. If it could be argued, somehow, that newspapers in different Retail Trading Zones were, nevertheless, in the same market, a good deal of policy research could be done to justify application of some antitrust provisions to chain acquisitions of daily newspapers.

Another area of interest may be in trying to use product performance standards in policy formation. Administrative law may be designed to alter newspaper structure and conduct in order to bring about better product performance. At this time, antitrust laws have little concern with restricting structure and performance activities that affect product quality. Since product performance seems so much more important for newspapers than for other industries, this may be a productive way to proceed in the policy area.

Summary

The industrial organization model posits that the *structure* of economic markets affects the *conduct* of participants in those markets, which, in turn, affects the *performance* of those markets. This perspective is valuable in the study of newspaper economics because it provides a framework for identifying key market elements, proposes a set of theories about how these elements interact, and suggests ways in which certain components can be manipulated in order to improve performance while keeping a good degree of freedom in the marketplace.

Studies of newspaper concentration should attempt to come to some agreement over the definition of a daily newspaper market, and use the definition consistently. Without a consistent and correct definition, it is not even possible to measure newspaper concentration. Here the daily newspaper market is defined as daily newspapers distributed within a given Retail Trading Zone. This definition excludes chain ownership of newspapers from being a concentration issue. One important point of difference in applying the industrial organization model to dailies is the much greater emphasis that should be placed on the product performance goal in evaluating overall performance of daily newspaper markets. The industrial organization perspective provides a rich framework for research by mass communication scholars.

CHAPTER 3

Pricing Behavior of Newspapers

Robert G. Picard

Mass Communication Division
Emerson College
Boston, MA

Pricing behaviors of newspapers are influenced by a variety of factors—industry structure, the nature and amount of inter- and intra-media competition, circulations of specific newspapers, the sizes of the primary markets in which papers circulate, demand for advertising, and general economic conditions.

In economic terms the newspaper industry is unusual, because it produces one tangible product, but it participates in two separate markets. And its performance in each market affects its performance in the other.

The tangible product of the newspaper industry is, of course, information that is packaged and delivered in the form of the printed newspaper. This product is marketed to media consumers. The second market in which newspapers are involved is advertising. While some observers may casually conclude that the papers sell space to advertising purchasers, a more precise and descriptive explanation is that the newspapers sell readers to advertisers. The industry delivers readers to advertisers, and the amount charged for advertising is more dependent upon the sizes and characteristics of audiences than the sizes of the advertisements themselves.

The dual markets of the industry are problematic because the primary information product—news, features, and other information sold to readers—produces only about one-third the amount of revenue for the papers that the secondary product—media consumers sold to advertisers—produce for the papers.

There are also differences in the demand for the two products. Media consumers' demand for newspapers is relatively inelastic—that is, consumers do not respond to changes in price by significantly changing their purchasing patterns. And the number of papers purchased remains relatively stable over time.

Demand for advertising space varies over time, however. Days of the week, seasons, and general business climates affect demand, even when price is not a factor. Demand for space by retail advertisers is relatively inelastic, however, except in large markets where competing media are more prevalent. The same is generally true for national advertising. Most daily newspapers, then, do not induce significant changes in advertising consumers' purchasing decisions by raising or lowering their prices, because most papers are located in relatively small and moderately-sized markets and do not experience much inter- or intra-media competition.

In larger markets, demand for space is more elastic, especially that of national advertisers. Demand is especially sensitive to price changes when there is another competing daily paper available and its audience demographics are similar, and the disparity in circulation between the two papers is not great.

How Rates Are Set

In marketing information to readers and readers to advertisers, newspaper managers must plan pricing strategies and set rates in much the same manner as producers of goods that will be marketed to the general public. Since advertising accounts for nearly three-fourths of total newspaper income, one would assume that the pricing of advertising space would be of considerable importance to newspaper publishers and owners. But the opposite appears true, for pricing strategies receive little consideration in industry publications and newspaper management materials.

Pricing strategies and rate setting are not even viewed with the same importance attached in other industries, where admittedly—despite the acknowledged importance and study given to pricing policy—"most companies do not handle pricing well" (Kotler, 1980, p. 381).

In the newspaper industry, where the overt lack of interest in price strategy appears epidemic, pricing appears to be handled in even worse fashion. One observer noted charitably in 1958 that "rate setting is not as much an integral part of the over-all marketing strategy as it might be" (Dunn, 1956, p. 512). His admonition has not yet been heeded, and the need for attention to be paid to rate setting has increased tremendously as newspapers have become more dependent on advertising revenue and competition for advertising dollars has grown.

The lack of concern about rates within the industry is reflected in, and is perhaps promoted by, the lack of concern about the issue in major newspaper management texts.

Leslie McClure's 1950 text, *Newspaper Advertising and Promotion*, widely regarded as a major work on the business side of newspaper operations, spends little time on the subject of rate setting, merely noting the influences on rates and providing an argument for differential rates.

Frank Rucker and Herbert Williams also virtually ignore the issue in their widely used and enduring text on newspaper operations, *Newspaper Organization and Management*. Although they acknowledge the importance of advertising and suggest ways to increase advertising sales, they do little more than McClure in the way of helping publishers or would-be publishers learn how to establish and maintain rates for advertising.

Economist Jon Udell's 1978 work on newspaper economics, *The Economics of the American Newspaper*, which was produced with the financial support of the American Newspaper Publishers Association, was a long-awaited and needed work on the economic side of publishing. Despite its importance it includes no significant discussion of rate structure or how rates should be set. Udell, in fact, pays much more attention to circulation prices—as did McClure and Rucker and Williams—even though circulation revenue has much less impact on newspaper economics than advertising revenue. It must be acknowledged, however, that the size of the circulation does have an influence on advertising sales.

Publishers seeking substantive information to help them make rate-setting decisions are also left without help by such organizations as the Newspaper Advertising Bureau, American Newspaper Publishers Association, and National Newspaper Publishers Association, which do not have publications on the subject and have not published journal articles that can be helpful to newspaper managers.

Academic researchers have not helped the situation either. Their literature is devoid of information helpful to publishers and contains only a few studies analyzing existing price behavior.

Because of the lack of information and studies on setting advertising rates, most publishers apparently set and adjust their rates by using intuition, adapting pricing strategies used by other industries, or blindly stumbling along with a let's-try-it-and-see strategy. In the nation's largest newspapers and newspaper chains, marketing and pricing strategies are gaining some consideration, however, and some firms now have departments which are beginning to analyze rates and make comparisons of rates in various markets among their other duties.

It is clear that there are numerous influences on the pricing of advertising space. John McKinney (1977, p. 54) has observed that "advertising rates are generally determined by considering the paper's total circulation, its expenses, and the rates charged by competing publications, if any exist."

Rucker and Williams (1974, p. 211) concur that the accustomed standard has generally been circulation, but, they add, "the business public is beginning to realize that something more than paid subscribers determines the value of a newspaper as an advertising medium."

The prestige of a paper, the quality of its circulation in terms of potential results for advertisers, the locations of readers, the production services rendered by the paper, and the local economy also play roles in the setting of advertising rates.

For the most part, strategies used in setting rates in the newspaper industry appear to take the forms of target return pricing and competition-oriented pricing or some combined variations of the two. Occasionally, a demand-oriented policy may be selected, but the two dominant policies remain target return and competition-oriented pricing.

Target return pricing is the strategy of determining the price that will give a specific rate of return on total costs, based on estimated volumes of business. In competition-oriented pricing, prices are set with the greatest emphasis being placed on competitors' prices, often after a review of what the going rate is for the product. Demand-oriented policy sets prices based on the perceptions and demand intensity of consumers. Richard Brown (1967) has argued that the target return model is most useful in explaining behavior of chain-owned papers and that a profit maximization model can be used to explain the behavior of the largest firms and the few local competing newspapers. Over all, however, models of oligopoly (see Chapter 1) best explain the market behavior of most papers, he argues.

In their basic strategies, newspapers have traditionally set different rates for different classes of advertisers. National advertisers usually pay higher rates than local advertisers, an occurrence not looked upon favorably by national advertisers. Newspapers also set different rates based on services rendered to the advertiser, placement, and the amount of advertising space purchased during a year.

James Ferguson studied the rate differential between national and retail advertising in a study sponsored by the Ford Foundation. He found no evidence to suggest that the differential could be laid upon higher costs to the paper for national advertising. The main factor, he said, is the value of retail advertising to the paper.

"Newspapers have held down retail rates relative to national rates in an attempt to attract retail advertising and thereby increase circulation and attract still more advertising," Ferguson (1963, p. 39) wrote. "In order to maximize profits, the interrelationships among circulation, retail advertising, and national advertising make it necessary to charge retailers less than national advertisers, despite the more inelastic demand of the retailers."

Compared with the prices of products, the rates of advertising space have been unusually rigid over time, perhaps reflecting the view promulgated by McClure (1950, p. 130)—that to operate profitably and "hold the confidence of advertisers," newspapers must keep fairly rigid rate structures.

"Publishers of individual newspapers and their business staffs have been forced to make rate decisions based almost entirely on their own analyses, however good or poor these may be," says S. Watson Dunn (1956, p. 489), a professor of advertising who has devoted considerable attention to newspapers. "In general they have played it safe by keeping their rate structure fairly rigid in spite of ups and downs in the business cycle and changes in operating costs."

Competition and Ad Rates

How competition for advertising dollars affects advertising rates is the major consideration in any serious discussion of newspaper advertising issues. In its broadest sense, newspaper competition for advertising involves competition with all media, including broadcast media, direct mail publications, posters, coupons, and vehicle-borne ads. For the purposes of this chapter, however, discussion of competition will be limited to the battle for advertising dollars between units of the newspaper medium, mainly daily papers, but also including weekly and shopper publications serving the same general marketing area.

Circulation, as was shown earlier, is a prime determinant of the attraction of a particular newspaper to an advertiser. But advertisements in a newspaper also play a role in increasing circulation, because newspaper readers are attracted to the information provided by advertising.

The newspaper with the largest circulation in a given marketing area has advantages which enable it to gain ground in both circulation and advertising, at the expense of papers with lower circulation and advertising revenues, forcing them into less advantageous situations, says Lars Furhoff, a researcher in newspaper economics. Publishing a large amount of advertising is one of those advantages.

"That newspaper which has achieved the highest density of distribution also enjoys the largest market potential, i.e. the largest number of readers within the territory in which advertisers are interested," Furhoff (1973, p. 9) contends. "This attracts an increased flow of advertising and thus larger resources to support the competitive strategems and low copy prices by which new readers and further advertising income will be gained."

The leading newspaper also has the advantage of determining the standards of advertising, editorial, production, and distribution quality expected by advertisers and readers. It therefore puts increased pressure on competing papers to live up to these standards. As those papers attempt to meet the demands, their economic difficulties increase, trapping them into a vicious circle or "circulation spiral" which aggravates the problems of selling advertising space and the rates which can be charged for that space.

Furhoff's contentions were later borne out by Karl Erik Gustafsson (1978, pp. 1–14) who showed that in Scandinavia only a household penetration of at least 50% made a competing newspaper indispensable to advertisers in a given market. More recently, a review of Furhoff's and Gustafsson's work (Engwall, 1981, pp. 145–154) argued that theories of oligopoly help explain their observations, and that, in competitive situations, the only way for a newspaper that does not have market leadership to survive is by pursuing policies that differentiate the product from the leading newspaper in terms of content and readership.

In this symbiotic relationship between circulation and advertising are the makings of a vigorous battle for advertising dollars when more than one paper competes for the available advertising. When this type of competitive situation exists, the setting of advertising rates plays an important role in the advertising marketing process.

"In a highly competitive field, newspapers operate on narrower margins of profit and tend to pay lower salaries and trim expenses wherever possible," says McClure (1950, p. 130). "As a result, they frequently offer their customers relatively low rates to prevent loss of lineage to competitors and to take business away from those competitors."

Udell (1978, p. 109) concurs that low-rate policy attracts business away from competitors and that the setting of rates determines whether lineage is large or small. "A low-rate newspaper will sell more advertising lineage to an advertiser than a high-rate paper because of the relatively fixed ratio of advertising expenditures to retail sales," he says.

The realities of publishing make it more likely that the largest paper in a community will be able to offer the lowest advertising rates, attracting more advertisers than it would if it had a higher rate, thus making up for any revenue that was lost when lowering the rates. The low-rate policy does not necessarily gain a paper more advertising revenue, but it can harm the competitor and thus may, in the end, have the effect of reducing the competition for advertising dollars.

This effect was shown starkly in Salem, Oregon, where the Gannett Co. sharply reduced advertising rates for its *Oregon Statesman* and *Capitol Journal* and actively pursued strategies to attract advertisers away from a successful weekly newspaper. As a result of the ensuing advertising war, the weekly paper was forced out of business and the Gannett papers were able to raise rates—increasing revenue—without fear that advertisers would move their business to the weekly newspaper (Winski, 1981, p. 155).

The fact that large papers *can* sustain low prices longer than smaller or poorer competitors, and that conventional economic wisdom indicates competition *should* hold down prices, does not mean publishers actually keep prices low, as will be shown below. Large publishers have other forces working for them, besides the ability to lower prices, that aid them in competitive situations.

Jon Udell (1978, p. 109) has observed that "the largest-circulation newspaper in a given market generally gets a disproportionately large amount of newspaper advertising revenue in that market. A competitive second paper, while it may be behind only slightly in circulation, is often a more distant second in advertising revenue."

Such a situation is well illustrated by the newspaper situation in Washington, D.C., where the second paper, the Washington *Star*, ceased operation for financial reasons. The Washington Post had a daily circulation of 578,831 and the *Star* a circulation of 342,760 (*Editor & Publisher International Yearbook*, 1980).

While the *Star* accounted for nearly a 40% share of the daily circulation, it received only a 24% share of the advertising lineage (Gordon, 1981, p. 1).

The disparity between advertising and circulation shares is illustrated in Figure 1.

Many of the newspapers competing in the few remaining multinewspaper markets are facing problems similar to those in Washington, D.C. Newspapers in Detroit, Denver, Los Angeles, and other major cities are experiencing this problem.

Competitive situations generally result in papers pursuing low-rate, competition-oriented pricing policies, sometimes artificially low, to carry out marketing strategies to dominate the advertising market. But the low-rate strategy generally covers only retail advertisers. Firms wishing to place national advertising are still saddled with higher rates because of the common rate differential between national and retail advertising rates.

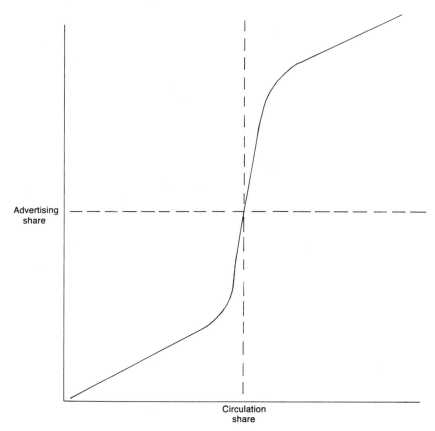

Figure 1.   Disparity Between Ad and Circulation Shares

The situation obviously aggravates national advertisers, but publishers are aware that the demand for space by national advertisers is relatively inelastic and therefore would not be likely to increase as a result of lowering national rates, even in a competitive situation.

In situations where daily suburban and regional papers compete under the "umbrella" of a large daily metropolitan paper, competition differs from head-to-head competition within a single market. While the suburban and metropolitan papers compete for the local media consumers, there is little competition between the papers for local retail advertising. Local suburban advertisers generally prefer to reach only local readers and do not wish, or cannot afford, to pay the higher prices of the metropolitan paper. As a result, the metropolitan paper cannot compete with the local paper for that advertising in a significant manner.

Noncompetitive situations, which represent the largest percentage of all newspaper markets, place newspapers at an advantage when it comes to rate setting, since less attention must be paid to the rate card than in competitive situations. Since there is no other daily newspaper competition for local advertising, publishers need only avoid price gouging so significant that advertisers are driven to other media or weekly papers. Publishers in these situations can choose any reasonable price and circulation quantity combination to yield optimal results.

Price Behavior Studies

In the past two decades, researchers have begun to consider seriously the pricing behavior of newspapers under various market and ownership conditions. These studies provide important insight into the effects of concentration of ownership, concentration, and monopoly on price behavior that aggregate studies of the newspaper industry have not. And they raise important issues about the treatment of newspaper and advertising space consumers.

In order to obtain a clearer understanding of the results of these studies, we will consider the various conditions individually, exploring studies of price behavior in competitive and monopoly situations and in chain ownership, joint operating agreement, and cross ownership situations.

Competing Papers and Prices

Competition lowers the prices of products, according to classical economic theory. One would thus assume that consumers benefit from papers operating in competition with other papers. The literature of newspaper economics, however, does not bear out this contention fully.

Studies considering the effects of competition on advertising prices have not supported the "benefits of competition" theory. Blankenburg (1980, pp. 663–666) found that competing weekly papers were, in fact, "modestly related" to higher prices for advertising. Ferguson (1983, pp. 635–654) revealed that competing dailies are associated with higher daily run-of-paper (ROP) milinch advertising rates and that competing Sunday papers result in significantly higher national and retail ROP milinch rates. Picard (1986) found that competing papers had significantly higher actual advertising rates than monopoly newspapers, but that, when circulation was controlled through the use of milline rates, their rates were lower. That study found, however, that competing papers raised their milline rates at a rate nearly double that of monopoly newspapers between 1972 and 1982.

In terms of circulation pricing, competition has also been shown not to be fully beneficial. Picard (1986) discovered that competing papers have marginally significant higher rates for subscriptions than do monopoly papers. An earlier study only partially supported the "benefits-of-competition" theory, revealing that competing papers charge less for single copy sales than joint operating agreement papers, but that the difference in price for monthly subscriptions was not significant (Picard & Fackler, 1985).

Why competing papers' prices have not been found to be significantly lower than those in other types of market situations is not clear from the existing literature. The result may arise, of course, because competing papers do not enjoy the economies of scale made possible by monopoly, chain ownership, joint operating agreements, and similar situations. It may also exist because the few competitive situations left in the United States—less than 5% of cities with newspapers have competing, locally produced newspapers—tend to be in large markets where there may be less price resistance than in smaller markets. Or it may result from the cooperative oligopolistic situations.

The higher unit costs of production and distribution in those situations may also be a cause. Average unit costs for monopoly papers decline as circulation increases (Figure 2). But competition splits the available consumers, thus reducing the size of circulation available to each, retarding achievement of the optimal points on the curve for one or both papers.

Monopolies and Prices

Newspapers that operate as monopolies have several advantages. They can adjust prices upward without significant fear of competition, because the barriers to entry into newspaper markets are extensive. Intermedia competition is not a significant deterrent unless the rate increases for advertising are exorbitant. If, however, a new competitor should seek to enter the newspaper market, the existing paper enjoys economies of scale that the new paper will not enjoy, and the existing paper can use these economies to compete vigorously with the new entry.

In addition, papers operating in monopoly situations can select their optimal quantity of circulation and price per copy or subscription to maximize revenue

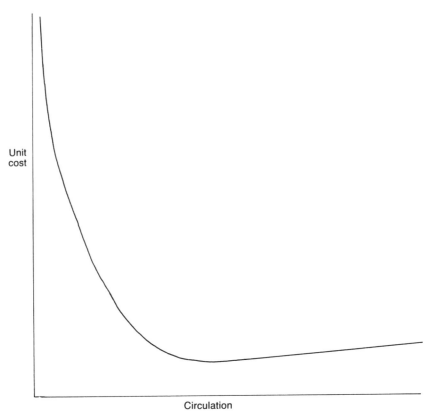

Figure 2.   Cost of Production

and minimize expenses. This can be done without concern about the behavior of competitors that would otherwise affect the economic decisions involved (Figure 3). This engineering of profit is also found in the pricing of advertising.

The literature strongly supports the view that monopoly papers have higher advertising rates than other papers. Only one significant study (Bowers, 1969) has found that monopoly status does not have a major effect on advertising rates. Since that study, researchers have consistently disagreed with its findings.

Grotta (1971) found that papers which become monopolies in a market due to mergers with, or suspension of, a competitor did not pass on the benefits of the new economies of scale to the consumer, but used them for their own enrichment. In fact, the study indicated that the advertiser paid significantly higher rates after consolidation.

Mathewson (1972) found that prices for advertising were slightly higher in monopoly papers than in competing papers and Kerton (1973) found monopolies

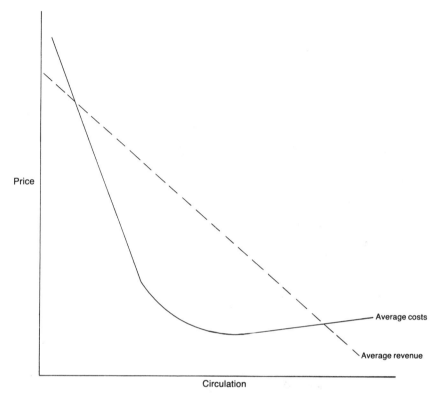

Price

Circulation

Average costs

Average revenue

Figure 3.   Average Cost Curve and Return for Monopoly

had a significant upwards effect on price. Charette, Brown-John, Romanow, and Soderlund (1983) reaffirmed Grotta's 1971 finding that the creation of a monopoly by suspension is associated with higher rates at the surviving paper. A similar result is reported in the Candussi and Winter chapter of this book. Picard (1986) found that monopoly papers had higher milline rates than did competing papers, even though their average circulation was higher and the rate should thus have been lower.

Few circulation price studies comparing monopoly papers with competing papers have been undertaken, and those available are not conclusive. Grotta (1971) indicated that subscription price increases were significantly associated with changes from competing to monopoly situations, as have Candussi and Winter. Picard (1985) found that monopoly papers have significantly lower subscription prices than joint operating newspapers, but that no difference in prices for single copies existed. His study of competing and monopoly papers found monopoly papers had lower subscription rates than competing papers, however (Picard, 1986).

Pricing in Chain-Owned Papers

Studies of the effects of chain ownership on advertising prices brought mixed and conflicting results until the mid 1970s. Definitive conclusions about the effects of chain ownership on the pricing behavior of such papers could not be reached until recent years.

A variety of studies concluded that multiple ownership of papers by a firm or individual did not lead to higher prices. Bowers (1969), Lago (1971), Grotta (1971), and Mathewson (1972) could find no influence of group ownership on prices for advertising. A study of weekly papers under group ownership also found no influence on ad prices (Blankenburg, 1980) and Charette et al. (1983), in a study of Canadian chain-owned papers, found no effect on prices immediately after a paper was acquired by a chain.

As early as 1969, however, Owen found that chain ownership affected national advertising rates, increasing them an average of seven percent. Subsequent studies by Kerton (1973) and by Bloomfield (1978) also found that chain-owned papers had higher prices. John Soloski, in a 1979 study on the effects of chain ownership on newspaper managers, found that the chains set economic goals for papers that led to higher advertising prices and efforts to engineer profit by reducing unprofitable or undesirable circulation to come closer to the optimum point on the cost curve. This, in effect, reduced the number of media consumers the advertisers got for their money and thus resulted in higher prices for reaching consumers, since actual prices did not go down as well.

By the 1980s, studies began to reveal that chain ownership was associated with higher prices. This may have been the result of the increasing profit consciousness of chain operations or better measurement by media researchers.

Studies of Gannett Company papers found that the chain reduced circulation in many of its papers to engineer profit, thus effectively raising prices (Blankenburg, 1982), and that Gannett was associated with higher retail (local) advertising rates—from 7.9% to 18.2% higher depending on the rate considered—than non-chain-owned papers (Blankenburg, 1983). A study that divided chain ownership by the number of papers owned found that size was not an important difference in the behavior of chains. Both small and large papers had higher retail and national rates than independent papers (Ferguson, 1983).

It must be noted that there is an intervening variable in these studies that should be considered and controlled in future research. The fact that chains tend to own monopoly papers needs to be considered, because the price effects measured for chain papers may be due, at least in part, to their monopoly status.

The preponderance of evidence today indicates, however, that chain ownership has in recent years been associated with higher advertising prices—prices that are from 3% to 18% higher than those in nonchain papers. Clearly, the issue of ownership has implications in terms of price behavior.

Studies of the effects of group ownership on circulation prices have been noticeably lacking, but two studies on the topic have concluded that chain ownership leads to higher circulation prices. Blankenburg (1982) concluded that Gannett ownership leads to higher circulation prices, and a 1984 study by Hale concluded that chain-owned papers as a whole charged 14% more for monthly subscriptions than independent papers.

That chain-owned papers charged more for circulation and advertising should not be surprising, since their managers emphasize pricing behavior more than managers of independent papers. In recent years, Allen Neuharth, CEO of Gannett, has urged his executives and those of other companies to raise circulation prices, noting the relative elasticity of demand on circulation. His company has also been especially sensitive to performance issues relative to cost of shares of the firm and has aggressively pursued profits in each of its markets.

Joint Operating Agreement Pricing

Despite the significant amount of discussion of the effects and propriety of joint operating agreements, little study has been made of economic effects of these arrangements. This is surprising, since the agreements violate antitrust laws by permitting price fixing, profit pooling, and market allocation among two papers in a single market.

When the courts found these arrangements a violation of antitrust law, the affected papers petitioned Congress and received an exception to legal prohibitions against anticompetitive practices. Since that statute passed in 1971, little research has explored its effects.

Two recent studies, however, suggest that both the media consumer and the advertiser are being economically disadvantaged by the joint operating agreements. Picard and Fackler (1985) found that joint operating agreement papers charge advertisers more than competing papers. The milline rate for JOA papers was 80% higher for JOAs than for the competing papers, despite the fact that JOA papers had larger average circulation and should thus have had a lower milline rate. The second study compared JOA papers to other monopoly newspapers and found that JOA papers raised their advertising rates 4 1/2 times faster than did monopoly papers in the period 1972–1982 (Picard, 1985).

These two studies also considered the effects of joint operating agreements on circulation prices, but the findings were mixed. Picard and Fackler (1985) found that JOAs had significantly higher single copy prices than competing papers, but Picard (1985) found that the prices were not significantly higher than other monopoly papers. The first study also found the JOA prices for monthly subscriptions were not significantly higher than those for competing papers. The second study, however, concluded that subscription rates for JOA papers were higher than those for other monopoly papers.

These findings about pricing of advertising and circulation for joint operating agreements suggest that the operators of these papers are making significant use of the market and monopoly power available to them by raising prices, and that the public is being economically disadvantaged by this behavior. The limited number of studies and inherent limitation on such studies warrant more research in this area before this evidence can be fully accepted, however.

Cross Ownership and Prices

Research into the question of whether different media owned by the same company leads to higher prices has brought mixed results, but the greater weight of evidence now suggests it does not.

Mathewson (1972) found prices for newspaper ad space in Canada were 24% higher when the paper also owned a television station. Busterna (1976), however, found that such cross ownership did not lead to higher television ad prices and Ferguson in 1983 explored the impact of such cross ownership on newspaper prices. He found that local television and newspaper cross ownership was associated with significantly *lower* daily and Sunday national and retail run-of-paper milinch rates. Wirth and Wollert (1984) also found that ad rates were not higher for combinations and concluded that the cross-media combinations in the same market do not lead to more market power or that the operators of such combinations do not exercise that power that exists.

Summary

Newspaper ownership and market conditions have effects on consumers of newspaper and advertising products that cannot be ignored. While it has been shown that competing newspapers do not necessarily guarantee lower prices, there is greater evidence that various types of noncompetitive situations result in higher prices.

In considering the existing price study literature, one encounters significant variations in advertising rates due to the great number of rates available to different purchasers. In addition, different researchers use different measures of rates, so all studies are not immediately comparable. But some conclusion about the effects of market and ownership conditions are possible:

First, that chain-owned newspapers, joint-operating newspapers, and single-newspaper monopolies generally charge higher prices than newspapers engaged in direct competition.

Second, that economies of scale created through chain ownership, joint operating agreements, and single newspaper monopolies are not passed on to the advertisers or newspaper consumers, but are retained and used to boost profits to owners.

Third, that cross ownership of media does not seem to affect pricing behavior.

These findings raise significant issues that must be considered. Monopolies, joint-operating agreements, and concentrated ownership all run counter to the free marketplace ideal of capitalist society, in that they place great market power and economic control in the hands of the newspaper owners involved.

Since price studies indicate that these individuals are using that market power, one must consider their behavior as possible violations of antitrust legislation.

Chain ownership has the potential of violating such legislation if power is concentrated in the hands of a single or a few companies. Today, however, while economic concentration does not exist in great enough quantities to induce government action in the U.S., the situation is quite different in Canada, as Chapter 6 and other chapters will reveal.

Joint operating agreement papers have been judged to be operating in violation of antitrust laws, and special interest legislation—in the form of the Newspaper Preservation Act—has made it possible for them to continue doing so. If further significant evidence shows that these papers engaging in joint operations are using their power to disadvantage readers and advertisers, it may be appropriate to amend the NPA to provide some overview of their pricing behavior.

Single-newspaper monopolies present the most significant threat to consumers today, since they encompass most of the newspaper industry. Since the newspaper product in one market is not comparable to that in another—in terms of local news and advertising, at least—those produced outside the primary market area of the "monopoly" paper are not directly substitutable.

Should the monopoly situations continue and pricing behavior consistently disadvantage consumers, it may be necessary to oversee the business operations of these papers in some manner. This might come through significant enforcement of antitrust laws regarding the papers' behavior toward weekly competitors or any new daily newspaper that might try to enter in the market.

Tax and other fiscal advantages that papers enjoy might be removed from monopolies or those which behave in a manner injurious to competition that are not subject to current antitrust enforcement.

CHAPTER 4

Limits of Competition

Diana Stover Tillinghast

Department of Journalism and Mass
Communications
San Jose State University

Economic factors affecting newspaper production have led to concentration in the press, and a rush to chain ownership has resulted in a decline in independent ownership (Bishop, 1972), as well as a final phase of concentration where there was a rush of larger chains buying smaller chains (Bagdikian, 1977). As a result of chain ownership and the economic conditions under which papers operate, readers in most communities have the choice of only one daily newspaper. Critics of increasing economic concentration and concentration of ownership of the press charge that an effect of chain ownership is mediocre monopoly newspapers interested more in profits than in serving their readers or the communities in which they operate. However, the story of newspaper concentration has had a different ending in Southern California where there is vigorous competition among chain newspapers. Rosse's (1975) "umbrella theory" will be used to explain the extent, nature, and limitations of this competition. Rosse developed his layer or "umbrella model" of newspaper competition in media-rich metropolitan areas, noting that competition exists between papers in different layers, rather than within layers. In descending order, the four layers are metropolitan papers, satellite city papers, suburban dailies, and less-than-daily newspapers and shoppers. He found that newspapers in each layer compete with higher-layer newspapers for audience attention and advertising dollars. Rosse noted that the circulation of metropolitan newspapers, which forms an umbrella over the market, becomes less dense as one moves away from the center of the market. As a result, the metropolitan papers are at a comparative disadvantage in serving advertisers and readers with more localized interests. Rosse also noted that vigorous intercity competition can result in audience and advertising shifts from layer to layer; these shifts can result from small changes in advertising or subscription prices as well as from increases or decreases in the amount of local news.

The Rosse model has been useful in explaining competition among newspapers in urban areas. Lacy (1984), who studied competition in 13 large metropolitan areas in the Southwest, found partial support for a hypothesis stating that competition from layers above is greater than competition from layers below, and support for a hypothesis stating that interlayer competition is a threat to the survival of some lower-level newspapers. But Lacy questioned Rosse's contention that the economic base of metropolitan dailies would eventually be eroded by suburban newspapers. His study supported the view of Roberts (1968), who predicted that metropolitan dailies would eventually drive suburban newspapers out of business. Lacy noted, however, that his results may have been different had he not combined the satellite city and suburban layers of newspapers.

In a later article, Lacy (1985) reiterated his concern about the possibility of metropolitan dailies expanding their markets through umbrella competition at the expense of small daily and weekly newspapers. He found that umbrella competition for circulation appears to be greater in metropolitan areas with monopoly-control city papers than in those with competitive central city papers. However, he found the opposite for advertising competition, suggesting that advertisers appear to be more affected by distance than readers.

This chapter examines the competition among newspapers in one of the most affluent and fastest growing areas of the country—Los Angeles, Orange, and San Diego Counties. Newspapers in these three Southern California counties are increasing their staffs and expanding their suburban coverage in their battles for the affluent suburban reader. As a result, readers can receive local news in more than one daily newspaper.

Rosse's umbrella theory will be used as a framework to examine the extent, nature, and the limits of competition in the first three layers of newspapers. The primary focus of this chapter will be on newspapers in Los Angeles and Orange Counties since they comprise the primary market area for the *Los Angeles Times*, the major metropolitan paper.

Ownership of Southern California Dailies

The battle for readers and advertisers in Los Angeles, Orange, and San Diego Counties is primarily a battle among large, well-financed newspaper chains. All but one of the daily newspapers, the *Daily News*, is owned by a newspaper chain.

The major players are Times Mirror Company with the *Times*, Freedom Newspapers in Orange County with the *Register* and the smaller suburban dailies in Anaheim and La Habra, Knight-Ridder Newspapers with the Long Beach and Pasadena papers, and Copley Newspapers with the *Union* and *Tribune* in San Diego and three South Bay newspapers in Los Angeles County—the papers in Torrance, Santa Monica, and San Pedro. Although it is not considered much of a competitive threat in the three-county market, the Hearst Corporation with its *Herald-Examiner* is still an important competitor. The Tribune Co., which publishes the (Escondido) *Times-Advocate* in San Diego County, was a major player before it got out of the newspaper business in Los Angeles County when it sold the *Daily News* for $176 million in 1985, making a hefty profit of about $152 million on the 4-day-a-week free distribution paper it purchased in 1973 (Endicott, 1986; Reinhardt, 1986; California Newspaper Publishers Association, 1986). By the time it sold the paper to Jack Kent Cooke, Washington Redskins' owner, the *Daily News* had carved out a market niche in the San Fernando Valley and was providing stiff competition to the *Times*. Cooke is not a novice when it comes to the newspaper business. He acquired his wealth, estimated at $800 million, through Canadian newspaper and broadcasting ventures with Roy Thompson.

Other chains in the three-county area include Thompson Newspapers with the San Gabriel Valley and Whittier papers, Ingersoll Publications with the *Orange Coast Daily Pilot* and the Glendale and Burbank papers, the Donrey Media Group with the Pomona paper, and Scripps Howard with the paper in Fullerton. In San Diego County, Howard has its corporate headquarters in Oceanside where it publishes the *Blade-Tribune*; it also publishes the paper in San Clemente, which is in Orange County just north of Oceanside. Also in San Diego County, *The Daily Californian* in El Cajon is a Landmark Communications property.

The 12 chains with newspaper properties in the three counties read like a list of Who's Who among chain ownership. Three of the chains rank among Fortune 500's largest American corporations, with Times Mirror ranked 135th, The Tribune Co. ranked 187th, and Knight-Ridder ranked 213th (Taylor, 1986). Advertising Age ranked all 12 of the chains among the top 100 media companies in the United States in total media revenues (Endicott, 1986). The chains ranked from 5th through 63rd in total media revenues, with Times Mirror ranking 5th and Howard 63rd. The Tribune Company ranked 9th, Knight-Ridder 10th, and Hearst 11th. All 12 of the chains ranked among Advertising Age's top 39 chains in the total amount of newspaper revenues, with Times Mirror 2nd, Knight-Ridder 3rd, the Tribune Co. 4th, Hearst 8th and Scripps Howard 9th. In addition, all but two of the chains rank among the top 20 chains in the country in daily circulation, with Knight-Ridder 2nd, the Tribune Co. 4th, Times Mirror 5th, Scripps Howard 9th, and Thompson 10th (American Newspaper Publishers Association, 1986). The only major chain not active in the market is Gannett.

The *Times'* Umbrella

The *Times*, with a daily circulation of 1,057,533 and a Sunday circulation of 1,374,642,[1] forms an umbrella over the Southern California newspaper market. The *Times* dominates an 11-county area from San Luis Obispo on the north to San Diego on the south, San Bernardino on the east, and the Pacific Ocean on the west. Its penetration is 18%, as compared with 6% for the Copley-owned *San Diego Union* and *Tribune*, 5% for Freedom's Orange County Metro Group that includes the *Register*, 4% for the *Herald-Examiner*, and 3% each for the *Daily News*, the *Press-Telegram*, the three Copley-owned suburban dailies in the South Bay area of Los Angeles County, and the *Riverside Press Enterprise* (Union-Tribune Publishing Company, 1986).

The 11-country marketing area, which has a population of 15.6 million, is extremely affluent. It outranks the New York and Chicago marketing areas in effective buying income and in total retail sales (Union-Tribune Publishing Company, 1986). In 1985, its effective buying income was $188.8 billion, and its retail sales were $92.9 billion.

The main battleground for surburban circulation in Southern California, however, is in the region's three most populous, affluent, and growing counties—Los Angeles, Orange, and San Diego. The three counties have 78% of the population of Southern California and 80% of all the business activity (Union-Tribune Publishing Company, 1986). In 1985, their effective buying income was $150.3 billion and their retail sales were $74 billion. In the three-county area, which has a population of 12.1 million, 24 daily newspapers were vying for readers and advertisers at the start of 1985. In terms of layers of competition, the *Times* and the *Herald-Examiner* are the metropolitan competitors, the *Register* and the *Union* and *Tribune* are satellite city papers, and the remaining 20 suburban newspapers comprise the third layer of daily newspapers.

Although the *Herald-Examiner* also shares the metropolitan layer of newspapers with the *Times*, it has steadily lost circulation and advertising linage, to the point that neither the *Times* nor the suburban dailies in the three-county area consider it much of a threat. As Gottlieb (1977) noted:

> The *Herald-Examiner* . . . is but a pale imitation of a metropolitan daily. It is a paper that for more than a decade has lost an average of 35,000 readers and a million lines of advertising each year. What was once (briefly) the biggest-circula-

---

[1] Unless otherwise specified, circulation statistics in this chapter are based on the annual Audit Bureau of Circulations' "ABC Audit Report: Newspaper" for 1985 for all but 4 newspapers. Circulation figures for the (Fullerton) *Daily News Tribune* and the (Downey) *Southeast News Signal*, which ceased publication in 1985, are based on the latest ABC reports available—the 1984 "ABC Audit Report: Newspaper" and the "Newspaper Publishers' Statement" for six months ending March 31, 1985, respectively. The Glendale and Burbank papers—which are not ABC papers—provided 1985 VAC figures and other necessary circulation data.

tion afternoon daily in the country has lost half its readers; its ad linage has fallen below the levels of the papers in, say, Shreveport, Louisiana, or Huntsville, Alabama. (p. 34)

In the 20-year period from 1966 to 1985, the paper's daily circulation dropped from 718,963 to 235,138, and its Sunday circulation dropped from 707,141 to 214,705 (Audit Bureau of Circulations, 1966 and 1985). The *Herald-Examiner* is a thin paper that runs little advertising. In 1985, the *Times* ran almost six times as much full-run linage as the *Herald-Examiner*.[2]

In the second layer of newspapers, two satellite city papers—the *Orange County Register* and the *San Diego Union* and *Tribune*—are the dominant papers in their respective counties. The *Register* has a daily circulation of 288,261 and a Sunday circulation of 321,365, and the *Union* and *Tribune* have a combined daily circulation of 356,354 and a combined Sunday circulation of 371,517.

The Register, the flagship of Freedom Newspapers, a chain of newspapers that once openly promoted the owners' libertarian philosophy in its news columns, improved dramatically in the late 1970s, particularly after the arrival of a new publisher, R. David Threshie. The paper switched to offset, invested in color printing technology, underwent a typographical redesign, and expanded and improved its news coverage. In 1985 it won a Pulitzer Prize for its photographic coverage—all in color—of the 1984 Los Angeles Olympics. It has established 32 "Neighbors" sections—weekly tabloids that provide local news and advertising.

In San Diego, the *Union* and *Tribune* have also expanded and improved their coverage. In 1986, based on an extensive readership study directed by the news department, the paper created a weekly television magazine and established five zoned daily news sections for both the morning and afternoon editions. The zoned sections provide San Diego news and news from four separate areas in the county. The two north county sections are aimed at attracting readers from one of the fastest growing regions in the country. The San Diego Association of Governments estimates that the population of north county will double between 1980 and the year 2000, reaching more than one million (Weintraub & Ray, 1983).

Twenty suburban dailies form the third layer of newspaper competition in the three-county market area. Of these, two newspapers have circulations of well over 100,000 and have generally been successful in keeping the *Times* at bay in their primary market areas.

The *Daily News* rose to journalistic respectability from a throw-away shopper, the *Valley News and Green Sheet*, which had a good reputation as the best place to sell one's old refrigerator. The *Valley News*, founded in 1911, developed its

---

[2] Calculated from Media Records Inc. year end figures from "December and Annual 1985" report for Los Angeles.

foothold in the San Fernando Valley by providing residents of the rural and sparsely populated area with local news. Although the Valley is in northern Los Angeles and is within the city limits, it is physically separated from the rest of the city by the Santa Monica Mountains. By 1959, when the paper began publishing 4 days a week, it was being delivered to more than 117,000 homes in 15 Valley communities. After the Tribune Company purchased the *Valley News* in 1973, it began converting to a paid circulation paper; it added a fifth day of publication in 1976, a sixth day in 1977, and a Sunday edition in 1979. In 1981, the name was changed to the *Daily News* and, in 1982, it achieved 100% paid circulation. By the mid-1980s, the *Daily News* had matured into a very typographically attractive, full-service newspaper that emphasized local news to the point that it almost belied the fact it was being distributed in a metropolitan region of 1.8 million residents. With a total daily circulation of 143,228 and a Sunday circulation of 162,360 in 1985, the paper was the largest suburban daily in the Los Angeles–Orange County newspaper market.

Although the *Times'* circulation and penetration have always been low in Long Beach, matters were not helped much by the Knight-Ridder merger in 1974, which resulted in improved editorial quality at the *Press-Telegram*, a Ridder newspaper. In recent years, the *Press-Telegram* has expanded its local coverage. It provides partial zoning of its local news section 3 days a week. It has divided its market into a north and south zone, permitting it to use the front page and the jump page of the local section for hard news from each of the areas. In addition, it publishes a weekly "People" section, containing features, youth sports, and a crime watch, that is delivered to readers in five zones. The *Press-Telegram* controls more of the weekday and Sunday circulation in its city zone than any other newspaper in the Los Angeles-Orange county market. It controls 71% of the daily circulation and 65% of the Sunday circulation in its city zone, as compared with 25% and 28%, respectively, for the *Times*. Its weekday penetration in its market area is 31% and its Sunday penetration is 34%, as compared with a 15% weekday and 21% Sunday penetration for the *Times*.

The *Times'* Push for Suburban Circulation

Since the *Times* does not do well among the low income, largely minority residents in central Los Angeles, it has pursued an editorial and marketing policy that links its survival and growth to its ability to expand, not only into the suburbs that ring its city zone, but also into the growth areas of Southern California, particularly Orange and San Diego Counties. Two of the Times' corporate goals for the 1980s are to expand circulation among a quality demographic audience and to undertake market expansion into contiguous areas (Times Mirror, 1979). This policy has meant that readers in central Los Angeles are the only readers who do not receive a zoned section especially designed for their area. In contrast, the *Times* publishes zoned sections for suburban areas in the rest of Los Angeles County as well as its separate San Fernando Valley, Orange County, and San Diego County editions.

Although the *Times* has been in the suburban market since 1952 when it began its first suburban sections, the quest for the suburban reader did not begin in earnest until the late 1960s. In 1968, the paper began publishing a separate Orange County edition from a satellite news and production facility in Costa Mesa. By 1972, the editorial expenditures for the edition were $868,023. By 1984, editorial costs had risen to more than $414 million. Ten years after it established the edition in Orange County, the *Times* crossed the county line into San Diego County and established its second edition there. By 1980, editorial costs were almost $1.7 million in San Diego and, by 1984, they had risen to almost $2.3 million. Although it created a separate news and advertising operation in San Diego, it published the edition from its Orange County plant.

When its $96 million satellite printing plant in the San Fernando Valley, which also houses news, advertising, and circulation, was completed in late 1984, the *Times* established a Valley edition. It added 25 staffers, bringing its Valley editorial staff to 37. By the start of 1985, editorial costs for the Valley edition were almost $1.3 million. In comparison, the costs to produce the suburban sections containing Valley news were $195,017 in 1972, $219,415 in 1976, and $402,541 in 1980, when the *Times* had only 12 full-time staffers.

By the late 1970s and early 1980s, it was clear to anyone watching the growth and improvement of the surburban dailies that the *Times* would have to fight for any circulation gains it hoped to get in its primary market areas (Malan, 1982; Haerle, 1984). At the time, Tom Johnson, *Times* publisher, noting that the paper's suburban competition used to be largely advertising products, stressed that this was no longer the case:

> They are improving. They are becoming legitimate news products, and they can be improved even further. We know that they can be improved further. . . . The *Los Angeles Times* is up against increasingly more professional competition out of newspapers in the San Fernando Valley—the *Valley News* (now the *Daily News*), *The Register* in Orange County, Knight-Ridder in Long Beach.[3]

The *Times* viewed its goal of pursuing suburban readers as so crucial to its survival that, in 1980, it committed $215.6 million to improve its printing quality and to increase its press capacity to enable it to expand its coverage of the suburbs and to deliver the paper to suburban readers more quickly and efficiently. On many heavy advertising days, its press capacity was strained to the limits as the result of two market segmentation strategies—topical and geograph-

---

[3] From interview with Tom Johnson, publisher of the *Los Angeles Times* and vice chairman of Times Mirror, conducted at the *Times*, Dec. 10, 1980.

ical segmentation. In 1980 it introduced two new daily topical sections—Calendar and Finance. At the same time, in addition to the Orange County and San Diego editions, it was improving and expanding its suburban coverage in its zoned sections for suburban readers in Los Angeles County. The *Times*, even if it wanted to, could not print much more than it was already printing, much less introduce new topical or suburban sections. Although the *Daily News* was making inroads in the San Fernando Valley, the *Times* was not able to establish an edition there until after its satellite printing plant in the Valley was completed in 1984.

The *Times* committed tremendous resources to news coverage during the 1970s and early 1980s. During the period from 1972 through 1984, the *Times*' editorial budget increased from $13.3 million to $56.4 million, a 324% increase. Even after accounting for inflation, the increases represent actual increases in editorial expenditures, since the consumer price index for all urban consumers (CPI-U) rose only 173% during the period. The *Times* expanded its suburban and topical coverage without abandoning its financial commitment to traditional hard news. Unlike other metropolitan newspapers that have cut their hard news to pay for the expansion of suburban and topical news, the *Times* pursued a strategy that assumed that upscale suburban readers wanted metropolitan, national, and foreign news as well as topical news and news about what was going on in their local communities. The *Times* expenditures for hard news went up 363% during the 13-year period, increasing from $3.9 million in 1972 to $17.9 million in 1984. The paper spent more than five times as much for suburban news in 1984 than it had spent 13 years earlier. During the 13-year period when spending went from $1.9 to $11.9 million, suburban news operations gained a larger share of the *Times* total editorial budget, increasing from 14% to 21%.

Although similar financial data were not available for the *Times*' three largest competitiors, all have met the *Times*' challenge by increasing their staffs. The editor of the *San Diego Union*, Gerald Warren, reported that the *Union* began gradually increasing its staff in 1975 when he became editor, explaining that the decision predated the *Times*' 1978 foray into San Diego County. However, Warren added that the *Times*' move probably speeded up the paper's timetable for staff expansion. From 1975 to 1978, the staff increased from 162 to 177; and from 1978 to 1986, it jumped to 259.[4]

One of the first things R. David Threshie did when he came to the *Register* as publisher in 1979 was to increase the newsroom staff. The *Register's* editorial budget quadrupled, and the number of news staffers increased from 118 to 296 in 1986.[5] A steady and extensive growth in circulation and advertising led to the

---

[4] From interview with Gerald Warren, editor of *The San Diego Union*, conducted at the *Union*, July 24, 1986.

[5] From interview with Chris Anderson, editor of the *Orange County Register*, conducted at the *Register*, June 27, 1986.

construction of a $25-million building to house the *Register*, in which newsroom space was more than tripled when the building was completed in 1986. Like the *Union* and the *Register*, the *Daily News* also increased its newsroom staff. The paper had 120 staffers when it added a Sunday edition in 1979. In 1984, when the *Times* started its Valley edition, the *Daily News* had 175 editorial staffers; by 1986, the number had increased to 215.[6]

Intercity Competition

Intercity competition is found throughout the Southern California newspaper market of Los Angeles, Orange, and San Diego Counties. In the three counties, readers and advertisers have their choice of at least three daily newspapers. In Los Angeles, the choice is between the *Times*, the *Herald-Examiner* and, for residents of the San Fernando Valley area of the city, the *Daily News*. In addition, Spanish-speaking residents of Los Angeles can subscribe to *La Opinion*, which serves 37,013 daily and 27,568 Sunday readers. Long Beach residents can choose from the locally published *Press-Telegram*, the nearby (San Pedro) *News Pilot*, the *Times*, the *Herald-Examiner*, or the *Register*.

In Orange County in the Disneyland city of Anaheim, the choice of papers includes the *Anaheim Bulletin* and the *Register* as well as the Los Angeles metros. In northern San Diego County, where many residents have moved south from Los Angeles or Orange counties, the choice is between one of the two fast-growing local dailies—the (Escondido) *Times-Advocate* or the (Oceanside) *Blade Tribune*—the *San Diego Union* or *Tribune*, the *Register*, and the *Times*.

Rosse (1975) noted that, when vigorous intercity competition occurs, it can result in audience and advertising shifts from layer to layer. The shifts in the Los Angeles–Orange County market have ranged from the movement of newspapers from a higher level to a lower level and vice versa, and layer-to-layer shifts in circulation and advertising.

The competition has led to market consolidation, resulting in a net decrease in the number of dailies. Although there were 22 dailies in Los Angeles and Orange Counties in 1980, by 1986 there were only 17 dailies. In 1985 alone, three small newspapers went from Monday–Friday publication to less than daily publication. They were the (Downey) *Southeast News Signal*, which controlled less than one-third of the circulation in its city zone, giving up almost half of the total daily circulation to the *Times* and 18% to other suburbans. The picture was even grimmer for the Burbank and Fullerton papers. The *Burbank Daily Review* controlled only 20% of the circulation in its city zone, and the *Daily News*

---

[6] From interview with Ali Sar, managing editor of the *Daily News*, conducted at the *Daily News*, June 26, 1986.

Tribune controlled only 23%. Although the three newspapers are no longer daily, they were included in the circulation analysis in this chapter because the data illustrate the competitive problems they had in trying to exist as third layer newspapers.

The *Register* and the *Daily News* are good examples of newspapers that have moved from a lower layer to a higher layer. The *Register* moved from the suburban paper layer to the satellite city newspaper layer. For many years, the *Register*—formerly called the *Santa Ana Register*—did not have much circulation outside of the Santa Ana area. It then expanded throughout Orange County and now has the second highest circulation in the Los Angeles–Orange County market. The *Daily News*, once a throw-away shopper, moved up to become part of the suburban daily newspaper layer and the fourth largest daily in the two-county market.

Circulation and advertising data also show that the intense competition has resulted in reader and advertiser shifts. A comparison of circulation data for the *Times*, the *Register*, and the 17 suburban dailies in the *Times'* primary market area for 1980 and 1985 indicates that there have been slight shifts. Although the *Times'* share of weekday newspaper circulation (48%) remained the same in 1985 as it was in 1980, its Sunday share decreased from 56% to 53%. Two percent of the *Times'* 3% decrease went to the suburbans, and the remaining 1% went to the *Register*. In 1985, the suburbans controlled 37% of the daily circulation and the *Register* controlled 15%. From 1980 to 1985, the *Register*, was able to increase its weekday market share from 13% to 15%—at the expense of a 2% loss for the suburban dailies.

In Orange County, there has been an unmistakable weakening of the *Times'* role as an effective umbrella for the county's 780,600 households. There has been a circulation shift away from the *Times* toward the *Register*. In 1970—2 years after it began its Orange County edition—the *Times* had a daily circulation in Orange County of 121,607 and a Sunday circulation of 162,207. The *Register's* 1970 daily circulation of 140,916 in Orange County was 19,309 more than the *Times'*, but its Sunday circulation of 142,339 was 19,868 less than the *Times'*. By 1985, however, the *Register* had clearly become the dominant paper in Orange County. Its daily circulation increased by 92% to 270,663, and its Sunday circulation increased by 111% to 300,867. During the same period, the *Times'* daily circulation increased only 33% to 161,532, and its Sunday circulation increased only 27% to 206,453.

In the San Fernando Valley, although the *Daily News* has not surpassed the *Times* in circulation, it has been gaining ground. In 1985, in the *Daily News* primary market area, the *Daily News* had a daily circulation of 112,084 and a Sunday circulation of 124,230, as compared with the *Times'* daily circulation of 129,311 and its Sunday circulation of 164,932.

Advertising data show that the intense competition has resulted in shifts in advertising from layer to layer.[7] One indication of a change in the advertising market is simply the growth in advertising volume by the largest papers in the *Times'* primary market area. In 1975, although the *Times* topped the list of the top 10 newspapers in total advertising linage, none of the competitors in its market made the list. In 1985, however, the *Register* was ranked 4th nationally in total inches of full-run advertising, and the *Times* ranked 2nd. The *Daily News* and the *Press-Telegram* also made the 1985 list of the top 50 newspapers in full-run advertising inches; the *Daily News* ranked 19th and the *Press-Telegram* ranked 44th.

Much of the growth in advertising volume for the *Register* and the *Daily News* has occurred in the 1980s. From 1980 through 1986, the *Register's* inches of full-run advertising increased from 4.6 to 5.3 million, and the *Daily News'* inches of advertising increased from 2.8 to 3.4 million. The *Press-Telegram* increased its advertising from 1.9 to 2.1 million inches. During the same period, the *Times'* full-run advertising inches showed a decrease of about 115,000 lines. In the intervening years, to compete with the *Register* and other suburban dailies that could offer advertisers local buys, the *Times* had to offer more advertisers part-run advertising.

Advertising figures for the five largest dailies in the Los Angeles–Orange County market show that, between 1979 and 1986, the *Times'* share of full-run advertising decreased from 37% to 33%. The *Register*, which—like the Times— had to compete for advertising dollars with suburban papers and the proliferating less-than-daily publications in Orange County by offering more part-run advertising, had a 30% full-run advertising share in 1979 and a 31% share in 1986. The *Daily News* gained the most in terms of market share—helping to keep the *Register's* share from going up and cutting into the *Times'* share. It went from a 16% share in 1979, when it started its Sunday edition, to 20% in 1986. The *Herald-Examiner* had a 5% share in 1979 and 1986. The *Press-Telegram's* share of the advertising market dropped from a 13% share in 1979 to a 12% share in 1986.

For years the *Times* had a virtual lock on the very lucrative department-store advertising because its regional circulation was attractive to department-store chains with outlets throughout Southern California. In recent years, however, Freedom's Orange County Metro Group, the Copley papers, the *Daily News*, and Knight-Ridder's *Press-Telegram* and (Pasadena) *Star News* have become much more aggressive in selling advertising to store chains. Rather than automatically positioning their papers as the second buy, they have shown advertisers that they can buy a combination of suburban papers and get coverage that is

---

[7] The advertising data in this section are based on a combination of Media Records figures and summaries and/or measurements provided by the *Times*, the *Register*, the *Daily News*, and the *Press-Telegram*.

better than, or equal to, that of the *Times.* There is evidence that the str. gy may be beginning to work Advertising lineage figures for the six largest news-papers in the Los Angeles–Orange County market as well as the *Star News* show that the *Times'* share field is decreasing while the *Register* and the *Daily News* are increasing their share of department store linage. The *Press-Telegram's* depart-ment store advertising share remains about the same.

The Limits of Competition

Although there is extensive competition in the Southern California market, it is important to explore the nature of the competition and the limits of the competi-tion. The competition in Southern California conforms to the three important limits outlined by Rosse (1975):

(1) The circulation of metropolitan papers becomes less dense as one moves away from the center of the market, and, as a result, the metropolitan papers are at a competitive disadvantage in serving advertisers and readers with more localized interests.
(2) The competition is primarily between layers, not within layers, with news-papers in each layer competing with higher layers newspapers for audience attention and advertising dollars.
(3) Within a given layer, the circulation zones of similar sized newspapers in that layer overlap very little, if at all.

Limits on the *Times*

Even the tremendous outlay of funds for capital investment and expanded news coverage have not allowed the *Times* to overcome market limitations to growth in areas away from the center of its market. One example is its inability to dominate the market in Orange County. But the best example of this limitation is the *Times'* 1978 move to San Diego, an expensive proposition in terms of news-gathering expenses alone. In 1978, the *Times'* daily circulation in San Diego County was 27,612, and its Sunday circulation was 37,410. During the next 7 years, the *Times* gained only 21,419 daily and 16,839 Sunday circulation. Dur-ing the same period, the *Union* and *Tribune* gained 24,919 daily and 45,531 Sunday.

The *Times,* with only 6% daily and 7% Sunday penetration in San Diego County, simply cannot deliver the readers that advertisers want to reach in their local city and retail trading zones. One reason is that the three largest local newspapers in the county have penetration rates that are considered high for Southern California. The *Union* and *Tribune* have a daily penetration of 46% and a Sunday penetration of 48% in San Diego County, the highest of any newspaper in the three-county area. In northern San Diego County, the Escondido paper has a 34% daily and a 36% Sunday penetration in its market, and the Oceanside paper has a 35% daily and a 36% Sunday penetration in its market. Although Rosse (1975) noted that metropolitan newspapers have a comparative advantage over smaller papers in attracting national and regional advertisers for whom their entire circulation is valuable, he indicated that they are at a comparative disadvantage when they compete with smaller papers for local advertisers. Although "their larger circulation makes profitable a higher level of editorial quality (better features, reporters and editors) which gives them an advantage in attracting audiences with less localized interests" (p. 13), Rosse noted that they simply cannot carry as many local stories per community as their smaller competitors. Rosse added that, as the advertising market shifts away from national and regional advertisers to local advertisers, "the comparative advantage in competing for audience attention shifts away from audiences interested in a 'quality' paper and towards audiences with more localized interests" (p. 14). Tichenor, Donohue, and Olien (1980) suggested that reading about one's community in a neighborhood section of a metropolitan newspaper may be a far different experience from seeing it in a suburban newspaper. They found that regional dailies do not address local concerns the way a hometown paper would, and that their readers see their community through the lenses of a distant city, rather than through the eyes of neighbors and local institutions. Like Bogart and Orenstein (1965), Tichenor et al. suggested that perhaps a metropolitan daily may attract a "quite select audience for news purposes, a relatively sophisticated segment of the total population which views life in a more cosmopolitan way than is true for the average socioeconomic level in the population" (p. 58).

Newspaper Layers and Limits

All of the newspapers in Los Angeles and Orange Counties have their largest share of the circulation market in their city zones and are not able to control as large a percentage of circulation outside their city zones.[8] This holds for both weekday and Sunday circulation.

---

[8] The following analysis of competition in the primary market areas of newspapers in Los Angeles and Orange Counties is based on ABC or VAC data as noted in Footnote 1. City-by-city circulation breakdowns for each newspaper were used to calculate the extent to which other newspapers also circulated in a newspaper's city and retail trading zones. A majority of newspapers divide their primary market areas into two zones—city and retail trading zones. However, for the 7 newspapers that have newspaper designated market areas as their primary market areas, their markets were divided into city zone and retail trading zone equivalents for analysis purposes. Since the *Times* has only a designated market area, its market was divided into a city zone equivalent consisting of the same area included in the *Herald-Examiner's* ABC Los Angeles city zone and a retail trading zone that includes the remainder of Los Angeles County and all of Orange County. The *Register's*

More important, the competition among the newspapers is primarily between layers—not within layers. This holds across circulation zones—city and retail trading—and across days of publication—weekdays and Sundays. All newspapers feel the competition from the umbrella paper, the *Los Angeles Times*, and—although it is not much of a competitive threat—the *Herald-Examiner* picks up a small amount of circulation on weekdays and Sundays in the city zones of all but three newspapers and in the retail trading zones of all newspapers. And, in Orange County, although the *Times* is a strong competitor, the *Register* is even a stronger competitor against the suburban dailies.

The *Times* controls a majority of the circulation in its city zone—52% on weekdays and 58% on Sundays—but slips to 40% on weekdays and 48% on Sundays in its retail trading zone. The *Times* competes with the *Herald-Examiner* in the metropolitan layer of newspapers and with newspapers in the two levels below it. In both its city and retail trading zones on weekdays and Sundays, however, the *Times* has managed to hold the *Herald-Examiner* to 18% or less of the total circulation. The *Herald-Examiner* is competitive only in the *Times'* city zone since it controls 18% of the weekday and 15% of the Sunday circulation, as compared with only 6% of the weekday and 5% of the Sunday circulation in the *Times'* retail trading zone. The *Times* is faced with fairly heavy competition from suburban dailies, giving up a market share that ranges from 27% to 33% of the weekday and Sunday circulation in its city and retail trading zones.

The *Times'* single largest competitor and its major competitive threat is the *Register*, a satellite city newspaper. Although the *Register* does not circulate in the *Times'* city zone, it controls 21% of the weekday circulation and 19% of the Sunday circulation in the *Times'* retail trading zone, which includes Los Angeles County suburbs and all of Orange County. However, since the *Register* circulates only in Orange County, it is important to determine how the *Times* fares against the *Register* there. In the *Register's* city zone, the *Times* has 30% of the weekday circulation and 32% of the Sunday circulation, as compared with the *Register's* 62% weekday and 57% Sunday circulation. In the *Register's* retail trading zone, the *Register* is not quite as strong, gaining only a 41% share of the weekday circulation and a 48% share of the Sunday circulation. In comparison, the *Times* has a 35% weekday share, and a 45% share of the Sunday circulation in the *Register's* retail trading zone.

---

designated market area was divided into a city zone equivalent consisting of Santa Ana and 14 nearby cities and a retail trading zone that includes the remainder of Orange County. The *Daily News'* designated market was divided into a city zone equivalent of San Fernando and all 15 unincorporated communities in the San Fernando Valley that are within the City of Los Angeles and a retail trading zone consisting of the remainder of the designated market area including Burbank. For the other four newspaper designated market papers, the following cities of publication serve as city zone equivalents and the retail trading zone equivalents consist of the remainder of the designated market: Pomona, *Progress Bulletin*; Anaheim, *Anaheim Bulletin*; La Habra, *Daily Star Progress*; Torrance, *The Daily Breeze*.

The *Register* is thus in an enviable market position. It is more than holding its own against the *Times* and faces little competition from the second metropolitan paper, the *Herald-Examiner*. It has the home court advantage because its metro competitors and Los Angeles County suburban competitors have to cross city and county lines to come into Orange County, its primary market area. The *Register* faces few threats from the suburban dailies in Orange County since its largest competitor, the *Orange Coast Daily Pilot* has a daily circulation of only 32,281 and a Sunday circulation of 32,270, and since the *Register's* parent company also owns the Anaheim and Fullerton papers.

The *Times* represents the greatest competitive threat for the suburban layer of papers as a whole. This is true for all 12 of the suburban daily papers in Los Angeles County and the 5 suburban dailies in Orange County where the *Times* and the *Register* together create a significant barrier to circulation growth for the five suburban dailies. In Orange County, the *Times* and the *Register* together control 58 to 81% of the weekday and 70 to 97% of the Sunday circulation in the city zones of the five suburbans. Even worse is the market share of the Orange County suburbans in their retail trading zones. The *Times* and the *Register* together control 75 to 84% of the weekday and 77 to 97% of the Sunday circulation in their retail trading zones.

Although there is vigorous competition among the metropolitan, satellite city, and suburban layers of newspapers, there is little competition within the same layer of newspapers. The only significant within layer competition is between the *Times* and the *Herald-Examiner*, but, as the circulation and advertising figures indicate, the *Herald-Examiner* has fallen far behind the *Times* in the battle for readers and advertisers.

There is not very much competition within the suburban layer of newspapers. This result supports the umbrella theory that holds that there is little competition within newspaper layers. There is a virtual absence of competition within the suburban layer of papers on weekdays in the city zones of 8 of the 12 suburban papers in Los Angeles County and all 5 of the suburban papers in Orange County. As noted earlier, two of the suburbans in Los Angeles County have reacted to the extensive competition in their market areas by going to less than daily publication. The finding of little competition among suburban newspapers on weekdays in their city zones holds on Sundays for the suburban dailies that publish on Sundays. This is not the case on Sundays, however, in the city zones of newspapers that do not publish Sunday editions. The six largest Los Angeles County suburban dailies have been somewhat successful in moving into the Sunday circulation voids created by the six smaller Los Angeles County suburbans, capturing from 25% to 57% of the total circulation in their city zones. Despite these inroads, the *Times* is the primary beneficiary of the Sunday circulation void since it controls from 37% to 74% of the Sunday circulation in the city zones of the Los Angeles County suburban dailies without Sunday editions. In Orange County, the *Register* and the *Times* together pick up almost all of the circulation in the suburban city zones on Sundays.

As one moves away from the center of a suburban daily's market, there is a small increase in competition among suburban dailies. However, this competition is still minimal compared to the competition from higher-level newspapers. On weekdays in the retail trading zones of suburban dailies, this competition for all but two papers ranges from 0% to 16%. Only the papers in Long Beach and San Pedro are faced with more extensive competition from suburban dailies. Other suburban dailies control 27% of the daily circulation in the *Press-Telegram's* retail trading zone and 31% of the daily circulation in the San Pedro *News Pilot's* retail trading zone. On Sundays the *Press-Telegram* is able to hold other suburban dailies to a 11% share of the circulation in its retail trading zone, but the *News-Pilot*, which does not publish on Sunday, has 49% of the Sunday circulation in its retail trading zone going to other suburban competitors. However, with the exception of the *News-Pilot* case, suburban dailies make few circulation gains in the retail trading zones of suburbans on Sundays, picking up a market share that ranges from no circulation in the *Daily News* zone to 14% in the (Whittier) *Daily News* retail trading zone.

It is difficult for a third-layer paper to move outside its primary market area because there is extensive competition from other suburbans in the fringes of its market area—the area where the only major competition among suburban newspapers exists. Circulation figures for each paper's market fringe—cities where a paper has at least 200 paid weekday circulation—were compared with the total circulation of all their suburban competitors that also circulate in the paper's market fringe. With the exception of the Santa Monica paper, there is more weekday circulation in each paper's market fringe controlled by other suburban dailies than by the paper itself. On Sundays, this is true for all papers except the *Press-Telegram*, the (San Gabriel Valley) *Sunday Tribune News*, and the *Orange Coast Daily Pilot*. They are probably able to dominate the suburban circulation on Sundays because they fill the void left by other suburbans that do not publish on Sundays.

Conclusions: Umbrella Theory and Competition

The examination of circulation patterns in the Los Angeles–Orange County market provides support for the umbrella theory. The vigorous intercity competition has led to market consolidation and to shifts in circulation and advertising. Although the newspapers are aggressively pursuing readers and advertisers, they are playing by the rules of the umbrella model—the limits of competition. Although there is extensive competition between layers, this study revealed there is little direct competition within layers. In Los Angeles County, the competition is primarily between the *Times* and suburban newspapers although there is within-layer competition between the *Times* and the *Herald-Examiner*, particularly in their city zones. In Orange County, the battle for circulation is primarily between the *Times* and the *Register*, a metropolitan layer paper and a satellite city layer paper.

Circulation data clearly show the limits of competition for the suburban papers in the two-county market. Although they compete with the higher-level newspapers, there is little competition within the suburban layer itself. There is little overlap between a suburban newspaper's city and retail trading zones and the city and retail trading zones of other suburban newspapers. When there is overlap, it occurs generally only on Sundays, as the result of a void created by small dailies that do not have Sunday editions. In these cases, the suburban dailies with Sunday editions have been able to pick up some of the circulation that would otherwise go to the *Times* or the *Register*.

The limits of competition are greater for suburban newspapers than for the two levels of newspapers above them. Unless they can take advantage of unique market conditions, as have the *Register* and the *Daily News*, to become fairly large dailies, they are virtually locked into their market areas. Most enjoy a home-court advantage in their city zones and to a lesser extent in their retail trading zones because of the local news they provide. Their ability to carry news and advertising tailored to their city and retail trading zones puts limits on the competition from outside competitors, but it also limits their ability to expand outside their primary market areas. If they try to expand in the fringes of their circulation areas, they run into the market areas of other suburban papers.

Even a well-heeled chain newspaper like the *Los Angeles Times* must cope with limits. Despite a considerable financial commitment in both capital outlay and operating funds, the *Times* is achieving only modest gains in the primary market areas of the two largest competitors in its market—the *Register* and the *Daily News*. And its move into the San Diego market has not produced the kind of circulation and advertising numbers that would even begin to cover its cost. Although it is a metropolitan newspaper with a suburban strategy that has kept suburban papers from seriously eroding its market, it does not fit Roberts' view of a newspaper that is directing its energies to squeezing out small competitors.

The concern that a metropolitan daily will lessen competition is not well founded in the Los Angeles–Orange County market. First, the *Times* is not a monopoly paper in its market layer. Second, its allocation of capital and operating funds is aimed primarily at containing its four largest competitors in the Southern California market—the *Union* and *Tribune* in San Diego, the *Register* in Orange County and the *Daily News* in the San Fernando Valley, and not at driving the smallest suburban dailies out of business. Third, all but one of the *Times*' competitors are owned by large newspaper chains that have the economic power to compete with the *Times* in the satellite city and suburban layer markets where they have the home-court advantage. Fourth, as long as the *Times* continues to spend huge sums of money to produce foreign, national, state, metropolitan, and suburban news, its competitors will also spend money to improve their newspapers. The struggle for readers and advertisers keeps the competitive and creative juices flowing at competing newspapers and ensures that most Southern California readers will have a choice of at least three newspapers—a prestige daily, a satellite city newspaper, or a suburban daily.

PART II

Influences on Management
and the Public

CHAPTER 5

Editors and Their Roles

Patrick R. Parsons

School of Communications
Pennsylvania State University

John Finnegan, Jr.

School of Journalism
and Mass Communication
University of Minnesota

William Benham

Department of Communications
Loyola University of the South

The role of chain ownership in the distribution of news and information can be examined from a number of perspectives. Most scholars have looked at content differences between independent and chain newspapers, with inconsistent results.[1] Others have considered the role of organizational structure in the management and control of individual papers, where it is assumed that journalist behavior somehow affects newspaper content, and that important changes in one will lead to important changes in the other (cf. Soloski, 1979, pp. 19–24). This paper follows in the organizational tradition. It looks at the effect of organiza-

---

[1] A general evaluation of content studies of newspapers in various ownership situations may be found in Walter Baer, Henry Geller, Joseph Grundfest, and Karen Possner, *"Concentration of Mass Media Ownership: Assessing the State of Current Knowledge,"* Rand Corporation Rand Reports (R-1584-NSF), (Santa Monica, CA: Rand Corp., 1974). See also Daniel B. Wackman, Donald M. Gillmor, Cecilie Graziano, and Everette E. Dennis, "Chain Newspaper Autonomy As Reflected in Presidential Campaign Endorsements," *Journalism Quarterly* 52 (Autumn 1975), pp. 411–420; Ralph R. Thrift, Jr., "How Chain Ownership Affects Editorial Vigor of Newspapers," *Journalism Quarterly* 54 (Summer 1977), pp. 327–331.; Ronald H. Wagenberg and Walter C. Soderlund, "The Influence of Chain-Ownership on Editorial Comment in Canada," *Journalism Quarterly* 52 (Spring 1975), pp. 93–98.

tional structure on individual communicators. It considers the extent to which communicator roles vary among different organizational structures and how such variation may affect roles assigned communicators by other important role sources.

A Role-Theory Approach to Journalistic Behavior

The framework for analysis is a model of communicator behavior based on role theory. The use of role theory in the analysis of communicator behavior is not novel. It has been used to examine the work of public relations professionals in their often difficult task of attempting to serve and please a multitude of publics with conflicting expectations (see, e.g., Broom & Smith, 1979, pp. 47–59; Dozier & Gottesman, 1982); Elliott (1977) has suggested it as a framework for examining the problems of those involved in the institutionalized production of culture; and the authors have used it in a previous study of newspaper editors in the upper Midwest (Benham, Finnegan, & Parsons, 1982). Role theory also has been implied in studies examining the commitment of journalists to professional values and/or organizational demands (cf. Becker, Sobowale, & Cobbey, 1979).

In fact, despite the lack of specific attribution to role theory, it is in the studies of professionalism, organizational commitment, and community journalism that this analytical perspective has experienced its greatest development. The value and power of role theory lies in bringing together various important influences on journalists and examining their interactive effect on communicator behavior.

Typically, the two chief sources of role expectations have been identified as coming from the individual journalist's organization and from a vaguely defined sphere of professional norms (cf. Becker et al., 1979; Elliott, 1977). To this one might add the individual's geographic community as a source of role expectations, as the importance of the community in helping forge journalist behavior has long been noted (Park, 1925/1980; Janowitz, 1952).

The general underlying concept of role theory is the effort of the individual journalist to satisfy various expectations about his or her role within each of these spheres of influence. *Role* as defined here means a set of behavioral expectations attached to a position within a social structure. Role definition is at the outset a socialization process that takes place through communication. Communication may be informal and personal, as when a superior comments on a subordinate's work, or formal and impersonal, as when a new employee receives an orientation lecture or reads a company house organ. In either case, role cues can be delivered both intentionally and unintentionally. Journalists, particularly those journalists new to an organization or community, may be highly interested in resolving uncertainties about their relationships with a complex environment and in avoiding unnecessary conflicts and risks. For example, organizational studies deal with journalists, not as autonomous individuals, but as occupants of positions within an organized structure who play roles associated with their positions. Journalists learn roles primarily by socialization—communication in which others indicate how they expect roles to be played. Social control is applied to ensure that these expectations are fulfilled.

Breed's classic 1955 study of social control in the newsroom concluded that newspapers seldom need to apply coercion to gain compliance with their policies. Although punishments such as firing or demotion were always an implicit threat, rewards such as status conferral and good fellowship with superiors and peers sufficed. Control was neither coercive nor overt; new newspaper recruits seemed anxious to learn their roles and did so from revisions and deletions in their copy, from the general style and tone of the paper, from the way their stories were displayed in its pages, and from comments made by superiors.

Although Breed found that the journalists he studied accepted organizational policy as part of the job, newsroom climates are not always so harmonious. Stark (1962) studied a metropolitan newspaper in which conflict continually occurred between professional journalists opposed to newspaper policies and editors charged with implementing those policies. In this case, reporters took role cues from their peers rather than from the organization. They frequently managed to thwart news policies because they were better informed than their editors about the news. Reporters were willing to take the risk of displeasing their superiors because of support from their peers and because they were confident in their skills and in their ability to obtain other jobs. Thus, journalists experienced role conflict, perceiving different expectations from their superiors and professional peers.

Sigelman (1973) identified a process that reduced the likelihood of such role conflicts. After studying journalists working on competing newspapers with opposing editorial policies, Sigelman concluded that a process of self-selection was at work in which journalists, given a choice, decided to work for the paper more congenial to their own views. Furthermore, after observing the same socialization processes that Breed had discovered, Sigelman identified them as processes designed to avoid conflict. Decisions made higher in the newspaper hierarchy were imposed on the working journalist by controls such as story assignment and final editing of copy, while superiors used "attitude promotion" to encourage habits and views that steered journalists toward making decisions advantageous to the organization.

The specific processes by which higher levels of news organizations' hierarchies influence decisions made by editors and reporters at lower levels have received little study, but Dimmick (1978, p. 7) has suggested that such influence is primarily informational:

Informational social influence occurs when individuals accept information . . . as evidence about reality in order to reduce their uncertainty. . . . In this form of influence, the source of the information is not conceived as consciously attempting to influence behavior.

The label "informational influence" appears to describe the processes that Breed identified as "socialization" and Sigelman alluded to as "attitude promotion." All of these processes involve the definition and learning of role expectations as part of the dynamics of the organizational setting.

But organizations are not the only influences on journalist behavior nor the only sources of socialization. Tichenor, Olien, and Donohue (1980) have amassed considerable empirical evidence that community settings influence the roles played by newspaper organizations as a whole, as well as by individual editors and reporters. Newspapers, these scholars suggest, are an integral part of the community social systems they serve, carrying out different information functions for small and homogeneous communities or large and pluralistic ones.

The concept that newspaper performance is related to community needs is not a new one. More than 50 years ago, Park (1925/1980) discussed how newspapers change as their community environments change, and, some three decades ago, Janowitz (1952) studied how a city's neighborhood newspapers fit a particular social and economic niche, meeting community needs unmet by city dailies. In different community settings, the expectations of the community about the appropriate role of an editor and journalist will be different, depending on the particular needs of the area, and those expectations will be communicated, generally by informal means, to the reporter.

Finally, studies of professionalism and professional commitment, the degree to which individual journalists exhibit professional traits and behaviors, can be examined within the framework of a role theory model. Johnstone (1976), for example, identified two different professional types, the neutral and the participant orientations. Adoption of a given type implies the adoption of different professional roles by the journalist. Becker et al. (1979) suggested numerous variables may play a role in the development of professional commitment, including education, training, and social background.

The question of professional role expectations is clouded, of course, by definitional fuzziness. A precise definition of professionalism has yet to be specified; only broad, general attributes exist to guide us.[2] And in terms of socialization, both the organization and the community have more efficient mechanisms— reward and punishment systems—with which to channel behavior. Nonetheless, journalists do seem to strive to be seen as "professionals," and so consideration must be accorded this aspect of communicator behavior.

In short, each sphere of influence has an established set of behavioral norms: expectations about the appropriate behavior of the individual. Such expectations

---

[2] A summary of the problem of definitional clarity may be found in Johnstone et al. (1976; pp. 97–102).

may be codified as in a professional code of ethics (cf. Society of Professional Journalists/Sigma Delta Chi, "Code of Ethics," adopted 1928 revised 1973), or as informal as the generalized expectations of the small town about the appropriate role of the local newspaper editor.[3]

The starting point for the model of behavior arising from this perspective is the suggestion that an individual will strive, to a greater or lesser degree, to satisfy the role expectations of all the differing sources. The problem for researchers, then, is multiform. One must first consider the nature of the differing role expectations and how such expectations might change according to different structural precursors. For example, professional expections may be different depending on whether a neutral or activist position is adopted, or, while professional role expectations might remain relatively constant, community role expectations might vary according to the structure of the community, with larger, heterogenous communities sending out role cues substantially different than smaller, homogenous communities (Tichenor et al., 1980).

After considering the variable nature of the role expectations, one must look at the degree to which an individual will strive to satisfy some or all of those expectations in varying situations. For example, when the role expectations of all sources are congruent, the individual communicator will have no trouble in satisfying each with the same behavior. When role expectations conflict, however, the communicator must choose among them. Obeying a direct order from a publisher, therefore, might result in the violation of some professional ethical code. It is at this point of conflict that researchers can begin examining the variables that come into play in the decisions of communicators to adhere to one set of expectations or another. Typically, such research has focused on the "commitment" of journalists to organizational or professional goals (cf. Stark, 1962; Becker et al., 1979). The entire field of professionalism studies might be considered as being subsumed under this broader approach. The notions of *role conflict* and *role commitment* then become important in this approach to communicator analysis. Also important, although not as prevalent in the literature, is the concept of *role salience*. It is defined as the degree to which adherence to a given set of behavior expectations is inherently important to the individual. Like role satisfaction or role ambiguity, it can be thought of as a precondition of role commitment. Therefore, the need to make a living (or fear of being fired) may lead to strong organizational role salience.

Finally, and importantly, the role-theory model provides a panoramic view for the examination of the interaction of role sources, a benefit missing from the more limited, particularlistic studies of community, organization, and profes-

---

[3] E.g., Clarice N. Olien, George A. Donohue and Phillip J. Tichenor, "The Community Editor's Power and the Reporting of Conflict," *Journalism Quarterly* 45 (Summer 1968), pp. 243–252, suggest editors within the community power structure exhibit different editorial behavior than those outside the power structure.

sionalism alone. The suggestion is that role sources interact, and that such interaction modifies the role expectations of each that are subsequently communicated to the individual. In other words, a change in the structure of the community might bring about a change in community role expectations, but that change might also affect the organization and bring about related changes in organizational expectations. This interaction of role sources might, therefore, affect the commitment of the individual to different role expectations and might affect the chances of role conflict in various situations.

Overall, the approach is broad and complex, but necessarily so, for it addresses a broad and complex problem: the understanding of communicator behavior within his or her career context. It establishes a framework for the study of most of the aspects of journalistic behavior, encompassing organizational, community, professional, ethical, and other related studies. And it is within this framework that the question of communicator behavior within chain and independent papers may profitably be considered.

Application of the Model

It has been suggested that changes in structural variables of role sources may lead to changes in communicator commitment to those sources. This is the point of departure for the examination of the chain–independent debate within the role-theory context. The question is whether structural changes in the organization will lead to changes in commitment levels, not just for the organization, but for professional and community sources as well.

It was noted earlier, for example, that Tichenor et al. have posited a role for the media, and by extension the individual communicator, that varies according to the size and complexity of the community. The differing role expectations of the different-sized communities might, therefore, affect the commitment of an individual to professional norms. Such might be the case if the goals and mechanisms of role socialization were more coherently focused in the small community, the communicator's role was more closely defined, and the feedback processes were more direct and personal. In the presence of the strong socializing atmosphere, communicators might be less apt to orient toward alternative or noncongruent professional norms.

Similarly, changes in organizational structure might affect commitment to competing role norms. More specifically, communicators in chain and independent papers may display differences in commitment to their organization due to differences in the structural natures of the organizations, and, concurrently, may display differences in levels of commitment to role expectations from other sources.

The literature suggests that a number of variables interact to affect organizational commitment. The size of the organization, for example, has been found to influence commitment (see Johnstone, 1975; Becker et al., 1979). It is suggested that increased organizational size reduces the effectiveness of communication between the individual and management, leading to role ambiguity. Role ambiguity, a lack of direction or definition in one's job, in turn, leads to job dissatisfaction and ultimately to reduced commitment (Johnstone, 1976).

This might lead one to the conclusion that chains would be more likely than independents to manifest employee dissatisfaction, since chains tend, by nature, to be larger organizational structures. Such a supposition is complicated, however, by other commitment-related variables. A simple but powerful one is salary; Johnstone (Johnstone et al., 1976) has unsurprisingly shown a strong positive correlation between salary and job satisfaction. It follows that larger and richer organizations might be able to offset any problems of role ambiguity through monetary compensation. Of course, this would not hold for organizations which have become rich by exploiting labor, or by realizing high "employee productivity." An example would be the Thomson chain, a relatively minor chain in the U.S., but with about 21% of Canadian daily circulation.

The point is that, while some variables might act to decrease commitment in the large organization, others intervene to increase it, and the sum total of these forces must be considered in gauging overall communicator commitment.

The implication for the chain–independent debate is that the structural differences between the two organizational forms will be an important variable in degree of commitment of the individual to the organization and, further, that this difference will also act to alter the nature of individual commitment to community and professional role expectations. The directionality of commitment, whether it increases or decreases overall for larger organizations relative to smaller organizations, given the mixture of interacting forces mentioned above, can be addressed by a closer examination of the process of organizational socialization within chain and independent papers.

The starting point for this analysis is the previously noted observation that individual journalists are subject to a variety of socializing agents which move the individual toward acceptance of, and adherence to, organizational norms and goals. This process of socialization occurs in all organizations at most levels. The model suggested by role theory, however, implies a qualitative difference between chain and independent papers with respect to the socialization process. This difference is embedded in the nature of the entity toward which the individual is being socialized. That is, the source of role expectations on an independent paper flows from the management of that single newspaper, a newspaper with limited organizational boundaries. The source of role expectations on a chain newspaper, alternatively, may not be the journalist's individual paper but rather the larger chain organization. The chain, as such, transcends the local geographic and interest boundaries of the individual newspaper. Socialization to organizational norms here is not socialization to the distinct newspaper for which one works but to the norms and expectations of the regional or national chain.

From the perspective of the role theory model, two somewhat paradoxical ramifications follow. First, the differing structural situations might lead to differing potentials for role conflict, specifically, conflict between organizational and community role expectations. In the case of the independent newspapers, the geographic and hence interest boundaries of organization and community might substantially overlap, leading to a certain degree of congruity in the role expectations. A given behavior by the journalist might satisfy the role expectations of community and organization. The same degree of congruity in role expectations may not be apparent in the chain ownership situation, however. While some degree of geographic and interest overlap does exist due to the interaction of the community and the individual chain paper, both the geographic and interest boundaries of the chain organization sweep beyond the local community. Organizational role expectations may take on a broader horizon, therefore, and increase the potential for community–organizational role conflict.

By itself this would suggest the possibility of increased role conflict and subsequently decreased commitment, in all areas, for individuals in chain situations. This would assume, however, that the process of socialization takes place with equal efficiency in both the organizational and community spheres. It would assume that there is equal opportunity for the individual to orient toward the expectations of both role-cue sources. But this may not be the case. There may exist differences between chain and independent papers that, in addition to changing the nature of the socializing process in the organization, at the same time change the process of socialization toward community role expectations. By decreasing the possibility of congruity of role expectations, the chain situation may also decrease the potential for the realization of processes that reinforce commitment to community role expectations. The result is that, while the potential for role conflict situations might increase with chains, the actual perceived role conflict of the individual might be less as a result of the decreased salience of community role expectations.

Two important conceptual caviats must be noted here. First, it would be a mistake to assume the role-theory approach considers chain employees to be somehow less desirous of meeting all the role expectations imposed on them. Structural forces that lead to increased or decreased role salience should not be confused with communicator intent. It is probable that individuals honestly seek to serve their various publics to the limits of their ability. For chain personnel, those limits may be circumscribed by structural constraints, however, and the best intentions cannot be realized without the appropriate supporting context for such realization.

Secondly, this general notion of chain–independent differences must be modified to recognize differences within the chain itself. That is, it may be likely that publishers and editors are subject to lower community role salience than are reporters because they are more likely to have closer links to corporate headquarters than are individual reporters. This, in turn, suggests some mechanisms by which these differences in salience and commitment between chain and independent papers might be realized.

Soloski (1979) has identified a number of methods by which chains maintain control over their member papers. The control of newspaper budgets and the mandated use of chain wire copy are examples. Another, and one relevant to this paper, is the movement of management personnel within the chain from one paper to another. The chain Soloski (1979, p. 24) studied reportedly had one newspaper which was used as a "proving ground for new publishers." If the publishers did well there, they were presumably promoted to another position within the chain but outside that particular newspaper. Soloski also noted the existence of a centralized group personnel office that helped facilitate movement of workers from one paper to another within the chain (p. 20).

In the context of the model, then, this potential intraorganizational mobility might encourage the development of organizational role expectations that extend beyond a given community. Part of the socialization process in such organizations might be the acquisition of company norms and expectations through job training at different sites and even in varying corporate roles. For chain communicators, this means movement through the organization by progressing from one paper to another. The result might be sustained organizational pressure to conform to role expectations but, importantly, weakened pressure to conform to community expectations. This weakened community-based socialization process would be the result, then, of repeated interrupted movement from community to community. The social situations that might lead to increased community commitment, such as the development of strong community ties, are simply not given the chance to develop in this type of organizationally dominated situation. The product would be increased salience of, and commitment to, organizational role expectations at the cost of decreased salience and commitment to community role expectations.

Again, while this extension of organizational role expectations beyond potential congruent community expectations may set the stage for increased role-conflict situations, the real potential for individual role conflict is reduced by reducing the relevance or salience of the community role expectations.

To test some of the assumptions of this model of communicator behavior, the authors conducted a survey of managing editors of daily newspapers in the upper Middle West. Questionnaires were mailed to 129 editors in the five-state region of Minnesota, Wisconsin, North Dakota, South Dakota, and Iowa. Of those who represented (N=79),[4] 58% worked for chain papers (N=46)[5] and 42% worked for independents (N=33).

Managing editors were selected for study as being both an integral part of the daily reporting process, more so perhaps than publishers, yet still high enough in

---

[4] A 61 return rate.

[5] Chain newspapers were defined as two or more noncompeting papers owned by one company.

the management hierarchy to demonstrate some of the corporate attachments attributed to publishers. As previously noted, reporters would seem to be less likely to be subject to noncongruent role expectations, although such a proposition remains to be tested.

Results and Discussion

To try to get at the question of editor commitment to organizational versus community role expectations, the survey sought information on career aspirations. According to the model, chain editors should express a greater desire to move out of the community and the local paper in order to advance within the broader organization. At the same time, the survey sought information on the history of editor job mobility and current ties with the community. The model would suggest greater job movement by chain editors, with some indication of movement within the chain, and less evidence of attachment to the present community as a part of that history of mobility.

In the first instance, editors were asked if they intended to remain with their current paper until retirement. The independent editors expressed a greater expectation of staying in their current jobs, with 46% responding "yes" compared to 24% of the chain editors, $\chi^2 = 3.9$, p = .04. More to the point, chain editors expressed a greater anticipation of working for a paper in another town, with 85% of them saying they expected to do so compared to 34% of the independent editors, $\chi^2 = 8.5$, p = .01.

The important related question for chain editors was whether their career ambitions were centered on remaining with the group. Soloski (1979, p. 24) reported anecdotally that the publisher of the newspaper he studied admitted to seeing his position as a stepping stone to an upper management post within the group. Of the chain editors surveyed for this study, 80% said they hoped to be promoted to a higher editorial position within their organization but outside their present newspaper.

Looking to the past as well as the future, the job history of the editors gave some indication of the organizational differences between the chains and independents. For example, editors on independent papers were somewhat more likely than chain editors to have held a previous job on that paper. About 71% of independent editors worked on the paper prior to their promotion, compared to about 59% of the chain editors, $\chi^2 = 12.25$, p = .01. Similarly, independent editors had been with their paper longer than chain editors. About 40% of the chain editors reported being with their present paper for less than 5 years, compared with 25% of their independent colleagues, $\chi^2 = 2.13$, p = 10. (These data were underscored by findings from a survey of managing editors conducted in 1979 by the American Society of Newspaper Editors.[6] Nationwide, the ASNE study found independent editors to have spent a median of 19.1 years with their respective papers, compared to only 9.1 years for chain editors.[7]) Further, 31% of the responding chain editors said they had never worked for another paper, compared to 18% for the chain editors.

For those editors studied, there does appear to be a history of movement and expectations of continued movement within the cain organization. This is organizational activity that supercedes activities restricted to the paper for which they currently work. The career horizons for chain editors may therefore extend beyond the local paper and the community which it serves.

This in turn may imply decreased community salience and commitment. Findings from the survey of Midwestern editors suggest that, concomitant with shorter average tenures at their newspaper, came shorter average residence in their community and a related decrease in general community ties. More than 50% of the chain editors surveyed had lived in their community less than 5 years; only 24% of the independent editors had lived in their respective towns less than 5 years, $\chi^2 = 4.32$, p = 04. (The ASNE study reported independent editors had been living in their communities a median 21.8 years compared to only 10.2 years for chain editors; American Society of Newspaper Editors, 1980, p. 22.)

Independent editors, in short, have lived up to twice as long in their communities. Independent editors also were more likely to have lived in their community before going to work for the paper. More than 41% of the independent editors had lived in the community before joining the paper; only 22.7% of the chain editors had done so, $\chi^2 = 2.28$, p = .10. These figures suggest the potential for deeper community ties for independent editors.

All this probably should not be taken to imply that there was any less desire on the part of the chain editors to serve their communities in the role of newspaper editor, however. In fact, the data suggest an intention of trying to meet with various role expectations from all sources. For example, independent and chain editors in the sample spent similar amounts of time meeting with and talking to members of the community. A number of questionnaire items probed for the frequency of meetings the editors typically had with community leaders to discuss newspaper activity. These items were used in constructing an index of interaction between editors and community leaders, and the results showed chain editors to have the same regular formal and informal contact with community leaders as did independent editors.[8] Such activity should not be confused

---

[6] American Society of Newspaper Editors, Ethics Committee, "News and Editorial Independence: A Survey of Group and Independent Editors," unpublished report, April 1980. A mail questionnaire sent to 1,682 managing editors; 398 responses from chain editors, 249 from independents, about a 38% response rate in both categories, p. 3.

[7] Mean scores were not available, p. 22.

[8] As a measure of community interaction, a Likert-type scale was constructed from questionnaire

with indicators of community ties and, in fact may suggest a greater need for chain editors to reach out to the community because of the lack of such ties. It is indicative of the desire to attempt to satisfy all role expectations whenever possible.

The point is that the nature of the different structures may make it less likely that community and organizational roles will be equally salient in times of role conflict. This in turn may lead to resolution of the conflict in favor of the organization. In short, the structure may tend to decrease community commitment on the part of chain editors in times of conflicting role expectations.

While the questionnaire was not specifically designed to gather information on professional role expectations, some items did raise questions in this area. It was found, for example, that chains were more likely to have written codes of behavior that discouraged membership in organizations not connected with the professions. This is interesting because it can be seen as in keeping with professional guidelines that suggest a journalist maintain some distance from activities that might generate a conflict of interest (see Society of Professional Journalists, 1928/1973). This behavior was reinforced by written code in only a minority of the Midwestern papers (32%), but, among those editors reporting the existence of such formal codes, 62% were from chain papers and 38% from independents.

For chains, at least, the combination of movement within the organization and the existence of the codes might serve to doubly reinforce insulation from the community. This, of course, could be seen as in keeping with professional norms and reinforcing professionally inspired codes. But it should not necessarily suggest adoption of the codes by chains (or the independents for that matter) only to help maintain professional standards. Such codes also could serve, according to the model, to help increase organizational commitment at the cost of community and professional commitment. This could be accomplished by decreasing the likelihood of community interaction—which the organizationally mandated codes seem to do—and, perhaps, by co-opting the role of professional norm provider, that is, assuming the function of establishing and maintaining professional goals, a function previously assigned to a less-well-defined but nonetheless distinct peer group structure.

---

items, asking about the frequency of formal and informal contacts with community members. Three questionnaire items were used for the scale of informal contacts, and four items for the scale for formal contacts. Each item requested the editor to estimate the number of meetings of a specific types he or she had had during a given period of time. For example, editors were asked the number of scheduled meetings they had had with community leaders since the beginning of the year, and how many times in the past month they had been stopped by people on the street to discuss the newspaper's performance. Responses to each item were ordered into six weighted groups (0–2 contacts = 1 point; 3–5 = 2; 6–9 = 3; 10–14 = 4; 15–19 = 5, 20 or more = 6). Points were then totaled for the index scored. For formal meetings, chain editors scored slightly higher (7.06, compared to 6.57 for independent editors), but the difference was not significant (df = 76, t = −.90, p = .37). For informal meetings, chain editors had a higher score than did independent editors (8.04, compared to 6.96; df = 76, t = −1.74, p = .09).

The possibility that the organization might act in some cases as a surrogate for a professional organization calls to question many of the assumptions about the use and effectiveness of professional norms. Unfortunately, this study generated only enough information to suggest the possible need for a closer examination. Much additional information is needed on the role of codes and other informal constraints relating to concerns of professional role expectations.

Conclusions

A role-theory approach to communicator behavior leads to the development of a model suggesting three important sources of role expectations for the journalist: the newspaper organization, the local community, and the profession.

The internal composition of each of these role providers, how these sources interact, and how role cues are communicated to the journalist all will have an impact on journalistic behavior.

The question of the effect of ownership and the general chain–independent debate can be examined within this role-theory framework by considering how organizational role expectations vary from one ownership situation to another and how the differences affect the role expectations from other sources.

The model of communicator behavior derived from this role-theory approach suggests that chain editors will be socialized into organizational role expectations that transcend the local community and therefore reduce the salience of community role expectations. In situations of role conflict, this may result in greater organizational commitment and resolution of the conflict in favor of the organization. Data gathered in a survey of managing editors in the upper Midwest suggests initial support for several basic assumptions of the model, including a tendency for chain editors to move from paper to paper within the chain organization and thus spend less time than independent editors on any one paper. The decreased tenure at individual papers is subsequently reflected in a decrease in the amount of time editors have lived in a given community and also in the types and number of ties they have forged with that community.

Additional information on editor commitment to community and organization still needs to be gathered, especially in situations involving role conflict. The investigation also needs to be extended to include deeper consideration of professional role expectations and their effect on the interaction of community and organizational commitment. It is still unclear how increased or reduced organizational commitment will directly affect service to the community, and the role of professional norms in the outcome will undoubtedly be pivotal. The extent to which different organizations and individuals adhere to professional norms must be considered in the broader question of ownership. The usefulness of the role-theory approach is in its ability to include all these aspects in an attempt to answer questions about communicator behavior.

CHAPTER 6

Interlocking Directorships and Economic Power[1]

James P. Winter

Department of Communication Studies
University of Windsor
Windsor, Ontario
Canada

Concentrated ownership and monopolies in the private sector were a part of Canadian history long before Confederation in 1867. Anthropologist Bruce Trigger (1985, p. 303) asserts that Jacques Cartier's nephew Jacques Noel obtained a monopoly on furs and mines in Canada in 1588. This was one of the earliest monopolies granted by the French Crown, which was anxious to see established settlements in New France. By eliminating competition, the Crown hoped that profits would accrue, which could be used to establish a true colony, rather than simply a trading base.

Oligopolies and monopolies built into the fabric of Canadian economic life continued through the Hudson's Bay Company charter in 1670, and the Canadian Pacific Railway monopoly clause in 1880, and, as will be shown, to present-day mass media. Harold Innis (1970) argued that it was mainly the socioeconomic impact of the fur trade that was responsible for the historical development of this centralized institutional control in Canada.

The Canadian industrial revolution took place between the 1840s and the 1890s (cf. Pentland, 1959, p. 4; Ryerson, 1968; Langdon, 1975, cited in Lauriston, 1986). By the 1880s the consolidation of the railroad in central Canada and the power of the CPR to establish rates produced an outpouring of protest by farmers and shippers in the west (Bliss, 1974, pp. 40–41). The period between

---

[1] The author expresses his appreciation to Paula Takacs, Toni Lauriston, and Michelle Hall for their research assistance.

1900 and 1914 saw mergers in such industries as textiles, tobacco, brewing, milling, and paper (Canada, 1978). Between 1908 and 1912, 58 industrial mergers included approximately 275 firms with a total capital of $5,490 million (Leadbeater, 1984, pp. 1–76, cited in Lauriston, 1986). For example, between 1893 and 1923 in the canning business alone, 76 firms merged to provide Canadian Canners Ltd. with 75% to 80% of the market (Traves, 1983, pp. 19–44). Reynolds (1940, p. 5) detailed the extent of concentrated control in six major industries by the 1930s. Imperial Tobacco had cornered 70% of all tobacco production, for example, while five firms controlled 90% of pulp and paper production, two meat packing firms accounted for 85%, one cement company 90%, four copper companies 93%, and four agricultural machinery firms 75%.

Another example of concentration over time may be taken from the banking industry. Between 1875 and 1960, the number of banks fell from 50 to 9 (Urquart, 1965, p. 246; Carroll, Fox, & Ornstein, 1982, p. 46). Today, about 90% of all bank assets and revenue in Canada are in the hands of the five largest banks: The Royal Bank of Canada, The Bank of Montreal, The Bank of Nova Scotia, The Canadian Imperial Bank of Commerce, and The Toronto Dominion Bank (Neufeld, 1972, pp. 77–81). Concentration continues apace in all corporate sectors today, both consciousness-industry related and otherwise. An example of the former, in addition to newspapers to which we will turn momentarily, is that of pay television. An indigenous Canadian pay-TV industry was established in March 1982 by the Canadian Radio Television and Telecommunication Commission (CRTC), following much deliberation and delay. In 1984 the industry was restructured to create regional or linguistic monopolies, eliminating competition. In the spring of 1986, the three remaining companies, First Choice, Superchannel, and Premier Choix told the CRTC they could not afford Canadian content requirements of 50% and wanted them reduced to 15% for the English services and 10% for the French service. All three of these corporate monopolies reported profits in 1985. But as with the banking example and those from other industries, this pay-TV example demonstrates that, in all industries, concentrated ownership has been a natural outgrowth of free-market competition, as well as an indelible part of the Canadian mindset.

According to the *Globe and Mail*, as of 1984, 46% of the value of the most important companies on the Toronto Stock Exchange was controlled by nine families: Ken Thomson, Edward and Peter Bronfman, Paul Desmarais, the Reichmanns, Galen Weston, Conrad and Montegu Black, Ron Southern, and the Siemen Brothers of Calgary. In 1986 a federal member of parliament told the House of Commons that, between 1977 and 1984, 500 corporates mergers had taken place yearly, a 100% increase over the annual mergers in 1960.

Concentration in the Newspaper Industry

Growth in the daily newspaper industry paralleled other sectors during the industrial revolution, with the number of dailies increasing from 23 to 91 between

1864 and 1891 (Kesterton, 1967, p. 3a). The number of dailies peaked at 138 in 1913, compared to a current figure of about 117. But, in 1913 almost all newspapers were independently owned. Perhaps Southam, with four of the 138 papers, was the largest chain (Lauriston, 1986, p. 49). By 1958 three chains— Southam News, Thomson, and FP Publications—controlled 20% of daily circulation. By the time of the Special Senate Committee on the Mass Media in 1970, these three chains controlled 47% of daily circulation. The senate committee, popularly called the Davey Committee after its chairman Keith Davey, commented:

> This tendency (toward concentration) could . . . lead to a situation whereby the news . . . is controlled and manipulated by a small group of individuals and corporations whose view of What's Fit to Print may closely coincide with What's Good for General Motors, or What's Good for Business, or What's Good for my Friends Down at the Club. There is some evidence, in fact, which suggests that we are in that boat already. (Canada, 1970, p. 4)

When the Royal Commission on Newspapers reported in 1981, the Thomson chain had swallowed FP publications, and the two chains of Southam and Thomson controlled 50% of national daily circulation and 60% of English language daily circulation (Canada, 1981, p. 2).

In August, 1985, the Southam chain effected a merger or "share swap" with the largest independent daily in Canada, *The Toronto Star*. Ostensibly arranged to avoid a "hostile takeover" by an unnamed corporation, the share swap gave *The Toronto Star* 20% of Southam shares, and Southam 30% of Torstar Corporation shares. As part of the arrangement, the two companies also exchanged members on their boards of directors. This effective merger means that the Southam chain itself now controls about 38% of Canadian daily circulation, or 48% of English language circulation, and that, together, the two largest chains of Southam and Thomson control 70% of English language daily circulation (by comparison, three Quebec chains control 90% of French language circulation).

It has been argued, of course, that this—at best—oligopolistic control of the newspaper medium in Canada does not bode well for the newspaper reading public. This was precisely the question addressed by the Royal Commission on Newspapers (The Kent Commission) in 1980. The Kent Commission was set up by the Trudeau government in response to prima facie collusion on the part of the two big English language chains, in apparent violation of anticombines legislation. The two chains conspired to simultaneously close one competing daily each, ending any competition between the chains, and leaving each chain with yet another city-wide monopoly. Southam closed its *Winnipeg Tribune* and Thomson its *Ottawa Journal* on the same day in 1985, leaving Thomson's *Winnipeg Free Press* and Southam's *Ottawa Citizen* as local monopolies. Competitive tabloids have since challenged both papers, and the *Winnipeg Sun*, with a much smaller circulation, continues to publish in competition to the *Free Press*.

Although the federal government pressed charges under the Anti-Combines Act, the newspaper chains were not convicted. Nor for that matter have many companies been successfully prosecuted under that act, which is a sterling example of toothless legislation.

While, for some, the debate continues over the evidence for harmful effects of concentrated ownership and monopolies in the press, this chapter examines a related, but different, problem with similar roots: corporate interlocks, specifically, interlocks between the two major Canadian chains themselves and with other segments of the corporate sector. This is a related problem because, obviously, the extent of corporate interlocks is a function of the degree of concentration in the industry.

It is, simultaneously, a different problem because, rather than focusing on the lack of diversity in information, or at least the diminished number of sources for that information, we are indirectly addressing the impact on the news of directors' potential conflict of interest.

This chapter examines the extent of interlocks between the two press chains themselves and among these chains and other businesses. Evidence for harmful effects of these interlocks, or even for their potential danger, is to a great extent intuitively obvious. Rather than documenting additional examples of problems, such as conflicts of interest which arise out of interlocks, as have authors such as Ben Bagdikian (1983) and Peter Dreier and Steve Weinberg (1979) using U.S. examples, this chapter is more concerned with the broader implications that extensive interlocks hold for popular notions of a pluralistic, rather than a monolithic elite structure, in our society (cf. Clement, 1975). The pluralist position holds that, through checks and balances, power tends toward an equilibrium of elites. As Porter (1965, p. 247) noted,

> An important element of the "western" model is that elites do not fill power roles in more than one system at the same time. It is assumed, for example, that political elites will relinquish any directorships in corporations.

Hence, evidence of extensive interlocks contradicts a pluralistic view of society and questions the true nature of power elite relationships, the status quo, and the role of the consciousness industry in sharing in and maintaining these.

Interlocking Directorates

The theory of managerial control of modern corporations stems from Berle and Means' 1932 book, *The Modern Corporation and Private Property*, in which they posited control by groups of top executives rather than stockholders or individual entrepreneurial industrialists (Kerbo & Della Fave, 1983, p. 201). Others have propagated some variation of a ruling-class thesis; i.e., the corporate economy is controlled by a capitalist class, based on ownership and control of property (Mills, 1956; Domhoff, 1979; Anderson, 1974; cited in Della Fave, 1983). If one subscribes to "managerial control" theory, then directors exist essentially to rubber stamp decisions made by management, and it could be argued that interlocking directorships are thus largely meaningless. The position taken here, on the other hand, is that boards of directors are crucial, both within the firm itself and as vehicles for coopting important external independent organizations. As Pfeffer and Salanick (1978, p. 161) note:

> Interlocking directorships . . . are one form of a more general tendency to manage the environment by appointing significant external representatives to positions in the organization. Known as cooptation, this is a strategy for accessing resources, exchanging information, developing interfirm commitments, and establishing legitimacy. Of all forms of interorganizational coordination it is one of the most flexible and easiest to implement, two advantages that have made its use pervasive.

As evidence, these authors cite Dooley (1969), who examined interlocking directorates among the 200 largest manufacturing corporations in the U.S., and found that interlocks with financial institutions consistently have been maintained since the 1930s. The mutual benefits are apparent: the bank representative on a board helps obtain financing for the firm, and also helps the bank to place loans. Such interactions represent attempts to stabilize the transactions of organizations through interfirm linkage. This is termed the *negotiated environment* of organizations (Cyert & March, 1965, cited in Pfeffer & Salanick, 1978, p. 183). According to Pfeffer and Salanick, director interlocks do not occur randomly, but rather in situations where a lack of coordination would adversely affect both companies' performance.

In Canada the only laws pertinent to interlocks prevent bank directors from serving on the board of another bank or trust or loan company. U.S. laws prohibit interlocks between the boards of companies which compete in any way. For some, these restrictions do not go nearly far enough. Nader, Green, and Seligman (1976, cited in Peterson & Heath, 1977), for example, propose that interlocks between any companies be prohibited; that no director should serve on more than one board at a time, and that no executive, legal counsel, or agent of one company should serve on the board of another company. Even directors interviewed as part of a study for the conservative Conference Board of Canada proposed that a self-regulating profession, similar to accounting, be established with a code of ethics which could forbid interlocking directorates with a potential for restricting competition or for other conflicts of interest (Peterson & Heath, 1977, p. 14). However, prominent members of the business community who were interviewed for the Peterson and Heath study disputed inferences that corporate power is concentrated in too few hands, and that directors form elitist groups with vested interests (Peterson & Heath, 1977, p. 64).

While there are differing interpretations in the literature for the meaning of interlocks, there is consistency in the reported extent of those interlocks. In American research, for example, Levine and Roy (1975, cited in Carroll, Fox, & Ornstein, 1982) found that 724 of 797 of the largest firms were connected in a single network. Clement found Canadian networks more densely interlocked than American networks, and also that Canadian financial firms play a more central role. Almost all Canadian firms have at least one interlock with a financial firm (Ornstein, 1984).

Carroll et al. (1982, p. 49) provided a quantitative description of interlocks among the top 100 Canadian firms, finding that 97 out of 100 firms formed a single connected subnetwork. The "degree" of interlocks, that is, the mean number of relations network members have with other networks members, was 11.8. The "density" of interlocks, the proportion of theoretically possible directorate links that in fact exist, was 12%; and *interfirm distance*, the length of the shortest path through the network connecting two firms, had an interpolated median distance of 1.72. The greatest distance (or *diameter* of the subnetwork) was 6. Thus the network was highly integrated: nearly two-thirds of all pairs of firms could reach each other through one intermediate board at most, and nearly 90% of the pairs were connected through no more than two intermediaries. There was no evidence of disconnected subgroups based on nationality or ownership, sphere of economic activity, or any other criterion examined. Carroll et al. (1982, p. 58) concluded through the use of smallest space analysis that banks and other financial firms occupy central positions in the network of corporate interlocks, serving to integrate the network as a whole. They asserted that large scale capital in Canada is socially integrated in a densely connected network of directorship interlocks, and that high integration and multiple interlocks provide a base for intercorporate cooperation and social solidarity among directors.

This recent research evidence supports the classic work by the late sociologist John Porter (1965, p. 234), who concluded that interlocking directorships crystallized control within small collegial groups. Porter pointed to the evidence that, in the mid-1950s, fewer than 1,000 individuals shared 81% of the directorships of the major corporations, as well as 58% of the directorships in the nine chartered banks. Porter's former student, Clement (1975, pp. 325–326, 341), conducted an empirical examination of the separation between the media and economic elites, suggesting that the greater the overlap the more evidence of a monolithic structure at the elite level, which lowers the opportunities for alternative ideologies and values. He found that 69% of members of the media elite held important corporate positions outside the media, concluding that the media are class institutions run by and for the elite, and that the media and economic elites are in fact the same people.

This question of the ramifications of interlocks between media and other corporate elites was pursued by Dreier and Weinberg (1979) in their study of the

25 largest newspaper corporations in the U.S. The authors noted the double standard by which many newspapers insist their reporters develop no ties to outside organizations which might affect their objectivity: yet no such precautions are taken for the more influential board of directors.[2] These authors found that the top 25 newspaper companies, with more than half of the U.S. daily circulation, have over 200 direct interlocks with the Fortune 1300 companies, and "untold" indirect interlocks (Dreier & Weinberg, 1979, p. 52).

Dreier and Weinberg (1979, pp. 52–53) also discuss the "chilling effect:" self-censorship of reporters, knowing their publisher is on the board of some local firm. They quote one reporter who said, "We're taught, subtly, not to cover the corporation sector and other private institutions the way we cover city hall."

Historical Overview of the Southam and Thomson Chains

Before examining the corporate directorships and interlocks of the Southam and Thomson chains, a brief history of the two chains is in order.

The history of Southam Press began in 1877, with the purchase of *The Hamilton Spectator* for $6,000. Two printing firms were subsequently added, followed by the *Ottawa Citizen* in 1897. By 1923 four more dailies had been purchased, and the Southams also invested in steel and iron companies (Rutherford, 1978, p. 108). By the 1980s, Southam was publishing 14 major dailies, with a 48% share of the independent Kitchener-Waterloo *Record*, and a 49% share of the independent *Brandon Sun*. Southam also has a sizable interest in Canada's largest daily, *The Toronto Star*, with one-tenth of the national daily circulation. Southam also owns Coles Bookstore Ltd., and through Torstar Corp. has an interest in Harlequin romance novels. The company publishes 39 business publications, 24 annuals and directories, and has a major interest in Selkirk Communications, which has radio, television, and cable interests in Canada and abroad. With the merger with Torstar Corp., Southam is the largest newspaper chain in Canada, with almost half of the English language circulation in the country.

The Thomson empire began in 1931, when Roy Thomson purchased a radio station in North Bay Ontario. His first newspaper was *The Timmins Press*, purchased in 1934. By 1943, he owned eight radio stations and five newspapers (Bradden, 1965). By the mid-1960s he was recognized as the biggest newspaper publisher in history, with 124 papers in eight countries. Today, under Roy

---

[2] In its 1983 annual report for example, Southam Inc. states: "Officers, editorial personnel and all other key employees of the company are expected to remain free from political and other outside activities when such activities might influence or appear to influence the editorial freedom or independence of any of the company's publications." The report also states that "Officers of the company and its subsidiaries, and senior publishing executives, may not act as directors of other firms." As we will see, apparently neither of these statements refers to company directors.

Thomson's son Ken, the chain owns 143 newspapers in Canada and the U.S. Forty of those papers are in Canada, including the prestigious *Globe and Mail*, and the 40 papers account for slightly more than one-third of all dailies published in Canada. The Thomson International Organization, with 1984 sales in excess of $3 billion, ranks among the largest multinationals in the world, with major retailing, travel, oil and gas, trucking, and insurance interests in addition to the newspapers. According to the 1985 edition of *The Blue Book of Canadian Business*, Thomson Newspapers is ranked number 106, or two ahead of Honda Canada Ltd., while International Thomson Organization is ranked number 25, two ahead of IBM Canada. A subsidiary, Hudson's Bay Co., is ranked 14th. By comparison, Southam Press, Inc. is ranked 82nd.

The Thomson chain has a reputation for running a penny-pinching, profitable business, where reporters have been asked to buy their own copies of the newspapers, and memos have been circulated about too much toilet paper being consumed in the women's washrooms of newspaper buildings. This is in a corporation whose 1984 profits were up 22% over 1983, to $153.8 million. By comparison the Southam chain is noted for a relatively greater sense of public responsibility. In short, Southam could squeeze greater profits from its newspapers than does Thomson. The fact that it does not makes the company ripe for a corporate takeover, a situation which the company avoided through the share swap with Torstar Corporation.

One indication of the relative profitability of the two firms is employee "productivity." In 1984 it was established that each Thomson employee contributed $20,498 to operating profit and each Southam employee contributed $10,922 (Westell, 1984).

The Southam Board of Directors' Interlocks

Two types of interlocks are detailed here. The first is a direct interlock, where a Southam director[3] holds a position as director of another company; the second is a stage-one or *first-order* indirect interlock. For example, Southam board member Hugh G. Hallward also belongs to the board of the Canadian Imperial Bank of Commerce. His fellow Commerce board directors, in turn, have other board positions, and so Hallward has an indirect influence on these boards.

Southam Incorporated's 13-member board of directors has over 40 direct interlocks with major Canadian corporations. The five largest financial and insurance companies among these and the five largest firms listed in *The Blue Book of Canadian Business, 1985*, have been selected for study here. These firms are (with the nonfinancial/insurance firms' rankings in parentheses): Toronto

---

[3] The lists of directors referred to are taken from the 1985 edition of the Financial Post's *Directory of Directors*.

Dominion Bank, Canadian Imperial Bank of Commerce, Victoria and Grey Trust Co., The Royal Insurance Co. of Canada, North American Life Insurance Co., Canadian Packers Inc. (26), Macmillan Bloedel Ltd. (36), Canadian Utilities Ltd. (67), Algoma Steel Corp. (80), and Canfor Corp. (83). Through the boards of these companies, Southam directors have close contact with hundreds of directors of the largest firms in Canada. Altogether, through these 10 firms, Southam might be described as having a first-order indirect interlock with 614 corporations. A short list includes: Massey-Ferguson, Stelco, Labatts, Carling O'Keefe, Loblaw's, Dominion Stores, Power Corp., Argus Corp., Hudson's Bay, Wardair, CP Air, CFTO TV Ltd., CFRB Ltd., Bushnell Communications, The Royal Bank, and Mobil Oil Corp.

Of particular interest is the close contact with other media groups, such as the Sun Publishing Co., Selkirk Communications, TV Guide, and Coles Bookstores (direct), and Bushnell Communications, Baton Broadcasting, CFTO TV, and CKLW Radio (indirect). Most notable among the media links, of course, is that with Thomson Newspapers itself. Both Southam and Thomson have directors on the board of the Toronto Dominion Bank. Thus, in the terminology used above by Carroll et al. (1982) the *interfirm distance*, or length of the shortest path through the network connecting these two firms, is 1. It could only be shorter if Southam and Thomson directly shared one or more directors.

The Thomson Board of Directors' Interlocks

The 10 directors on the board of Thomson Newspapers Ltd. serve as directors for well over 50 different companies. Ken Thomson himself, perhaps the wealthiest man in Canada today, sits on almost 40 different boards. To examine the interlocks between Thomson Newspapers and other corporations, the ten largest companies on which Thomson directors sit were selected.[4] The five financial and insurance companies were: The Royal Bank of Canada, The Toronto Dominion Bank, Sun Life Assurance Co., The Mortgage Co. of Canada, and Manufacturer's Life Assurance Co.. The five other corporations (with their ranking in the top 500 Canadian companies in parentheses) are: Shell Canada Ltd. (12), Hudson's Bay Co. (14), IBM Canada Ltd. (27), Abitibi Price Ltd. (35), and Polysar Ltd. (63). To ascertain the first-order indirect interlocks, the company directorships of each of the other directors of these 10 firms were compiled. These are the companies with which the Thomson Board of Directors has indirect contact, and the list is very extensive, amounting to some 622 corporations.

---

[4] Corporation rankings were taken from *The Blue Book of Canadian Business*, 1985 Edition. Financial corporations are not ranked in the Blue Book, but obviously are among the very largest companies.

The interlocks of Thomson are pervasive. A few of the very largest corporations include: Bell Canada, Chrysler Canada, The Canadian Imperial Bank of Commerce, the Bank of Nova Scotia, The Bank of Montreal, Canadian General Electric, Canadian Pacific, B.P. Canada, Gulf Canada, Texaco Inc., Husky Oil, Imperial Oil, Olympia and York Developments, T. Eaton Co., Seagrams, Noranda, Westinghouse, RJR- Macdonald Inc., Nabisco, and Power Corp.

A number of interlocks in particular should be noted. First of all, there is a large number of interlocks with other consciousness industries: MacLean Hunter Ltd., Baton Broadcasting, Rogers Cablesystems Ltd., Torstar Corp.—which, in turn, is in partnership with Southam Inc.—and so forth. Another important link with Southam Inc., is through the Toronto Dominion Bank. It is also through the Toronto Dominion Bank Board that there are indirect interlocks with the Eatons, and Sears Ltd., the major competitors of Hudson's Bay Co. and Simpson's Ltd.—both owned by Thomson interests. One also should note that each of the five major banks is accessible to Thomson either through direct or indirect interlocks. Finally, indirect interlocks with Olympia and York Developments Ltd. and Power Corp. provide contact with two of the other "top nine" Canadian families: the Reichmann brothers and Paul Desmarais.

Turning to a more extensive comparison of the interlocks between Southam and Thomson, a comparison of the lists of company interlocks of Southam and Thomson was made. It revealed that there are at least 95 major indirect interlocks between these two giant newspaper firms. No effort was made to count every interlock, but rather just the major corporations: yet there is overlap on about one out of every six of the firms on the Thomson list. These simultaneous interlocks include all five of the major banks, the major insurance firms, and many top 100 industrial firms, including the top six firms: General Motors Ltd., Canadian Pacific Ltd., Ford Motor Co., Bell Canada Enterprises Inc., Canadian Pacific Enterprises Ltd., and Imperial Oil Ltd.. Southam and Thomson also indirectly interlock on firms ranked 12th through 17th on *The Blue Book of Canadian Business* list, as well as many others in the top 100.

These two major consciousness industry firms also overlap on a number of media boards: Baton Broadcasting, Bushnell Communications, CFCN Communications, CFRB Ltd., Kawartha Broadcasting, Roger's Cablesystems Inc., five different MacLean Hunter communication firms, The *Toronto Sun* Publishing Co., Torstar Inc., and also (again indirectly) on their "competing" boards of directors: Southam with Thomson, and Thomson with Southam.

Conclusions

This study supports earlier research pointing to the central importance of major banking institutions in the already close-knit group of Canadian corporations. Both the Southam and Thomson chains have direct or indirect access to the boards of all five major banks. Over all, the corporate directors form a very cohesive group: the constant reappearance of some firms' names among small numbers of directors was startling. The two major newspaper firms are intricately locked into, not only the financial and insurance institutions, but the major corporations generally. Their presence among the corporate boards is pervasive, serving to make them indistinguishable from the corporate sector generally, and from each other. Additionally, the cohesiveness of these pluralistic groups raises questions about the potential for conflict of interest for individuals on several different boards of directors. Of special concern here is the newspaper director who is on numerous outside boards. It is time to give serious consideration to proposals restricting interlocks among corporations, especially those in consciousness industries.

Of broader concern are the ramifications these extensive corporate interlocks hold for our notions of a pluralistic society. In Canada, and the U.S. evidence does not contradict this view either, there is now strong evidence to challenge the pluralist view. Questions about the impact of this apparently monolithic elite system on democratic society must be addressed, and solutions for the problems sought.

CHAPTER 7

Monopoly and Socialization

A. Carlos Ruotolo

School of Public Communications
University of Puerto Rico

The major point in the discussion about media monopoly and ownership concentration is the potentially damaging effect of such economic arrangements on media performance. The implied threat is that the market monopoly also may mean a monopoly of ideas—the media speaking in one voice.

For newspapers, the monopoly of ideas is of great concern because, historically, newspapers have been associated with freedom of expression, the very essence of democracy. Therefore, the lack of pluralism in newspapers is more readily associated with a threat to democracy itself.

Involved in this discussion are two fundamental points that need theoretical clarification: (a) the extent to which monopolistic ownership affects the contents, and (b) the effects of biased or homogeneous contents on readers.

On the first aspect, the relation between monopoly and newspaper content, the empirical evidence is rather inconclusive and scanty. Nixon and Jones (1956) did not find differences of content characteristics (i.e., news categories) between competing and noncompeting papers, although competing papers had a greater newshole. Borstel (1956) examined the amount of commentary in editorials, columns, letters to the editor, and cartoons presented by small dailies and found no difference between competing and noncompeting papers.

Other researchers examined the coverage of local issues, a content characteristic likely to be reduced by monopoly because it is costly. Rarick and Hartman (1966) studied a single paper, under the same management but operating in competitive and noncompetitive (after the competing paper closed) situations. They found that, in the competitive condition, the paper gave more space to the news and placed greater emphasis on local content. Similar findings were reported by Trim, Pizaute, and Yaraskavitch (1983) on the coverage of local government by Canadian newspapers in Winnipeg and Ottawa. Without competition (after competing papers closed down), the surviving papers reduced the coverage of local government affairs. Not only did the total space decline, but also the scope and emphasis given to local government stories. These results, however, are rather tentative. Rarick and Hartman themselves suggested that comparative studies need to take account of the intensity of competition. When a paper is competing from a strongly dominant position, one may expect almost no impact on its contents due to the presence of the smaller paper in the market. Slight changes observed in the dominant paper, after the small competing paper disappears, may be due to other factors, not to the absence of competition. Furthermore, other research points in the direction of increase in local coverage under monopoly. Schweitzer and Goldman (1975) found that a paper that was left without competition increased the local contents by 5% when operating alone in the market.

The finding that monopolies do not substantially affect the contents of newspapers in the U.S. comes as no surprise. Monopoly alone is not likely to be a major cause of content homogeneity. The economics of news production generally, and distribution, may constitute stronger forces toward homogeneity than monopoly itself. The need to cater to wide audiences, not marginal readers, appears to be a central influence that makes mainstream newspapers—competing or not—"rivals in conformity," as Bigman (1948) put it. Besides their orientation toward the same audience, newspapers rely on the same news sources and news gathering practices. Donohue and Glasser (1978) studied 12 dailies in Connecticut and found a great increase in the usage of wire copies from 1967 to 1976. Some papers had no staff-generated copy at all; all news came from the wire services. They concluded that "The economics of news production has the potential to create a situation where news homogeneity is not dependent on pluralism of ownership but pluralism in sources utilized in news collections" (p. 593).

Given that competing and noncompeting papers do not necessarily greatly differ, the second aspect that needs to be analyzed is the relation between content and its possible effects on readers. One would ask: Does it matter that newspapers' content is similar?

The issue of content effects cannot be properly addressed in terms of newspapers alone. The whole media context needs to be considered, since the audience is responding to the totality of available messages. Local newspaper monopolies and other forms of media concentration affect the audience to the extent that lower competition and diminished alternative sources of information reduce the scope, quantity, and quality of the messages available to the public.

One possible consequence of media concentration on their messages is the increase in content homogeneity. Research has shown that cross-ownership of newspaper and television outlets increases the similarity of coverage and of contents presented to the public (Gormley, 1977). Another form of concentration, newspaper chain ownership, increases the similarity of editorial endorsement of candidates by member papers and substantially reduces their editorial vigor (Wackman, Gillmor, Graziano, & Dennis, 1975). Chain papers present less argumentative, fewer controversial, and fewer local-topic editorials than independently-owned newspapers (Thrift, 1977).

From a social perspective, content homogeneity may pose a threat to the functioning of an open society. Without pluralism of information, the political process and many other social exchanges based on information may be impaired. Indicative of how homogeneity affects the audience are the findings that people living in an area of cross-ownership monopoly have access to less news, have lower levels of knowledge about current events, and make less use of outside media (Stempel, 1973).

Homogeneity may have broad implications, especially in developed societies whose complexity increases individuals' reliance on the media for information about their social and political environment. From the information purveyed by the media, individuals continuously extract and confirm beliefs, interpret reality, and form their worldview.

> The mass media force attention to certain issues. They build up public images of political figures. They are constantly presenting objects suggesting what individuals in the mass should think about, know about, have feelings about (Lang & Lang, 1966, p. 455).

This notion that the media are constantly providing information with which people construct their symbolic environment appears to have empirical support. Zukin and Snyder (1984) have presented strong evidence that, in a media rich environment, political information was learned in a passive, nonpurposive fashion. The simple availability of information was sufficient to produce learning. People living in a media-rich environment learned more political information about candidates than those living in a media-poor environment, even when interest in the election was held constant.

If the symbolic environment portrayed by the media is homogeneous, one may expect that individuals will have limited ability to make appropriate decisions. Homogeneity appears to be high when the media present cultural values and topics related to the preservation of the social order (Gans, 1978; see also Breed, 1958b). Because homogeneity limits people's choices, it also carries the potential of distorting other social processes that depend on people's judgments. As Tuchman (1981, p. 88) puts it, "News draws from life, transforms life, and reenters life."

Homogeneity and Political Cognitions

A fundamental concern about news homogeneity is the possible impact that it may have on the political system. In democratic societies, the press and the political system are in a symbiotic relationship. A self-governing people need information to make decisions. Therefore, without full disclosure of the political information, of the conflicting opinions, people's ability to govern themselves may be impaired, and democracy itself will not function.

The research accumulated in recent years suggests that the media play an important role in the distribution of political information. The impact of the media begins early in life as an agent of political socialization. Children learn about current topics primarily from the media. Other sources of political socialization—parents, friends, and teachers—play a smaller role than the media in providing current information. Initial knowledge of political information learned from the media later on leads to higher political knowledge among school children. Chaffee, Ward, and Tipton (1970) assert that, in political socialization, the media "constitute a major independent agency of personal political growth" (p. 658).

The relationship between children's public affairs media use and political knowledge has been found consistently in several studies. Gollin and Anderson (1980), for example, found that, among high school students, newspaper reading is related to knowledge of public issues. While 22% of the regular readers give correct answers to questions about issues, 17% of occasional readers reply correctly—whereas only 10% of nonreaders give correct answers.

Among adults, learning about politics takes more elaborate forms. The political knowledge adults gain from the media elicits a variety of cognitive effects that range from simple learning about current events to some behavioral consequences stemming from higher levels of political information holding.

Cognitive effects, at a simple level, begin with the role media play in providing information about current events. Studies on the diffusion of news stories have found that the media are the primary source of information for the majority of people. Deutschman and Danielson (1960) found that 58% of people learned about major events from the media as the first source, and that 50% used the media for supplementary information as well.

Exposure to the news media (newspapers and TV news) clearly is associated with learning about candidates' images. Newspaper reading, but not TV watching, has been found to contribute to learning about candidates' stands on the issues as well. Furthermore, people with high exposure to the news media tend to be more interested in presidential elections than people with low news exposure (Patterson, 1980).

Much of the information learned from the media is rather superficial, at the awareness level. However, when issues are of national relevance and when the media coverage of these issues is intense, some deeper level of learning occurs.

Palmgreen (1979) reports that, under these high relevance and high coverage conditions, media exposure is a stronger predictor of information holding than education and issue salience.

Political information learned from the media appears to have some consequences on the individual's political behavior. McLeod, Glynn, and McDonald (1983) found that presidential candidates' images are a predictor of voting. Image learned from newspapers affects early deciders, while the image from television is a stronger influence for voters deciding preferences during the campaign or closer to the election day. Aside from elections, political information holding is related to some other political behaviors such as discussing politics, going to political meetings, and contributing money to campaigns (Kessel, 1965).

Another cognitive effect, the relative salience of information, is implied in the agenda-setting perspective of media effects. The thrust of agenda setting is that, by emphasizing certain topics, usually issues, the media make these topics highly salient in people's minds. Thus, the political coverage would have the effect of telling voters what issues are important. The media agenda of issues and images and the public agenda are expected to overlap. The evidence suggests such agenda-setting effects are qualified by several "contingencies" such as topic relevance, audience characteristics, and timing.

The research on agenda setting, however, has done more than verify this hypothesis. Because it implies a close correlation between effects and the media content, agenda setting has uncovered the relatively homogeneous media coverage of political campaigns. The media agenda appears to be set very early in the campaign, and, after that, only a few topics and images dominate the coverage. "The basic structure of the race was determined very quickly, long before most voters were highly attentive to the campaign or had a chance to reflect and discuss the various issues and candidates that had emerged at the beginning of the campaign year" (Weaver, Graber, McCombs, & Chaim, 1981, p. 205).

From the homogeneity standpoint, it is highly significant that the media usually carry a very limited agenda of issues and images, let alone the fact that the horse-race coverage usually takes the majority of the news attention. The complexity of the issues, the full range of opinions, the fair representation of social groups, are all neglected. The implications of such a lack of plurality might be substantial in the alignment of public opinion. By limiting the available information at the time the people are supposed to provide their input into the political system, the media may actually lead, rather than serve, the public. The favored issues, parties, and images may indeed become a self-fulfilling prophecy, gaining legitimacy as representative of public consent when actually no real choice was available.

Homogeneity and Attitudes

The role of the media in shaping attitudes and opinions apparently is very limited. Since the early studies in Erie County and Elmira, the impact of the media on attitudes is best described as minimal. This conclusion is based on studies of media effects on conversion, the change of attitudes from one position to the opposing position as the result of exposure to persuasive messages.

Attitudinal effects, however, may occur in ways other than conversion. The media afford a high credibility status that may carry considerable weight in the formation of opinions. Community members rate the media as their highest influential institution. The media outrank all other community groups—including the church, business, and universities—in people's perception of influential groups (Smith, 1984).

A more direct influence, however limited, is found when newspapers endorse political candidates. Editorial endorsements influence undecided voters, especially in elections for high-level offices (McCombs, 1967). Robinson (1974) suggested that in presidential elections, endorsements have consistently affected independent voters. And in landslide presidential elections, endorsements have affected voters of the losing parties as well. A small but significant difference in voting for a candidate could be attributed to editorial endorsements. Reviewing five presidential elections, Robinson (1974, p. 591) found "a highly consistent relation between individual voting behavior and exposure to newspaper endorsements."

Intense commentaries carried by the media also may affect voters' evaluation of a candidate. Gerald Ford's erroneous statement about Eastern Europe during a presidential debate did not change voters' evaluation of his candidacy until the media elaborated on the topic. Negative reactions to Ford's statement did not emerge until the afternoon of the day after the debate. Negative public evaluations coincided with the great publicity given by the media (Steeper, 1978).

It is interesting to note that, in this instance, the media commentary was mostly negative toward President Ford, and public reaction was likewise negative. The fact that one-sided information dominated the news media and affected the audience is highly indicative of the dangers of homogeneity. In this episode, President Ford was in error, and one would expect the commentaries to be negative. Nevertheless, in many common situations—especially when prejudice and opinions are involved—error is not so clearly identifiable. In these cases, the potential danger of homogeneity to people's judgment may be substantial.

Political attitudes also may be affected by simple familiarity with the subject matter. Campaign themes, candidates, and images that are frequently portrayed in the media may become familiar to the audience. And familiarity itself influences people's evaluations.

This frequency of exposure effect is likely to occur in situations of low involvement, but many political decisions and many races for lower offices are only remotely relevant to the bulk of voters, and thus are low involvement. The frequency of exposure effect, already well established in laboratory experiments, was found to be applicable to low-involvement political behavior.

Grush, McKeough, and Ahlering (1968) found that voters' level of exposure to candidates was strongly related to electoral outcomes in congressional primaries. Candidates in the high-exposure conditions, either by prior exposure (incumbents and celebrities) or by media exposure (high advertising spenders), got significantly better electoral results than candidates in the low-exposure condition. These findings suggest that, often, moderate levels of homogeneity suffice to produce an effect; all that is required is that one piece of information be exposed with greater frequency than other pieces of information.

The implications of the frequency of exposure phenomenon may be far reaching. As a great many pieces of human knowledge, including most political information, fall in the category of low involvement, the potential of the media for shaping cognitions and then breeding favorable attitudes may be substantial. Learning and liking of ethnic groups, lifestyles, human traits, foreign countries, and similar subjects may be affected by the "bias" of the media in playing up some, but not other aspects of the information about these topics.

Homogeneity and Conformity

Content homogeneity, especially in extreme cases in which no opposing views are available, may have a conformity effect on people's behavior. The social psychological literature shows that homogeneous information influences people's behavior toward conformity with the group. In his pioneering research, Asch (1951) found that, when faced with unanimous opinions, subjects showed a clear tendency to conform to the majority perception, even against their own personal perception. People find it easier to contradict their own perceptions than to disagree with majority opinion.

Conformity to the majority opinion increases when the number of different sources of information agreeing on the same judgment increases (Wilder, 1977, p. 253). However, the presence of a partner—either present or absent—reduces the pressure for conformity (Allen & Wilder, 1977, p. 187).

Because the pressure for conformity to the majority does not require the physical presence of the influencing individuals, the mass media may well work as a channel through which homogeneous majority opinions (or dissenting opinions) are vicariously conveyed to the audience. Elizabeth Noelle-Newman, in her "spiral of silence" theory of public opinion, posits that, indeed, people assess the prevalence of majority opinion primarily through media exposure. When the perceived predominant opinion is contrary to the individual's own opinion, the individual will be less inclined to express his or her views for fear of isolation. "To the individual, not isolating himself is more important than his own judgment" (Noelle-Neumann, 1974, p. 43).

In the same way that individuals in the minority are inclined to refrain from expressing their opinions, those in the majority will be more inclined to speak out. This spiraling process will result in the almost absolute prevalence of a dominant opinion—a situation of very high homogeneity in which opposing views are considered deviant. Noelle-Newman (1980) claims that, under this high consensus circumstance, the selective perception mechanisms that usually lead to reinforcement effects of media exposure do not operate. The end result is that the media will have powerful effects since no alternative information is available.

Although high consensus situations are rare, the fact remains that media homogeneity can foster the process of spiraling silence, and, by doing so, the media may induce conformity. Thus, without plurality and proper balance, the media may mold rather than mirror public opinion.

Conclusions

The literature reviewed in this chapter suggests that the media may affect public opinion in several ways: shaping the symbolic environment, providing political information, facilitating the formation of attitudes about low-involvement matters, and inducing conformity to majority views. From the knowledge of these potential effects, the issue of monopoly and ownership concentration can be placed in proper perspective: the relationship between effects and these modes of media ownership and operation. Neither monopoly nor concentration in itself is harmful or dangerous to democracy—as the argument usually goes—unless monopoly and concentration result in adverse consequences to the public due to content control.

It appears that the fundamental concern ought to be centered around news homogeneity, since the content output of the media is what affects the public. And homogeneity is caused by several factors. Monopoly and ownership concentration may be forces toward homogeneous content, but the economics of the marketplace, journalists' orientations, and bureaucratic news practices are powerful factors that need to be considered as well.

So far the research on the effects of monopoly has failed to show that it is a strong factor in homogeneity. It appears that the economics of the marketplace (newspapers' reliance on advertising as the main source of revenue) is a driving force behind homogeneity and behind newspaper monopoly itself—as advertising upsets newspaper competition by favoring papers with large, elite readership.

Whatever its cause might be, news homogeneity interferes with the democratic ideal of people governing themselves. Democracy requires that the citizens make decisions as informed participants. News homogeneity, even at low levels, amounts to informational bias which is likely to have adverse effects on people's ability to exercise sound judgment. The evidence is clear that, in many cases, the slightest preferential treatment elicits more positive public response.

Even more important than the publication of biased content is the highly homogeneous coverage of political campaigns. In this case, bias is not the problem, because political coverage tends to be balanced. The problem is lack of plurality of issues, images, candidates, and constituencies that are portrayed in the media. Moreover, all media tend to present highly similar coverage of the same few images and events. Such high levels of news homogeneity can hardly provide citizens with the full information they need to provide input to their government.

In such cases of limited, high-homogeneous content, what is *not* presented in the media may be more important than what is presented. Alternative views, minority groups, complex issues, and the like are often neglected information. Such neglect, however, may come with a high price for individuals and society. What is neglected cannot become part of the culture, cannot be evaluated, cannot be liked or disliked.

> Individuals make their own selection of materials through which to cultivate personal images, tastes, views, and preferences, and they seek to influence those available to and chosen by their children. But they cannot cultivate that which is not available (Gerbuer, 1973, p. 567).

The high homogeneity with which certain topics are presented may not only restrict people's choices but may actually impose the views, habits, and images that are overwhelmingly presented by the media. The research on conformity and on spiral of silence effects show that majority dominance may well occur under consensus conditions.

In a democratic system, media performance ought to be evaluated in terms of content pluralism and of fair representation of reality. Media homogeneity is dysfunctional to a democratic society, whatever the underlying causes, including monopoly and concentration. To counter the risks of homogeneity outlined in this chapter, new communication policies from the industry and from journalists—and perhaps from governments—are becoming necessary; new policies that ensure content plurality. As journalist Robert McNeil (1985, p. 8) put it in a speech at Columbia University, "The First Amendment does not require fairness, but I think the American public is beginning to."

PART III

Influences on Content

CHAPTER 8

Concentration, Monopoly, and Content

Maxwell E. McCombs

Department of Journalism
University of Texas

Some critics contend that the marketplace of news, entertainment, and commentary becomes significantly less diverse when suspension of publication by a
competitor leaves a city with only a single daily newspaper. Monopolies, of
course, have become the modal situation across North America. The disappearance of competition and the emergence of monopolies in all but a handful of
markets is the culmination of an economic trend set in motion well over a half
century ago.

Traditionally, the presence of competing daily newspapers in a market was
taken as prima facie evidence of diversity. But traditional assumptions in democratic political theory about competition and the diversity of news and opinion in
the marketplace need to be examined more rigorously. An important role of
social science is to make explicit and subject to empirical verification the assumptions only partially articulated in our social rhetoric. Even if traditional
democratic assumptions about competition and diversity were empirically true in
the eighteenth and nineteenth century, they need to be examined in light of the
social and economic situation in the late twentieth century. How much difference does the structure of ownership in a local newspaper market make to
what is available to local readers?

Or, alternatively, as the more recent literature on the sociology of news asks,
how much of what is available to local readers is determined by the traditions,
practices, and beliefs of journalists, regardless of the ownership structure? The
traditions of journalism center on news values and ethical standards, such as
objectivity and fairness. The homogenizing influence of these traditions on news
content has been traced back to the 19th century by Schudson (1978), Shaw

(1972), and Roshco (1975). Seminal research by Epstein (1973) and Sigal (1973) has documented the impact of work practices and organizational constraints on the final news product, influences which are more internal to the news organization and profession than to any external competition. The beliefs and social perspectives of journalists as centripetal forces for a centrist convergence also have been detailed for a variety of news organizations by Gans (1979) and Gitlin (1980).

In short, the sociology of news literature collectively creates the expectation that newspapers competing in the same geographic and demographic market will produce highly similar products. For example, a detailed content analysis of competing dailies in 23 U.S. cities found no statistically significant differences between "leaders" and "trailers" across the 22 content categories compared. Nor did Weaver and Mullins (1975) find any differences in the proportion of space devoted to editorial content. This null relationship between competition and message diversity also is reflected in the preponderance of evidence from the accumulated journalism research of the past five decades (see, e.g., Nafziger & Barnhart, 1946; Bigman, 1948; Willoughby, 1955; Nixon & Jones, 1956; Donohue & Glasser, 1978).

These assertions and questions about newspaper content and competition became far more than academic considerations when, in 1981, the Canadian government brought antitrust charges against the country's two major newspaper groups, Thomson and Southam. Among the issues in contention were the suspension of the Montreal *Star* in 1979, leaving Southam's *Gazette* as the only English-language daily in that city; and the suspension by Southam of the Winnipeg *Tribune* in 1980, leaving Thomson's *Free Press* as the only daily there.[1]

These suspensions also created a natural experiment for testing hypotheses about competition and diversity through content analysis. With the shift from competition to monopoly occurring in two widely separated markets, it is possible to do a detailed before-and-after study and to build in a replication.[2] Both in Montreal and Winnipeg, pairs of dailies can be examined in a period of vigorous competition, and the surviving daily can be compared before and after the

---

[1] As part of the defense against these charges, Thomson funded an extensive content analysis of the newspapers in Montreal and Winnipeg before and after the suspensions. While the study reported here was prepared for that adversarial procedure, it should be emphasized that Thomson maintained an arms-length relationship at all times. All decisions on conceptualization, hypotheses, operational definitions, analyses, etc. were independently made by the author and his research associates, Luis Torres-Bohl and Val Pipps. These details and the findings were revealed to Thomson executives and the defense team only upon delivery of the completed research report.

[2] It is important to point out that, following the demise of the *Star*, the *Gazette* was not a monopoly newspaper per se, but a monopoly English-language paper in Montreal. Another important distinction between these papers is that the *Gazette* has been regarded as an elite newspaper, a Montreal equivalent of the *Globe and Mail*. Additionally, in Winnipeg, the *Free Press* did receive competition, albeit minor, from the new tabloid daily, the *Sun*.

demise of its competitor. In both cities, the "before" period is 2 years prior to the suspension of competition, and the "after" period is 1 year after suspension, a total span of 3 years.[3]

Drawing from three intellectual traditions—democratic political theory, sociology of news, and journalism research—this content analysis of the daily newspapers in Montreal and Winnipeg framed two broad competing hypotheses to guide the numerous detailed comparisons of these newspapers. One hypothesis, based on traditional assumptions of competition and diversity, predicts differences during the period of competition in each city. As a corollary, the views of at least some critics also would lead to an expectation of major negative changes in the surviving newspaper. The opposing hypothesis, based on the sociology of news and journalism research, predicts no significant differences between the newspapers during the period of competition in each city. This hypothesis also would predict the lack of any significant changes in the surviving newspaper.

Comparing the Newspapers

Newspapers are the epitome of mass communication, with its broad array of messages for a vast audience. To examine the degree of diversity present in the

---

[3] To yield representative pictures of what these newspapers provided their readers, three criteria were set for selection of the actual months to be sampled before and after the suspensions in Montreal and Winnipeg:

1. Use of a "typical" news and advertising period to avoid special seasons, such as Christmas and the summer vacation period.
2. Selection of observation points far enough removed from the date of suspension to eliminate the perturbation of this change in the market, yet close enough in time to be pertinent.
3. Holding the observation month constant across time (before and after suspension) and across markets (Montreal and Winnipeg). This yields directly comparable replications and eliminates a major alternative explanation for any differences in the results.

Since the Montreal *Star* closed in September 1979 and the Winnepeg *Tribune* closed in August 1980, the simultaneous application of these criteria suggested observing each surviving newspaper in September of the year after the suspension in its city, September 1980 for the Montreal *Gazette* and September 1981 for the Winnipeg *Free Press*.

Use of an identical interval for the "before" observation period was complicated by an extended strike at the Montreal *Star* from June 1978 to February 1979. Therefore, the "before" interval was extended to 2 years, September 1977 for Montreal and September 1978 for Winnipeg. In short, each market was observed 2 years before and one year after the end of the competition.

For each of these Septembers, six issues of the newspaper(s), were measured in detail. While a full week's sample can adequately represent a much larger span of time, the contents of any particular week's issues of a newspaper are subject to the idiosyncracies of that week's news events and advertising campaigns. Therefore, a 6-day *constructed week*, consisting of one Monday, one Tuesday, etc., selected at random from the entire month, was used as the sample. During those periods when two newspapers were being published in the same market, the same constructed week was used for both newspapers.

newspapers of cities such as Montreal and Winnipeg, a content analysis should begin with broad comparisons of these newspapers and progressively narrow the scope of these comparisons. For example, the Montreal newspapers in both 1977 and 1980 published a wide range of news, entertainment, and commentary— 200 items or more a day in each newspaper, hundreds of pages a week.[4] But how different were these editorial products?

There were different news/advertising ratios in the competing Montreal newspapers of 1977. The newshole in the *Star* was 36% of its total space, while the *Gazette's* newshole was 48% of its total space. However, close examination of the figures also reveals a "fat" Montreal *Star* (420 pages per week) versus a *Gazette* less than two-thirds its size (256 pages per week). Under such circumstances it is hardly surprising that the "thin" *Gazette* found it necessary to maintain a proportionately larger newshole in order to compete with the *Star's* extensive contents. And after the *Star's* demise, the now "fat" *Gazette* (536 pages per week) displayed a news/advertising ratio identical to that of the *Star* when it dominated the Montreal market.

During the period of competition in Winnipeg, the *Free Press* was a substantially larger daily than the *Tribune*, averaging over 13 pages and over 50 stories a day more than its competitor. This practice of producing a "fat" daily persisted after the suspension of the *Tribune*. During the period of competition, however, the two newspapers in Winnipeg had different news/advertising ratios. While the *Tribune* maintained a 35/65 ratio of news to advertising, the larger *Free Press* was closer to a 30/70 ratio of news to advertising. However, after the suspension of the *Tribune*, the *Free Press* increased its newshole, both proportionally and in terms of actual news space. The newshole was now 35% of the total space—an increase from 157 pages in 1978 to 165 pages in 1981.

Of course, the design of each day's newspaper does not result from any set of precise calculations or specifications, but rather from a melange of long-term

---

[4] The September 10, 1977, issues of the Montreal *Star* and Montreal *Gazette* were analyzed using both frequency counts and space measurement. The correlations between these two sets of measures across the news categories adapted from Bruce (1966) were .97 for the *Gazette* and .99 for the *Star*. This is true whether the amount of space taken up by the headline was included in the space measure or not. Based on these findings, the decision was made to employ frequency counts as the measurement procedure in this study.

To ascertain the reliability of the frequency counts, two coders were employed. After discussion of the coding categories and procedures, each of the coders *independently* coded the September 12, 1977, issues of the *Star* and *Gazette*. At this point, there was substantial agreement between the coders, but, to further check the robustness of the coding procedures, the two coders next independently coded the September 10, 1977, issues of the two Montreal newspapers. Overall, 24 different comparisons were made as the two coders used the various category sets to content analyze the special sections, editorial and op-ed pages, and news of the day. Both the median and modal correlation was +.99, and only three of the 24 correlation coefficients were less than +.90. Comparisons of independent analyses of the September 11, 1978, issues of the Winnipeg *Free Press* and *Tribune* also revealed a high degree of reliability in the coding of those data.

and short-term decisions and judgments applied to the material available that day. Typically, the material published is no more than 10% to 20% of what is available and, of course, a much smaller percentage of the actual day's events.

Under such circumstances one would hardly expect identical editorial products. Some diversity in news and content is inevitable, but there are varying degrees of diversity! To take a nonjournalistic example, the numerous wineries of California's Napa Valley do not produce perfectly identical Cabernet Sauvignons. But their diversity is diminished in the eye of the observer when Bordeaux clarets are added to the comparison. Add some white Burgundies, and there is yet more diversity. Enough on the diversities of wine. The point is that the range of diversity in any set of comparisons may be minor or major in scope. Here the notion of diversity in newspaper content is taken to mean some degree of major scope. Such comparisons conform to what the average person would consider diversity.

Beginning with the general character of the Montreal newspapers, how diverse were their packages of news, entertainment, and commentary in 1977 and 1980? The research presents a picture of *rivals in conformity*. Detailed comparisons of the general content categories reveal only a few significant differences between the two newspapers. Most striking is the larger volume of general news in the *Star* when it dominated the market. Interestingly, the other two differences are from the editorial pages. In 1977 the *Star* ran more local editorials and more letters to the editor than did the *Gazette*. To the extent that a strong local editorial voice is indicated by the number of local editorials, the *Star* was the strongest newspaper in 1977. It also was the newspaper which provided more community participation on the editorial page through publication of letters to the editor. Neither the number of local editorials nor letters to the editor in the *Gazette* increased after the disappearance of the *Star*.

The *Gazette* did significantly increase its general news and sports coverage, and the number of comics, from 1977 to 1980. These three categories largely account for the increased number of items appearing in the *Gazette*.

Parallel to the pattern in Montreal, Winnipeg is another portrait of rivals in confomity. With only three exceptions, the rival *Tribune* and *Free Press* produced highly similar products. Detailed comparisons of the general content categories shows only three statistically significant differences in the amount of news published on a typical day: business news (the *Free Press* published more), lifestyle/food news (again, the *Free Press* published more), and nonlocal editorials (the *Tribune* averaged about one a day, while the *Free Press* concentrated exclusively on local editorials).

After the suspension of the *Tribune* in 1980, the *Free Press* remained much the same newspaper. Only one category, letters to the editor, changed significantly. The number of letters published during a typical week more than doubled, so that the *Free Press* of 1981 was running more letters each week than both newspapers together had published back in 1978. To the extent that a strong editorial voice also is indicated by the number of local editorials, the *Free Press* continued its established practice of publishing two or more local editorials daily.

News of the Day

Narrowing the focus of our attention, to take a detailed look at the news of the day, we can consider those items appearing principally on the front page and main news pages of a newspaper. In all four of the newspapers examined here, more than half of the news of the day falls in the category of political news, evidence for the sociology of news view that the sharing of professional news values across news organizations results in highly similar products.[5] In this case we see a high degree of similarity across two cities and across a variety of time periods.

Comparison of the Montreal profiles reveals no difference between the competing *Star* and *Gazette*. There was a statistically significant change over all in the news coverage of the *Gazette* from 1977 to 1980, a substantial decrease in crime news and a modest decrease in human interest material. Modest increases also occurred in the political and banking categories. Emphasis remained much the same from 1977 to 1980 on all the other categories of news.

Statistical comparison of the three Winnipeg profiles reveal no difference between the *Tribune* and *Free Press* in 1978, or between the 1978 and 1981 editions of the *Free Press* in their emphasis on various categories of news.

Geography of the News

Another way of examining the diversity of newspaper content is to consider the geography of the news, the daily map of the world presented in the news pages. Since all but a few American and Canadian newspapers are highly local in their news perspective, differences would be expected between Montreal in the east and Winnipeg to the west. But a sociology of news perspective would predict high similarity in the geographical focus of newspapers in the same city.

The *geography of the news* in the Montreal newspapers before and after the suspension of the Star was essentially the same. Examination of the patterns of geographic coverage reveals that about one story of every six was local news. Roughly a similar proportion of stories was news of Quebec province.

After the suspension of the *Star*, the *Gazette* had a more cosmopolitan emphasis. Local news and Quebec news coverage decreased, while news coverage increased for Ottawa, the Maritimes, western Canada, and foreign countries (other than the U.S.).

---

[5] It should be emphasized that this statement is made in the context of the quantitative approach taken in this study. *Amount* of political news may or may not reflect *quality* of that news. If, for example, the *Free Press* supported the Conservatives and the *Tribune*, before its demise, supported the Liberals, this latter perspective is obviously lost.

In Winnipeg there was a statistically significant difference in the geographic perspectives of the *Tribune* and *Free Press* in 1978. *Free Press* coverage placed a heavier emphasis on local news from Winnipeg. While better than one story out of four was local in the *Free Press*' news of the day, local coverage in the *Tribune* was closer to one story in five. The two papers' coverage of Manitoba provincial news was about the same.

Ontario receives major coverage in almost all Canadian newspapers regardless of their location in the country. While this is true in both Montreal and Winnipeg, the *Free Press* coverage of Ontario in 1978 was approximately double that of the *Tribune*. Interestingly, the *Tribune* placed much heavier emphasis on U.S. news than did the *Free Press* in 1978. Otherwise, all the papers examined here devote about one story in six to U.S. coverage.

With the demise of the *Tribune*, the *Free Press* cut back on the areas where it exceeded *Tribune* coverage (local news and Ontario news) and expanded where it had trailed the *Tribune* (U.S. news).

Sources of News

There were significant differences among the competing Montreal newspapers in their use of sources. The principal difference in 1977 results from the greater diversity in the *Gazette's* wire service sources for the news of the day. While both newspapers used CP and AP, only the *Gazette* also relied upon UPI. The other principal difference is in the use of syndicated material, more extensive in the *Star* than in the *Gazette*. Interestingly, the use of locally produced staff copy is almost identical in the two newspapers. For both it is about two news stories out of every five.

There were extensive, statistically significant changes in the *Gazette* from 1977 to 1980. Use of locally produced staff copy declined from 38.07% to 29.86%. Of course, the substantial increase in the newshole of the *Gazette* must be taken into account in interpreting this finding. In terms of actual stories, there were 122 staff stories published during a typical week in 1977, and 156 staff stories published during a typical week during 1980. Of course, in terms of the sheer number of local staff news stories, Montreal readers were receiving about 100 fewer stories per week after the *Star* closed.

There also were significant differences among the Winnipeg newspapers in their use of sources. The major difference is the much greater volume of staff produced news in the *Free Press*, a level of staff production maintained after the suspension of the *Tribune*. Otherwise, in 1978 the two Winnipeg newspapers were much the same in their relative use of CP, AP, and syndicated material.

There are statistically significant changes in the *Free Press*' use of news sources from 1978 to 1981, but all of these are in the relative use of external material. Use of CP declined and use of AP increased, bringing the two into approximate parity. Use of other external sources increased substantially. Both before and after the suspension of the *Tribune,* the *Free Press* staff produced about four stories out of every 10 in the news of the day. This was a significantly higher level of staff stories than appeared in the *Tribune.*

Summary

Traditional democratic assumptions about newspaper competition and the diversity of content are not well supported by these content analyses of the Montreal and Winnipeg papers. Comparisons of the general content reveal few significant differences between either pair of competitors; examination of the news of the day reveals no significant differences at all. There were some differences in the geographic emphasis of the Winnipeg competitors, and there were differences in both markets in the sources of news. But these latter differences, geography and sources, are no more than minor variations on a theme. Emphasizing U.S. news more, or local news less, are minor points of differentiations in essentially similar products. All four of the newspapers examined here represent the mainstream of North American journalism in style and content.

The "critics corollary" that the demise of a competitor will be followed by diminished quality in the survivor is totally rebutted by the evidence of these content analyses. Only a few changes from before to after the end of competition were found, and all of these were positive changes in the quality of the editorial product.

In short, these data support a sociology of news perspective that newspapers competing for the same geographic and demographic market will produce highly similar products due to the similarity of their professional values, beliefs, and practices. The increasing professionalization of journalism during this century has resulted in a convergence of views among journalists about what is the news of the day. For example, a qualitative analysis of the Montreal newspapers' coverage of a regional power blackout indicated that readers of both newspapers received essentially the same facts emanating from the same sources over a 3-day period.

Finally, these empirical findings undermine the notion that vigorous use of the antitrust statutes can insure a diversity of information in the marketplace. The principal conclusion to be drawn from this content analysis of Canadian newspapers during the last decade is one drawn over 25 years ago by Professors Raymond Nixon and Robert Jones after an extensive examination of 420 competitive and noncompetitive U.S. dailies:

differences in quality seem to hinge upon the "social responsibility and professional competence" of those who own and operate the papers, irrespective of whether they have competition. (Nixon & Jones, 1956, p. 313).

Professional perspectives on journalism, not the presence or absence of competition, determine the content of the daily newspaper. Competition does not insure diversity.

CHAPTER 9

Monopoly and Content in Winnipeg

Dores A. Candussi

Department of Communication
State University of New York,
Plattsburgh

James P. Winter

Department of
    Communication Studies
University of Windsor
Windsor, Ontario
Canada

On the same day in 1980 the two dominant Canadian newspaper chains closed competing papers in the cities of Ottawa and Winnipeg, leaving each chain with one monopoly city. The hue and outcry which followed these simultaneous closings led to charges against Southam News Ltd. and Thomson Newspapers Ltd. by the Canadian Federal Government, under the Anti-Combines Act. An additional outcome was the Royal Commission on Newspapers, chaired by Tom Kent, which reported in 1981. As a result of the Commission's report, a Canadian Newspaper Act was drafted by the Federal Government in 1982, which, if enacted, would have seen legislative control over newspapers in Canada.

The legislation drafted by Minister of State Jim Fleming, a former radio broadcaster, was never introduced in the House, as Fleming left the Cabinet and there has since been a change in government. As for the Anti-Combines Act, the court found Southam and Thomson not guilty of unduly conspiring to limit competition, to the public detriment. This fall 1983 decision by the courts that newspaper monopolies are not to the public detriment provides the impetus for a further examination of this question.

The arguments for and against monopolies may be summed up as follows: the promonopoly side says monopoly newspapers are not as sensational and trivial, as competition promotes sensationalism. They say so-called "competitive" newspapers are virtually rewrites of the same material anyway; in fact that competition as we know it does not mean diversity. They maintain that in multimedia society there is no such thing as a "monopoly," with burgeoning radio, television, cable, magazine, surburban, and satellite city dailies, and DBS satellite sources of competition. They argue that monopoly situations are more profitable, and that profit is reflected in greater editorial expenditures. Finally, the "pro" group argues that monopolies are an economic fact, an inevitable development of the marketplace. The antimonopoly side argues that in general, monopolies are not a good thing when compared to competition. Monopolies lead to price gouging of readers and advertisers, an inferior product due to lack of competition, and a focus on high profit yield rather than social responsibility. Unlike the family-run newspapers of yesteryear, the chains of today (many of which have monopoly cities as their preserve) focus on the bottom line. Hence, the concentration into chains is seen as being directly tied into the monopoly situation. They argue that monopolies reduce the diversity of information in the all-important newspaper medium, and that other media are in the headline, rather than the "in-depth," news business. The "anti" group further argues that concentration and monopoly heighten the homogenity of owners—essentially a small group of economic elites—and reinforce and legitimate the status quo with respect to ideology and consciousness.

Differences between these two sides may boil down to what has been described in the U.S. as a "central conundrum" in the operation of the press (Entman, 1985). The contradiction is between the logic of the free-market system, and that of First Amendment ideals (largely adopted in Canada as well, and enshrined in the 1982 Constitution). The free market system assumes it is only good market practice to be motivated by economic self-interest in cornering the market, including the newspaper market. First Amendment or "social responsibility" ideals on the other hand stress the search for "truth" and "objectivity," along with such notions as diversity, fairness, and other characteristics identified with the public well being.

Siebert, Peterson, and Schramm (1956) argued that the press system of a society is merely a reflection of the broader socio-political-economic system of which it is a part. The U.S. system (and to a somewhat lesser degree the Canadian) is a free-market one. Our expectation within the system is that competition will be to the advantage of the consumer, but also (classical economic theory aside) that competition means the "best person will win" and that eventually economies of scale and oligopolistic or monopolistic markets will accrue to the winner.

It is from within this state of consciousness, framework or *Weltanschauung* that we view the newspaper or monopoly situation generally and that fact has failed us in the formation of weak anticombines and trust-busting legislation and, for example, the Newspaper Preservation Act in the U.S.

Accompanying, and part and parcel of this, has been the growth of our faith in science and logical positivism. Hence we demand "proof" to convict those who stand accused of murder, as well as those accused of collusion to unduly limit competition. Were our world view different—if we saw the ultimate monopolistic outcome of an unregulated market as detrimental to the (at a minimum, economic) well-being of the public—then so-called scientific evidence of the sort to be found in this chapter would be unnecessary. Within this consciousness we would simply observe that private monopolies are not good, and set in motion policies which would eliminate them.

The point here is that from a certain perspective, the current level of discourse in the newspaper competition literature is regrettable. For while academics debate the varied findings of their various operationalizations of, for example, "quality," owners such as the Southam, Thomson, and Gannett chains gleefully go about their business. According to this other perspective we should be on a higher plane of discourse, looking at the broader ramifications concentration in industry holds for a monolithic rather than pluralistic elite system (Clement, 1975), or the role of the media/economic elite in influencing our consciousness (Smythe, 1981).

But just as we require the overview of broad generalists such as John Porter or C. Wright Mills, who occasionally gloss over the fine details in their emphasis on the larger picture, so too do we need the Warren Breeds and Ben Bagdikians who will supply the pigment for the paint of the broader picture. These latter authors fill in the gaps in the assumptions made by the broader theorists, and both perspectives are necessary to our understanding of this complex issue. However, no one studying the issue of newspaper concentration should be unaware of the argument by Mills and others that there is no diversity in the media on important dimensions, even under competitive situations.

At best, this chapter can address only a small portion of the above arguments: specifically, whether a particular monopoly led to an inferior editorial product and advertisement price gouging. In this manner, evidence may be provided in answer to the question posed by the court decision in the Southam and Thomson anticombines case: whether monopolies are detrimental to the public interest.

Winnipeg's Monopoly Paper

The current study consists of a pre- and post-monopoly examination of the Winnipeg Free Press to observe selected differences.[1] The Free Press became a monopoly in August 1980 when the Winnipeg Tribune closed its doors. The Tribune and the Free Press were competitive in 1979; thus, that year was used as the premonopoly test. The year 1983 was used to test the change in the Free Press after it ceased to compete with the Tribune, once it was in a virtual monopoly situation.[2]

---

[1] The authors express their appreciation to Dr. Gerry McPhail of the University of Windsor Mathematics Department for his able assistance.

[2] After the demise of the Winnipeg Tribune, the Free Press did not have local newspaper competition until the publication of the tabloid Winnipeg Sun. As time is needed to build circula-

A random sample was drawn and a content analysis conducted on two constructed weeks' content pre- and postmonopoly. The random sample was stratified according to the months of the year and the days of the week. Every month was represented in both 1979 and 1983, and the publishing days (Monday to Saturday) appeared twice. Twelve issues per year were studied, for a total of 24 individual issues.

Each entire newspaper was coded, with the individual story serving as the unit of analysis. The total number of stories coded was 4,208.

It was thought that the *Free Press* would experience a decline in newshole after the demise of the *Winnipeg Tribune*. There was in fact a 7%, statistically significant, decline in newshole. This is based on the absolute amount of space devoted to newshole. But on all newspapers, regardless of ownership, the total amount of space (i.e., the number of pages published) is determined by the amount of advertising available. Since the amount of advertising declined by 27%, it seems at first hardly surprising that the amount of space devoted to news declined by 7%. In fact, newshole as a percentage of total space (the usual measure of newshole) increased from 33% to 38%.

It also was expected that the proportion of local news to total news would decline in the monopoly period, and this was not the case. There was actually a slight but insignificant increase, from 22% local news in 1979 to 24% in 1983. Similarly, it was expected that the number and proportion of local stories would decline in the monopoly period, but this was not the case. Nor was it found that the length of the stories in column centimeters differed.

There was however a 34% reduction in the number of national stories published in 1983, compared with 1979, while the number of centimeters per story remained the same.

The number of international stories also decreased significantly between 1979 and 1983. These dropped from 617 to 552, an 11% reduction. Again, the amount of news per story did not change. Under normal circumstances, under a monopoly situation one would expect the amount of advertising to rise. However, probably due to the tail end of the recession in 1983, the amount of advertising in the *Free Press* actually declined by 27% between the pre- and postmonopoly periods. This compares, as has been mentioned, with a decline of 34% in national news coverage, and an 11% reduction in international news, but only a drop of 7% in the newshole generally. Thus, it appears that the newshole fared quite well overall in relation to the decline in advertising. However, although there was less advertising in the monopoly *Free Press*, as we will see this did not represent a drop in revenue.

---

tion, the *Sun* is far from a strong competitor. Therefore, the Winnipeg situation is treated as a virtual monopoly in the current study, although of course it technically is not. In January 1983 the *Free Press* had an average daily circulation of 189,865, while the *Sun* circulation was 40,877. The advertising line rate for the *Free Press* was $1.98 Monday to Friday and $2.48 Saturdays, compared to 95 cents for the *Sun*.

It was felt that the creation of a monopoly situation in Winnipeg would result in an increase in retail and classified advertising rates out of proportion to other newspapers, for example, *The Ottawa Citizen*, the Southam monopoly newspaper in Ottawa. This was thought to be the case because of the reputation for more social (rather than fiscal) responsibility on the part of Southam when compared to Thomson. In all, five newspapers were compared with *The Tribune*. Display advertising rates increased by 117% in *The Tribune* between January 1979 and January 1983. Classified rates increased by 98%, which produces an "average" increase of 108%. "Costs" in this period were determined by adding the cost of living increase of 45% to the percentage increase in circulation, and for *The Tribune*, this came to 83%. Here of course we are overestimating costs by ignoring economies of scale. Subtracting the costs from the average leaves a net plus 25 figure for *The Tribune*. Figures for the other dailies examined are as follows: *Ottawa Citizen*: 7; *Edmonton Journal*: 13; *Windsor Star*: minus 4; *Victoria Colonist-Times*: minus 13; Thunder Bay Times-News/Chronicle-Journal: 9. Thus, *The Tribune* had about twice the rate of increase of any other paper studied, the closest being *The Edmonton Journal*, with a plus 13 to *The Tribune's* plus 25.

It is apparent from the above discussion that although the amount of advertising declined in *The Free Press* between the pre- and postmonopoly periods, the advertising *revenue* did not decline but rather increased, even when taking inflation into account. As mentioned the average increase in advertising rates for the monopoly paper was 108%, with a cost of living increase of 45%, and a decline in advertising space of 27%. Taking these factors into account, it may be shown that advertising revenue in 1983 represented a 5% increase over 1979.[3]

Obviously, these calculations do not take into account costs associated with circulation increases. With the demise of *The Tribune*, *The Free Press* circulation increased by 35% by 1983. Over the same period the price of a weekday copy of the paper increased by 67%, and by 100% for the Saturday edition. The respective prices had been 15 cents and 25 cents in 1979, and these rose to 25 cents and 50 cents by 1983.[4]

Taking into account circulation and price increases by 1983 allows us to calculate the net increases in circulation revenue, adjusted for inflation. The weekly circulation revenue in 1979 was $142,140.50, and for 1983 was $344,377.50, a simple increase of 142%. Once again taking inflation into ac-

---

[3] If the advertising rate in 1979 is represented by X, then the 1983 rate is 2.08X, and the 1979 equivalent of the 1983 rate would be: 2.08X times (100/145) = 1.434X. If the volume of advertising in 1979 is Y, then the volume of advertising in 1983 is 73/100 times Y. The advertising revenue in 1979 dollars for 1979 is XY, and the advertising revenue in 1979 dollars for 1983 is (1.434X)(73/100Y). 1983 revenue as a proportion of 1979 revenue would be: (1.434X)(73/100Y) divided by XY, which equals 1.05.

[4] The average purchase price increase was thus 72.5%. The circulation increases were 45,031 to 180,174, or 33% for weekdays, and 75,167 to 238,320, or 46%, for Saturdays.

count, we find that the 1983 circulation revenue represents a 67% increase over that of 1979.[5]

Thus we see that despite the decline in advertising space, advertising revenue increased by 5%; and despite a 34% decline in national newshole, an 11% reduction in international newshole and an overall decline in newshole of 7%, circulation revenue increased by 67%.

As on average approximately 80% of newspaper revenues come from advertising, versus 20% for circulation revenue, this 5% increase in advertising revenue may be more important than it appears.

Conclusions

In Winnipeg the development of a monopoly situation does not seem to have benefited either the consumer or the advertiser. As did Trim, Pizante, and Yaraskavitch (1983) with respect to local news, the authors found that the overall newshole decreased by 7% during the period, but the newshole as a percentage of available space, increased. While the proportion and number of local stories remained the same, contrary to expectations, the number and proportion of national news stories decreased, as did the number of international news stories.

It should of course be pointed out that in this area as in others our pre- and postdesign does not allow us to draw causal inferences. In other words it is possible for example that declining national and international coverage is part of a broad trend and is unrelated to the monopoly situation under study. Such definitive causal inferences will await extensive time series analyses, with studies of control newspapers. Nonetheless, we have demonstrated here that *The Free Press'* advertising rate increases, for example, far exceeded those for other competitive and monopoly newspapers. Additionally, research by, for example, Hicks and Featherstone (1978) and Stemple (1973) has indicated that monopoly situations compare unfavorably with competitive markets *at the same point in time.*

The amount of advertising decreased by 27%, but the cost of advertising increased dramatically, taking into account such factors as circulation figures, inflation, and increases at other papers. In 1979, 49% of space constituted advertisements, versus 63% of space in 1983. While advertisers paid much more, consumers also paid much more and got much less news both proportionately and in absolute terms, for their money. Although we do not have adequate measures of the quality of the news product delivered to the reader, it would appear from the quantitative measurements used that the monopoly situation adversely affected what readers received. Certainly, lessened national and international coverage and a smaller newshole are indicative of undesirable changes.

---

[5] The 1979 value of the $344,377.50 earned in 1983 is $237,501.72 (344,377.50 × 100/145), which is 67% greater than the $142,140.50 earned in 1979.

The 5% increase in advertising revenue, especially when coupled with the 67% increase in circulation revenue, indicates that—in true monopolistic tradition—the Winnipeg market is being put through the wringer in pursuit of profit maximization.

In terms of news coverage, stories were shorter and fewer color photos were run. While there was an increase in the number of sources for local stories, there was also a notable increase in local stories focusing on city police possibly of a sensational nature. Coupled with this was a dramatic decrease in prestigious wire sources such as the *New York Times*, the *Los Angeles Times*, and the *Washington Post*.

The limitations of the quantitative approach taken by the current study should be emphasized. There is a great need for monopoly studies which include intensive interviews with journalists and other professionals about qualitative changes, to supplement studies such as this one. But the current findings support the critics who decry the development of one-newspaper towns, and that social science research which points to a detrimental impact of concentration and monopolies on the public.

CHAPTER 10

Content of Joint Operation Newspapers

Stephen Lacy

School of Journalism
Michigan State University

The Newspaper Preservation Act of 1970 has neither severely damaged the First Amendment nor saved the newspaper industry from its march toward single-newspapers cities. In reality, the act has had some success, but it has not been as successful as sponsors would have liked.

This Act of Congress exempts certain newspapers from some portions of antitrust law and allows two newspapers in the same city to pool their advertising, circulation, production, and business departments in order to promote competition between the two editorial departments, which must remain separate. This combination is called a joint operating agreement (JOA).

Twenty-two JOAs existed when the Act was passed in reaction to a court case that ruled the Tucson JOA had violated sections one and two of the Sherman Antitrust Act (Martel & Haydel, 1984). Remarkably, the underlying assumption that joint operating agreements would promote editorial competition was not tested empirically before the Newspaper Preservation Act was passed. Since 1970 JOAs have received only limited empirical examination. This chapter reviews the arguments concerning joint operating agreements in light of developments in the newspaper industry since 1970 and empirically tests the underlying assumption about JOAs and editorial competition.

History of the Joint Operating Agreements

The Albuquerque (New Mexico) *Journal* and *Tribune* formed the first joint operating agreement in 1933 when they combined all but their editorial departments. During the next 33 years, newspapers in 21 other cities entered similar agreements. In 1965 the Justice Department filed suit against the Tucson agreement for violation of the Sherman and Clayton acts. The federal district court found that the Citizen Publishing and Star Publishing companies had violated section one of the Sherman Act by price fixing, profit pooling, and market allocation agreement, and section two of the Sherman Act, because the joint operating agreement gave the newspapers monopoly power over the market. The court also held that Arden, a group of stockholders in the Citizen Publishing Company, had violated the Clayton Act by acquiring the Star Publishing Company. Arden was ordered to divest itself of Star stock, and the defendants were ordered to modify the agreement to eliminate the price fixing, profit pooling, and market allocation. The district court findings were upheld by the Supreme Court in 1969 (*Citizen Publishing Co. v. United States*, 1969). The Tucson newspapers argued they had merged, but the court said a merger had not taken place, because the editorial voices remained separate (Matsunaga, 1969).

Reaction to the Justice Department's suit came quickly. Even before the Supreme Court had ruled on the case, the Failing Newspaper Act was introduced in the Senate in 1967 (Martel & Haydel, 1984). Sixteen similar bills were introduced in the House in 1968, followed by 30 bills the next year. The Newspaper Preservation Act, which was ultimately passed in 1970, had 101 cosponsors during the 91st Congress (Carlson, 1982), most of whom were from states with joint operating agreement newspapers (U.S. Congress, 1969). The act allowed the 44 newspapers (in 22 cities) with joint operating agreements to be exempted from certain aspects of the antitrust laws, and it also set up standards for new agreements to be formed. The standards stated that the attorney general must give written approval to the agreements and that one of the newspapers in the agreement must be failing, meaning it must be "in probable danger of financial failure" (Patkus, 1984).

Since its passage, there has been disagreement over how the Newspaper Preservation Act should be applied. Publishers reacted against Attorney General John Mitchell's rule that applicants for JOAs must disclose their financial data (Keep, 1982). The constitutionality of the act was tested and upheld when the Bay Guardian Company filed suit against the JOA in San Francisco in 1970, charging that the *Examiner* and *Chronicle* were financially healthy and their JOA should be disallowed (Keep, 1982). The most recent JOA application to be approved has led to a refining of what constitutes a failing newspaper. In approving the application of the Seattle *Times* and the Seattle *Post-Intelligencer* for a joint operating agreement, the Attorney General ruled that the existence of an alternative purchaser was irrelevant to satisfying the "failing newspaper" test (Carlson, 1982).

Overall, the Newspaper Preservation Act has had little impact on the newspaper industry, except for legalizing the original JOAs. Twenty-two JOAs existed when the act was passed. Today 21 JOAs exist, but they are not all the original agreements. The two newspapers in Bristol, Tennessee, and the two newspapers in Franklin-Oil City, Pennsylvania, have been replaced with single newspapers, and St. Louis has become a competitive market again. Chattanooga, Tennessee, had an agreement until 1966, when it was dissolved, but another agreement was established in 1980. The Anchorage *Daily News* and *Times* joined in 1974, but the agreement dissolved in 1979 after the *Daily News* filed suit against the *Times* in 1977. The other two agreements existing in 1985 are in Cincinnati, Ohio, and Seattle, Washington. The agreement in Columbus, Ohio, expired in 1985 and was not renewed.

The 44 newspapers with joint operating agreements in 1984 had a total circulation of 4,915,990, which accounted for 7.8% of total daily circulation in the United States. The 60 competitive newspapers had a combined daily circulation of 13,692,977. The average circulation for JOAs was 109,244, while the average daily circulation for competitive newspapers was 228,216.

The Debate Over Joint Operating Agreements

The newspaper industry and newspaper scholars split during the congressional hearings about the Newspaper Preservation Act. The American Newspaper Publishers Association supported the Act (Keep, 1982), as did newspapers such as the *The Washington Evening Star*, Chicago *Sun-Times*, and Chicago *Daily News* (U.S. Congress, 1969). Raymond Nixon (1969) supported the act, while other scholars, such as Stephen Barnett (1969) and John R. Malone (1969) argued against the act. In addition to the U.S. Attorney General and the Federal Trade Commission, the Newspaper Guild and several independent publishers opposed the act (Keep, 1982).

The testimony of Barnett summarizes the arguments against legalizing joint operating agreements. In his testimony before the House Antitrust Subcommittee in 1969, he stated that the purpose of the act was not to preserve a second newspaper, but to protect existing publications from competition so they could reap monopoly profits. He also argued that the Newspaper Preservation Act would actually inhibit competition because it would make entry into a market more difficult for a third paper. Finally, Barnett said the NPA would violate the historic independence of American newspapers.

Arguments advanced by Malone (1969) were similar to Barnett's, although Malone was much more savage in his criticism of the bill. He, like Barnett, argued that the Newspaper Preservation Act would violate the independence of the press as set forth in the First Amendment. He described a dilemma for the public that would come from passage of the act:

> I submit that a government licensed monopoly must shortly become a government regulated monopoly, or else this nation must return to the seventeenth century where unregulated crown monopolies are granted. (p. 338)

He said the act would allow predatory practices to the detriment of the reading and advertising public.

William McCulloch (1969), as well as Barnett, expanded on the barrier-to-entry argument by saying that this would be particularly applicable to suburban newspapers that might want to move into central cities. Both also argued that the newspaper industry was in fact quite healthy.

Since the passage of the Newspaper Preservation Act, the same arguments have been advanced, with a few new ones added (see Chapter 11). David M. Rubin (Keep, 1982) argued that the government does not have similar laws for magazines, newsletters, or weekly newspapers, because these firms do not have as much clout. He also expressed concern about the permanent nature of JOAs. Once formed, they need not be reexamined if the market changes.

Humphrey (1970–1971) was lukewarm in his support, saying that the Newspaper Preservation Act would save those newspapers with agreements when the act was passed, but that it was limited in doing anything about future decline in newspaper competition. His argument, which has been supported by events since 1970, was that the cause of declining competition had not been addressed by the act. He suggested a progressive tax on advertising revenue.

The original arguments for legalizing joint operating agreements were based on an assumption that most cities could not support two daily newspapers. Rosse (1980) attributed the decline of competition to the economies of scale that come from large newspaper organizations. First-issue costs for newspapers are high, because the costs of equipment and staff just to produce the first issue are fixed. Costs of additional issues come only from the ink, paper, energy, and additional production-staff time. Thus, the average costs of newspapers decreases rapidly with the increase in the number printed. Decreasing costs result in increasing marginal profits over a wide range of production, as Nixon (1969) pointed out in the subcommittee hearings.

A second characteristic of the newspaper industry that also contributes to single-newspaper cities is the circulation spiral. As a newspaper acquires a majority of circulation in a market, it begins to attract a disproportionate percentage of newspaper advertising. This in turn helps to attract more readers, which also attracts more advertising. The trailing newspaper falls farther and farther behind in advertising and circulation, until it cannot survive (Gustafsson, 1978; Martel & Haydel, 1984).

Proponents of the act argued that the government must do something to preserve a second editorial voice in markets where only one newspaper can survive without external interference. Matsunaga (1969, p. 18) summarized the stand when he said:

> The real and vital issue before this subcommittee and the Congress is a free press versus the sanctity of our antitrust laws. The initial responsibility falls upon members of this subcommittee to decide which is in the best interest of the general public: a free press or the sanctity of our antitrust laws.

If one accepts the inevitability of one-newspaper cities, Matsunaga's statement becomes the justification for joint operating agreements. However, both proponents and opponents neglected to examine whether joint operating agreements actually preserve a second voice. Some critics used examples from particular JOAs (Carlson, 1971) to support the argument that the agreements do not provide separate voices, but anecdotal evidence can be found to support both sides. What was lacking during the hearings on the Newspaper Preservation Act, and is still lacking for the most part, was empirical evidence to support one side or the other.

Evidence Concerning the JOA Debate

At the heart of the whole controversy is the question of whether most cities can support more than one newspaper. When the act was passed in 1970, there were 45 cities in the United States with separately owned and operated newspapers. Twenty-nine such cities existed in 1984. Although these figures indicate a loss of 16 competitive cities, actually 26 cities have lost a second newspaper during these 15 years, and 10 cities have gained newspapers. Of the 26 cities that lost separately owned and operated newspapers, three become joint operating agreement cities. It appears that new newspapers can start, but the number is not keeping up with those that are going out of business. Most of the new second dailies were started in smaller cities, such as Manchester, Connecticut; Cookeville, Tennessee; and Green Bay, Wisconsin. Cities that lost newspapers tended to be larger, such as Fort Worth, Newark, Philadelphia, and Cleveland. There are exceptions, but the general trend is that larger cities are more difficult to enter because of the high start-up costs of a newspaper large enough to compete in a major city. A second conclusion suggested by the changes is that JOAs are not a way to ensure a second voice in most cities that are losing daily newspapers. The reason is simple. If a newspaper is truly failing, the dominant daily will be best served by letting it fail (Holder, 1982; Patkus, 1984). Why should a newspaper that can become a monopolist support a newspaper that will prevent it from being so? Experience indicates that most large cities, if not most cities, simply cannot support two dailies under present law and technology.

The second argument by the opponents, that JOAs are a barrier to entry, is difficult to assess. There is probably some validity to it, because no third newspapers have started where a JOA exist, but, at the same time, few if any third newspapers have started in U.S. markets with two separately owned and operated newspapers.

The opponents' argument that JOAs give publishers monopoly profits has little empirical evidence, but since monopoly newspapers make monopoly profits (Owen, 1969; Mathewson, 1972; Block, 1955; Grotta, 1971; Kerton, 1973) and JOAs have business organizations similar to monopoly newspapers, joint operating agreement newspapers probably make monopoly profits. A proponent for

JOAs would say the difference between the monopoly and JOA markets is not that they do not both make monopoly profits, but that in the JOA the profits are split between two organizations that provide two voices. Once again, this argument comes back to whether JOAs actually provide two voices.

A fourth argument is that JOAs hurt suburban newspapers. Here, at last, there is some evidence to test the validity of this argument. Niebauer (1984) studied six matched pairs of competitive and JOA newspaper markets for the impact on suburban newspapers. These areas were matched for number of households, income per capita, population, retail sales, and metropolitan daily newspaper circulation. Niebauer found no difference in the number of suburban newspapers in competitive markets and markets with JOAs. However, he found the suburban newspapers in JOA markets had more than twice the circulation of the suburban newspapers in markets with competitive metropolitan newspapers. He suggested the difference could be due to poor management, or to a lower quality product in JOA markets because the competition is not felt. The latter seems unlikely, because the circulation in some JOAs determines how the profits will be divided, plus editorial competition may be due to something other than economic factors. Whatever the reason, Niebauer concluded that JOAs have kept a second voice, even if it is weak, without hurting the suburban press.

The final argument against JOAs is that they are unconstitutional. As mentioned above, the act has been found to be constitutional (Patkus, 1984). It is in reality a narrow exemption to antitrust laws. Such exemptions existed for other industries, such as insurance, before 1970 (Matsunaga, 1969).

The important question really becomes whether JOAs allow two separate voices to exist in a market that would probably not have two without the agreement. Based on the trend toward disappearing second newspapers within a city, many certainly would not have a second newspaper without the JOA. Blankenburg (1986) studied newspapers that eliminated an afternoon or morning edition between 1970 and 1984 and developed a discriminant analysis function to classify newspapers that consolidated editions during this time. This function predicted five JOAs should have lost one of the editions, indicating that at least some cities would not have had two newspapers without JOAs. But does the JOA really provide a second voice? This is the subject of the next section and will involve two questions. First, do JOA newspapers more closely resemble competitive or monopoly newspapers in their content? Second, do the two newspapers under a joint operating agreement tend to be similar or different in content?

Ardoin (1973) concluded that JOAs did not appear to keep two different news voices in a market. He modified this conclusion by adding that there were some differences in the 36 newspapers he analyzed using 10 categories of news topics, but that the differences were not consistent. He also qualified by saying that, when his results were compared to earlier studies of competitive versus noncompetitive newspapers, the content of the JOA newspapers in his study seemed slightly more like the competitive newspapers.

Hicks and Featherston (1978) compared three markets; two had jointly owned morning and evening newspapers, while the third (Shreveport, Louisiana) had a joint operating agreement for the morning and evening newspapers. They found that, in all three situations, there was little overlap of content in the morning and evening newspapers.

Comparison of Competitive, Monopoly, and JOA Newspapers

In the absence of hard evidence about the effects of JOAs on newspapers within a city, this chapter attempts to answer with empirical data whether news and editorial content in joint operating agreement newspapers more closely resembles content in competitive or in monopoly newspapers. The similarity of news and editorial content in JOA newspapers published in the same city is also examined. The data came from a national sample of 114 newspapers, stratified for ownership and market structure (Lacy, 1986). Newspapers were randomly selected within the strata. Competitive and JOA markets were oversampled, because they constitute a small proportion of total newspaper markets in the United States. A constructed week from November 1984 was content analyzed for the newspapers in the sample. This final sample included 21 competitive, 21 JOA, and 72 monopoly newspapers, which was 35% of the competitive newspapers and 48% of the JOA newspapers in the United States. The monopoly papers in the sample equaled about 4.5% of all monopoly newspapers.

Three types of allocation processes were assumed to affect the content of the newspapers. A news space allocation process was assumed to affect the space allocation of the news sections. This process involves the day-to-day decisions made by the editorial staff about how the news space in the paper will be filled. An editorial space allocation process, which allocated space on the op-ed and editorial pages, was also assumed. While there may be an overlap in responsibility on smaller newspapers, these two processes are usually separate. The third allocation process assumed is the budgeting process, which is the regular allocation of money in order to produce the news-editorial portion of the newspaper. This involves money spent on wire and syndicated services, staff, equipment, travel, and other editorial expenses. Support was found for the existence of the budget and editorial allocation processes (Lacy, 1986).[1] The three-process assumption is used here for analyzing the content of the JOA newspapers.

---

[1] The budget allocation process was found through factor analysis to have two components; one involved space devoted to news and editorial material versus advertising, and the other dealt with editorial matters such as numbers of staff and wire services. The factor analysis also found three out of four types of editorial material had high loadings on one factor. The content measures assumed to be associated with the news space allocation process were spread through three different factors. These three factors did not share loadings with the other allocation processing factors and together accounted for less than 20% of the variance. A seventh factor loaded on only two variables, length of hard news stories and length of all news stories.

Five of the 22 categories considered in the study showed statistically significant differences at the p < .05 level when comparing joint operating papers with competitive papers. Two were in the budget allocation, two in news space allocation, and one in editorial–op-ed space allocation. Competitive newspapers tend to have a higher percentage of their news section given to the newshole and a greater number of reporters. The number of reporters is probably a reflection of the greater circulation of competitive newspapers, an average of 292,891 versus 126,021 for JOAs. There was no statistically significant difference in square inches per reporter, a measure that adjusts for the size of newspaper when considering differences in staff size.

The only differences in news space allocation were in length of stories. JOA newspapers tended to have shorter hard news stories and shorter stories overall. The only difference in the editorial space allocation is that JOA newspapers gave a higher percentage of total editorial and op-ed space to editorials than did competitive newspapers.

It is notable that the 21 JOA and 21 competitive papers were statistically different in circulation and city population. This difference may well have contributed to the budget allocation differences, but since the overall number of differences were few and the differences in circulation for the sample probably are reflected in the populations, circulation was not controlled for in this analysis.

The comparison of JOA and monopoly newspapers revealed the types of newspapers differ in nine of 22 categories. All six of the budget allocation comparisons show a statistically significant difference. Monopoly newspapers had fewer full-time reporters and more square inches of copy per reporter. They gave a higher percentage of total newspaper to editorial and news material and a higher percentage of the news section to the newshole. They had fewer wire services and a smaller proportion of the newshole given to in-depth coverage than did JOA newspapers.

The only differences in news space allocation were in percent of newshole given to staff copy and to county coverage. JOAs had a higher proportion of news section given to staff copy and a smaller proportion to county coverage. In the editorial–op-ed space allocation process, JOA newspapers gave a greater percentage of space to editorials than did monopoly newspapers.

Just as with the comparison of competitive and JOA newspapers, there was a statistically significant difference between monopoly and JOA newspapers in circulation and city population. Monopoly newspapers averaged only 29,501 circulation, compared to 126,021 for JOA newspapers. Because this substantial difference could account for the differences in budget allocation, circulation was controlled for by comparing the 21 largest circulation monopoly newspapers with the 21 JOA newspapers.

When controlling for circulation in the comparison of JOA and monopoly newspapers, no statistically significant differences in circulation between the

JOA newspapers and the 21 largest monopoly newspapers in the sample were discovered. But, as a result of controlling for circulation, only three of the six budget allocation categories are still statistically significant: square inches of news copy per reporter, percentage of news section used as a news hole, and number of wire services. In the news space allocation process, the proportion of staff copy and country coverage continued to be significant and the proportion of newshole given city coverage also became significant. JOA papers gave a high percentage of space to city coverage than did monopoly newspapers.

Controlling for circulation also changed the editorial–op-ed measures. Percentage of space given editorials was no longer significant, but the percentage of news and editorial space given to all editorial matter became statistically significant. JOA papers had a higher proportion of space given to all editorial and op-ed material.

In summary, JOA newspapers resemble competitive newspapers more than monopoly newspapers in the way they allocate funds to wire services and reporters and the way they allocate news space. There is little difference among the three in editorial and op-ed space allocation.

Comparison of Pairs of JOA Newspapers

The sample of 21 joint operating agreement newspapers contained pairs of newspapers from four cities. These newspapers from San Francisco, Albuquerque, Knoxville, and Charleston were compared to see if the newspapers within a particular town differ. While this analysis will not deal with the particular subjects of stories or the quality of the writing, editing, and graphics, it can give some idea about whether the newspapers differ in the allocation of space to certain categories of information and the allocation of revenue for the news-editorial product. This analysis is not meant to argue for the superiority of one newspaper over another, but rather whether they tend to be different.

Since JOA newspapers are similar to competitive newspapers, it would seem logical that the same market forces that affect content in competitive newspapers will affect content in JOA newspapers. Several scholars (Corden, 1952–1953; Reddaway, 1963; Rosse, 1967) have suggested that the theory of monopolistic competition (Chamberlin, 1950) applies to content competition in newspapers. Monopolistic competition treats the product as a variable in determining supply and demand. This theory holds that producers attempt to differentiate their product from other products in various ways to generate demand. Price is not the only variable in monopolistic competition because it is assumed to vary little. This type of price behavior is characteristic of newspaper subscription prices.

Monopolistic competition does not entirely explain newspaper behavior. If differentiation were carried to its logical end, newspapers would be segmenting the market with little cross-elasticity of demand for two newspapers in the same market. This could be said to be true for a market such as New York, where three newspapers compete, and the *Daily News* and *Post* are better substitutes for each other than for the *Times*. The reason this segmentation does not apply to most two-newspaper markets is the desire of advertisers to have the greatest audience for their advertisements (Rosse, 1980). As a result of this pressure to compete for the same audience, two newspapers in the same market tend to differentiate themselves while trying to remain substitutes for each other. This means the differences between two newspapers in a competitive or JOA market will not be great.

San Francisco Chronicle and Examiner

The total space in these newspapers differed by slightly less than 9,000 square inches for the week. The *Chronicle* gave 11,496 square inches of the newspaper to copy in the news and editorial sections, compared to 10,218 by the *Examiner*. The newshole in the *Chronicle* news and editorial sections was 51.1% of the total news section space, while the newshole for the *Examiner* was 48.9% of the total news and editorial section.

Looking at news space allocation, the *Examiner* gave significantly more space to staff copy and less to wire service copy than did the *Chronicle*. This applied to both total square inches and to the proportions. Otherwise, the two newspapers are highly similar in the allocation of news space.

The difference in editorial space allocation is much greater. The smaller newspaper, the *Examiner*, devoted more space, 2,094 versus 1,560 square inches, to the editorial and op-ed pages than did the *Chronicle*. This amounted to 9.6% of the news and editorial space for the *Examiner*, which was 3.2 percentage points more than the *Chronicle* gave to editorial and op-ed material. The allocation of editorial and op-ed space also differed. The *Chronicle* gave a much larger proportion of its space to letters to the editor and guest columns than did the *Examiner*, 25% compared to 9.3%, which indicates a paper more open to readers and nonstaff writers. The *Examiner* gave more space to editorial cartoons, 25.2% to 12.8% of the editorial and op-ed pages. The *Examiner* had slightly more of its space given to editorials than did the *Chronicle*. The *Chronicle* tended to write more editorials about matters concerning nearby counties than it did about San Francisco: the opposite was the case for the *Examiner*.

Overall, the editorial and op-ed pages appear to differ in emphasis, with the *Chronicle* being more open to outside sources, but the *Examiner* being more concerned with editorial comment by staff editorial writers and cartoonists.

For the constructed week in November 1984, the *Examiner* was a more locally oriented newspaper that used more staff copy and graphics and also gave greater emphasis to editorial comment. The *Chronicle* had more international news and more wire-service copy in the news columns, but made its editorial and op-ed pages more accessible to outsiders than did the *Examiner*. Generalizing to the entire month of November, there was a statistically significant difference between the editorial and op-ed page distributions of the two newspapers, but not between the news-space allocations. The readers may not have had two different news voices, but there appears to be some difference in the topics covered by the city's two editorial voices.

Albuquerque Journal and Tribune

If a JOA tends to force newspapers to be similar, it would seem the longer the agreement has been in force, the more likely the effect is to take place. Since the Albuquerque Journal and Albuquerque Tribune make up the oldest JOA, it would seem that they would have become more alike than any other JOA pair. This is not the case, however, especially on the editorial page.

The Tribune had much less space than did the Journal, which is attributable to the latter newspaper having more than twice the circulation of the former. The Tribune had a newshole of only 15,928 square inches, compared to a newshole of 25,553 square inches in the Journal.

There was some difference between the two newspapers in news section allocation. The Tribune had a higher percentage of its news section given to wire service copy, although the Journal actually had a larger number of square inches. There was also a difference between the newspapers in allocation of editorial and op-ed space. The Journal had more space devoted to editorial and op-ed matter, but the Tribune had a larger proportion of its news and editorial space allocated to this type of material. The Journal allocated 15% of its editorial and op-ed pages to letters to the editor and guest columns, while the Tribune gave only 7.1% of its editorial and op-ed space to similar material. The Journal depended more on syndicated columns, 54.9% to 47.9%, but the Tribune used more cartoons, 22% to 13.2%.

Overall, Albuquerque had two different editorial pages for the constructed week in November.

Knoxville Journal and News-Sentinel

As with Albuquerque and San Francisco, one of the newspapers in Knoxville dominates the circulation in the city. The News-Sentinel had 104,542 average daily circulation in 1985, compared to 60,219 for the Journal. The newshole for the News-Sentinel was 48.0%, compared to 49.9% for the Journal.

The differences in how the Knoxville newspapers distributed their editorial and op-ed space was noticeable. The larger newspaper, the News-Sentinel, had more space given all editorial and op-ed material, 1,530 versus 1,234 square inches, but the Journal had a greater percentage of total news and editorial op-ed space given its editorial material, 10.2% versus 8.3%. There was a slight difference in space given to letters to the editor and guest columns and space given to columns, but there was a greater difference in space given to cartoons and editorials. *The Journal* gave 31.2% of its editorial and op-ed pages to cartoons, compared to 11.1% for its competitor. The *Journal* gave only 14% of its editorial and op-ed space to editorials, while the *News-Sentinel* allocated 22.3%. The *Journal* editorialized more about issues involving the county, but the *News-Sentinel* gave more space to issues about the city of Knoxville.

As with the previous two examples, there were enough differences between the way the two Knoxville newspapers allocated their editorial page resources to indicate that readers had somewhat different newspapers at their disposal during the constructed week.

Charleston Gazette and Daily Mail

The two Charleston newspapers do not have the great difference in circulation found in the other three cities. The *Gazette* led in 1985, with an average daily circulation of 62,175, while the trailing *Daily Mail* had an average daily circulation of 52,993. The total amount of space given to news and editorial copy was about the same.

Just as with the previous sets of JOA newspapers, the allocation of editorial and op-ed space showed significant differences. The *Gazette* had considerably more space and a higher proportion of space, 24.7% versus 11.5%, devoted to letters to the editor and guest columns than did the *Daily Mail*. The *Daily Mail* had a higher proportion of space given to columns, cartoons and editorials. Neither of the newspapers was overwhelmingly local in its editorials, but the *Gazette* did give 1.9% of its editorial and op-ed space to city editorials, compared to zero % by the *Daily Mail* The latter paper gave a higher proportion to county editorials.

Summary

Considering just the issues examined for the constructed week, all four pairs showed some differences in news space and editorial–op-ed space allocation. The differences were not as great in the news sections as in the editorial sections. When considered as a sample for the month of November, the differences in the news space distributions were too slight in most cases to conclude they were not due to chance.

The budget allocation process did not show a great deal of variance in most pairs. Commitment to staff and wire services was fairly consistent.

The small differences were not surprising because of the nature of JOA newspaper markets. They must compete for readers because profit distribution is sometimes tied to circulation. This means that each newspaper must be a substitute for the competing newspaper, while being at the same time a differentiated product. It appears the JOA newspapers studied here were fairly good substitutes for each other in the news pages, although there were some slight differences, while differentiating themselves primarily in the editorial and op-ed section. Since this study did not examine the content of individual stories, it is inappropriate to conclude the editorial voices were entirely different in these JOA markets, but there is evidence that these pairs differed in their emphasis on types of editorial and op-ed material and in the subject matter of editorials.

Conclusions

The purpose of this chapter is to review joint operating agreements in light of 15 years of experience and to present empirical evidence concerning the underlying assumption that joint operating agreements will preserve a second editorial voice in the city in which it is in effect. An examination of events in the newspaper industry since 1970 shows support for two of the five main arguments advanced by opponents to the Newspaper Preservation Act. JOA newspapers may well charge monopoly prices for advertising. They may well be a high barrier to entry in a market, although the barrier may be more a function of the size of the market than the fact that the market has a JOA.

Evidence does not support the other three arguments against JOAs. First, the act is constitutional, according to the judicial system. Second, few cities can support more than one newspaper for an extended period of time, due to economies of scale and the circulation spiral. Third, there is evidence that JOAs do not interfere any more than competitive newspapers with suburban newspaper development.

The fact that the Newspaper Preservation Act led to some actions that would have otherwise been in violation of the antitrust laws is not a matter of dispute. Proponents of the act admitted before the law was passed that this might happen. The key to the whether the Newspaper Preservation Act should have been passed and should continue to exist is whether the people who live in cities with JOAs are benefitting from such agreements. The evidence presented here would indicate that readers in JOA markets are getting newspaper products they would not have without the JOAs.

Newspapers produced under joint operating agreements are more similar to competitive newspapers than to monopoly newspapers in the way they spend money and allocate news space. While they are not exactly like competitive papers, the difference is less than the difference between JOA newspapers and monopoly newspapers. This study also suggests that, in at least four of the 22 JOA markets for the period in this analysis, the readers had a choice between two different editorial and op-ed sections and, occasionally, between two slightly different news sections.

The fact that these differences between pairs of JOA newspapers and among newspapers facing different market structures were not greater should not be surprising or considered an argument against the importance of JOAs. Journalism education, group ownership, and professional norms often work to make newspapers similar. The point is that the Newspaper Preservation Act has preserved two newspapers for readers where there might have only been one, and it has created newspapers that spend more money on the product than do monopoly newspapers. Since the circulation of JOA newspapers comprises 7.8% of total daily circulation in this country, the overall impact is important.

Even though the Newspaper Preservation Act has had some success, modifications to the act that would open entry into the market would be consistent with the spirit of the act. Owen (1975) has suggested that means of producing newspapers should be separated from the editorial staffs of newspapers to break up the economies of scale enjoyed by large newspapers. The Newspaper Preservation Act did this, but went further to separate the advertising, distribution, and business departments of the newspapers. Reuniting the advertising and business departments with the editorial departments, while keeping production and distribution separate, might work to further make JOA newspapers similar to competitive newspapers.

A second modification would follow similar lines of breaking up vertical integration. Currently, joint operating agreements are limited to two newspapers. If JOAs were opened up to third newspapers in conjunction with the separation of advertising and business departments, entry into markets might be encouraged. This option was suggested by Humphrey (1970–1971). If a company did not have to make the huge capital investment necessary to buy printing equipment, more dailies might start.

The Newspaper Preservation Act has been at least partially successful in accomplishing what its sponsors wanted it to do. The cost has been higher advertising prices, which ultimately means higher prices for goods. The important questions now are whether fine tuning the act will help bring the benefits while lowering the costs, and whether such tuning will encourage entry into markets with already high barriers.

CHAPTER 11

Editorial Diversity and Concentration

F. Dennis Hale

Department of Journalism
Bowling Green State University

Fifty-six daily newspapers changed hands in 1985, making it a banner year for newspaper purchases. The New York Times Co. bought five daily newspapers, including the 30,600-circulation *Tuscaloosa News*, and the Gannett Co. bought 10 dailies, including the two Pulitzer Prize winners, the *Detroit News* and the *Des Moines Register*. Also in 1985, Ingersoll Publications bought the 37,600-circulation *Alton Telegraph* in Illinois and the Donrey Media Group purchased the 18,000-circulation *Norman Transcript* in Oklahoma. And a New Zealand chain with the unlikely name, Independent Newspaper Group, acquired the 9,400-circulation *West Warwick Pawtuxet Valley Times* in Rhode Island ("Daily Newspaper Sales," 1986).

Just what will happen to the quality of these locally owned and independent newspapers that were purchased by outside chains? There should be a simple answer to such a straightforward question. But there is not, because the policies and philosophies of media chains differ, and the perceptions and definitions of what constitutes quality in newspapers differ.

An example is the *Midland Reporter-Telegram*, a 20,000-circulation daily in West Texas which the Hearst Corporation purchased in 1978. Mrs. H. B. Johnson, a 30-year reader of the newspaper and a retired jeweler, said that, under Hearst ownership, the paper eliminated its sacred cows and improved: "It's not biased like it used to be. In the past, the newspaper slanted too much of the news. It seemed to play ball with the monied people. Now that's changed. There is a lot more local news in the paper now. The paper is larger, but of course there is much more advertising than in the past (Ghiglione, 1984, p. 106).

Hank Avery, an oilman and former mayor of Midland, disagreed: "We used to have a newspaper. The only good thing about it now is the rubber band around it." He added: "There's nobody there anymore who knows a thing about Midland. All of the old ties are gone, and it has hurt the newspaper. They don't know what Midland is today, and they certainly do not know about its past." Avery criticized an obituary that failed to mention that the deceased subject was the widow of a former mayor who had served 20 years on the city council, and that the family had donated the land for the city hall (Ghiglione, 1984, pp. 106–107).

Anecdotal evidence supports both sides in the debate about the influence of newspaper chains. Press critic Ben Bagdikian concedes that many of the 4,000 reporters and editors on Gannett's then 87 newspapers produce admirable journalism. But Bagdikian (1983, p. 78) says most of Gannett's empire "consists of vast silent domains where ruthless demands for ever-increasing profits crush journalistic enterprise and block adequate coverage of the news in their communities." Bagdikian also argues that, in 1966, when Gannett had 26 papers, it averaged 45 news employees per newspaper; this compared to 26 employees per paper in 1981 when the chain had 81 papers. Average circulation was the same in both years—44,000. Bagdikian never explains how he arrived at this conclusion, nor how he defines a news employee (p. 86).

Changes inevitably occur when a new owner takes over a commercial enterprise such as a daily newspaper. Liberal commentary took a beating in January 1984 when Rupert Murdoch purchased the *Chicago Sun-Times*. Celebrated columnist Mike Royko left the *Sun-Times*, as did prize-winning commentator Roger Simon. And the newspaper dropped from its editorial pages the columns of such liberals as Ellen Goodman and Garry Wills ("Roger Simon to Depart Sun-Times," 1984). Ownership definitely influences the content of the editorial page. Shortly after publisher Jeffrey M. Gluck took over the *St. Louis Globe-Democrat*, he endorsed the re-election of incumbent U.S. Senator Charles Percy. This reversed the endorsement a few weeks earlier of the previous owner, Newhouse Newspapers ("St. Louis Daily Shifts Support," 1984). Sometimes a chain owner finds himself outvoted or in the minority with other owners. Thus Harry Hoiles, whose father was founder of Freedom Newspapers, resigned from the chain's board of directors because of the alleged failure of the organization to promote the libertarian philosophy of his father. Libertarians favor minimal involvement of government in society ("Hoiles Leaves Freedom Group," 1984).

Often there are conflicting arguments about the effects of changes made by chains after they purchase a newspaper. Thomson Newspapers, which has the best profit margins of any publicly owned newspaper company in the United States or Canada, owns small-city newspapers which the Canadian government has characterized as editorially lackluster (Chaney, 1982b, p. 3). One year after Thomson purchased the *Kokomo Tribune* in Indiana, the editor was removed. The new publisher said that the old editor was insensitive to the needs of the local people. The departing old editor said that powerful people in Kokomo hoped to use the new newspaper ownership to reassert their influence over the news columns. An outsider observed that the newsroom changes could be interpreted in at least two ways: "Does it (Thomson) really suck all the profit it can from its new acquisitions without regard for journalistic quality or employee morale? Or does Thomson simply impose long-needed management reforms that cause resentment among lazy employees?" (Chaney, 1982a, p. 10). Following Gannett's takeover of the Pulitzer Prize winning *Detroit Evening News,* two dozen corporate executives lost their jobs and several executives were stripped of their vice-president titles (Radolf, 1986, p. 20). The impact of that and other changes made by Gannett will be debated for some time.

Some anecdotal evidence clearly is supportive of chain ownership. Ben Sargent (1978), editorial cartoonist for the *Austin American-Statesman,* said chain ownership improved his Texas paper: "A case can be made that chain ownership can render a paper more independent of the local pressures which reduce most small and medium-sized dailies, and many large ones, to anemic, blithering boosterism." *New York Times* columnist Tom Wicker and *Time* magazine critic William A. Henry III agree. Wicker, a predictable liberal who frequently decries concentration of economic power, commented: "I have not been one of the doom shouters about acquisitions, mergers and growth of publishing chains." When a chain buys an independent paper, Wicker said, "More often, it is a sound national chain taking over a shaky local paper and making it stronger" (Rockmore, 1986, p. 130). Similarly, *Time* critic William A. Henry III (1986, p. 16) observed: "Most independent owners run papers in ways that comfort them, their friends and their general social class." He concluded: "There's nothing automatically wrong with 'independent' family ownership of newspapers. But there's nothing self-evidently sacred about it, either."

The debate about the quality of chain-owned papers is likely to continue, because the number of chain papers and the size of newspaper chains continue to grow. Of the 39 papers that were sold in 1984, 33 went to chains ("Privately Held Groups," 1985, p. 46). This compares to 26 of 30 dailies in 1983 ("Foreign Publishers Top," 1984, pp. 40–42), 32 of 36 in 1982, and 30 of 38 in 1981 ("Group Ownership," 1983, p. 34). For a long time it appeared that chains would never create a problem in concentration of newspaper ownership. From the 1930s through the 1970s the size of newspaper chains remained stable, ranging from 5.1 to 5.6 newspapers per chain (Compaine, Sterling, Guback, & Noble, 1982, p. 39). However, by 1986 the average size of daily newspaper chains was close to 8 ("Group-Owned Dailies," 1986, p. 68) In 1984 there were 149 newspaper chains, down from 169 in 1978. The 149 chains controlled 69% of U.S dailies and 78% of Sunday papers, and 79% of U.S. weekday circulation and 88% of Sunday circulation. Over half of the chain papers were owned by 79 chains that controlled only two to four papers each ("Groups Still Own," 1986, p. 68).

It is inevitable in the United States that newspaper chains will continue to grow both in the average number of newspapers that each chain controls and in the proportion of all newspapers that they own. In February of 1985 the employee magazine of Gannett gleefully announced: "There is practically no limit on what Gannett may potentially acquire." The magazine noted that "The relaxed FCC limitations have also opened the door for acquisition of smaller diversified newspaper and media companies" (Lacy, 1985, p. 20). Not surprisingly, 1985 turned out to be Gannett's "biggest year ever in mergers and acquisitions," in the words of the corporation's chairman, Al Neuharth (1986, p.2). He boasted of the company's new grand total of 91 dailies and 5.7 million circulation: "That's by far the largest of any company in the USA, and no other company will catch us, because there are more to come." At about the same time, *U.S. News & World Report* concluded that "most experts see only more takeovers ahead as family ownership gives way to control by distant chains and conglomerates" (Sanoff, 1985, p. 60). Six years of government deregulation by President Reagan had given laissez faire a new respectability and had placed more daily newspapers in the hands of corporate giants.

And when a large corporate chain buys a newspaper, it has unlimited power to make changes. This point was emphasized in the 1981 report of Canada's Kent Commission which studied newspaper chains in that country ("Conglomerates," 1981, p. 57):

> No one who has been close to newspapers can doubt that, in fact, the power exercised by a chain, shaping the editorial content of its newspapers, is pervasive. Head office appoints the publishers, who appoint everyone else. They control budgets and, in some cases, control expenditures in fine detail. They operate with a string of interchangeable publishers and understood administrative norms. To suggest that they foster editorial independence is, as is said in French, to dream in color.

The process for fostering conformity may be quite subtle, according to press critic Bagdikian (1985, p. 104): "Individuals make their hourly and daily work decisions in conformity to observed conventions without receiving explicit written or spoken orders on how to treat their work. The same is true of news organizations."

Some of the conclusions from the research and literature concerning chain ownership have been mixed. In 1984 Loren Ghiglione (1984, p. xii) edited a collection of 10 case studies about newspapers purchased by chains. One of his conclusions was: "It's virtually impossible to generalize—good guys or bad?—about the groups' impact." Similarly, in the book, *Who Owns the Media?*, Compaine (1982, p. 44) concluded: "Whether or not group ownership improves or degrades a newspaper depends upon the criteria that are established for making such judgments, the state of the newspaper when the new owner arrives and, more importantly, which chain is doing the buying."

The purpose of the empirical study conducted for this chapter was to take a closer, more controlled look at how the form of ownership of a daily newspaper influenced the content and the information that was available to readers. More specifically, the study measured how the content of the editorial pages of 28 independent papers changed after the papers were purchased by chains.

Literature Review

A number of researchers have specifically compared the quality of the news in independent and chain papers. One of the earliest and most comprehensive studies was Grotta's comparison of 40 papers that had changed from independent to chain between 1950 and 1968 with 114 papers that remained independent or chain throughout the time period. The study used regression analysis to examine a variety of quality-related variables, including size of the editorial staff, size of the news hole, percentage of local news, size of the editorial page news hole, and percentage of editorials as content. Grotta (1971, pp. 245–250) found no significant differences between independent and chain papers. He concluded: "If there are indeed significant economic efficiencies from larger scale operation in the industry, this study indicates that those benefits are not being passed on to the consumer." Grotta discovered that chain papers are not inferior to independents. But they definitely are not superior either.

More recently, Donohue and other researchers measured conflict news in 1965 and 1979 in 83 newspapers published in Minnesota county seats. The sample was divided into papers owned locally and those owned by out-of-staters, and consisted of 21 nonmetropolitan dailies and 62 weeklies. For the most part, locally owned papers were independently owned, and out-of-state-owned papers were chain owned. Conflict news was defined as space devoted to differing positions about public issues from at least two persons. During the 14 years, locally owned papers increased their coverage of conflict by one third, and out-of-state-owned papers decreased their coverage of conflict by nearly one-half. The authors concluded that "these findings strongly suggest that the form of ownership has had an impact on local reporting of government issues" (Donohue, Olien, & Tichenor, 1985, p. 507). It should be noted that the locally owned papers in the study had smaller circulations than the out-of-state-owned papers. Thus, smaller circulation size did not explain the difference between the two groups of papers. The Donohue findings constitute a serious indictment of the influence of outside ownership on newspapers. The clear conclusion is that, when outsiders own newspapers, they encourage them to minimize the reporting of local controversy. Unfortunately, this means that local controversy goes unreported. Local radio and television, because of their abbreviated formats, provide no in-depth coverage of local events. So, if the local newspaper plays it safe and avoids in-depth or investigative reporting, local controversy simply goes unreported and thus is unnoticed by the public.

A study of television also is relevant to this discussion of media ownership and news quality. Baldridge (1967) measured one week of local programming by 11 nonchain stations and 18 chain-owned stations in 10 markets in 1965. The small sample size and the lack of matched pairs of stations prevented the use of more sensitive statistical tests. Thus, none of Baldridge's findings were statistically significant. However, nonchain stations broadcast 22 hours and 49 minutes of local programs, compared to 17 hours and 45 minutes by chain stations. And nonchain stations broadcast 3 hours and 49 minutes of local public affairs, to 2 hours and 33 minutes by chain stations. These certainly sound like significant differences. And they clearly point to a poor performance by the chain stations when compared to the independents. But because of the limited design and scope of the study, the apparent differences were not statistically significant.

No review of the research about the quality of the news and newspaper ownership should ignore the qualitative, nonempirical approach used in the book *The Buying and Selling of America's Newspapers*. The book consists of 10 in-depth case studies of newspapers purchased by chains. The papers range from 6,000 to 47,000 circulation, and come from 10 different states. Some of the papers deteriorated in quality. The small Kansas paper, the *Atchison Daily Globe*, lost circulation and had terrific staff turnover after it was purchased by the Thomson chain. *The Transcript*, in North Adams, Massachusetts, deteriorated just as abruptly under the ownership of Ingersoll Publications. The number of reporters dropped from nine to three, ad content soared from 35 to 50%, and newsroom expenses fell from 17% to 10% or 11%. Other newspapers in the study—such as the *Redlands Daily Facts*, a California paper purchased by Donrey Media, and the *Sante Fe New Mexican*, purchased by Gannett—seemed to remain about the same in quality under chain ownership. And a third group of papers improved under chains. Included are the Midland, Texas, paper which has already been discussed, and the Lynchburg, Virginia, *Daily Advance*. The author characterizes the Lynchburg papers as a "public shame—pariahs in the community they served," before they were purchased by Worrell Newspapers (Ghiglione, 1984, p. 136). Loren Ghiglione, who edited the book and wrote one of the newspaper profiles, draws no conclusions about the impact of chain ownership. However, the 10 papers fell into three categories: three improved under chain ownership, three remained about the same, and four deteriorated. These findings from qualitative case studies are consistent with Grotta's findings from empirical content analysis. On balance, chain ownership does not make much of a difference. Quite clearly, it does not improve newspapers.

The research that is most relevant to this chapter are seven studies that specifically examined the influence of newspaper ownership on editorials and the editorial page. The two most limited studies, by Wagenberg and Soderlund (1975) and Borstel (1956), found no differences. Canadians Wagenberg and Soderlund compared editorials about one national election in four papers, from one chain and three independent papers. They found no pattern within the chain and no difference between the chain and independent papers. Regionalism emerged as the most important factor that shaped themes of the 811 Canadian editorials. In the early 1950s Borstel compared the editorial pages of 20 small dailies. He found no consistent differences between the 6 chain and 14 independent papers in numbers of letters to the editor, local columns, and editorials about local or state subjects. Both of these studies have serious limitations. The Canadian study examined only seven papers and one chain. The Borstel study of 20 small papers was quite narrow when it was conducted; now it is quite dated.

More comprehensive studies of chain and independent editorials have found major differences. Wackman and Gillmor (1975) examined presidential endorsements by most American dailies for four elections, 1960 through 1972. They found that 6% to 10% more chain than independent papers made endorsements, that chain papers were more likely to favor the favorite candidate of the publishers, and that papers within a chain were overwhelmingly homogeneous in presidential endorsements. The researchers concluded that "Clearly these data run counter to the insistence of chain spokesmen that their endorsement policies are independent from chain direction" (p. 419). There are relatively more small dailies with less than 10,000 circulation among independent than chain papers. These small dailies have editorial pages that are limited or even nonexistent. This fact may have been responsible for the larger percentage of chain papers making endorsements than the independents.

Thrift (1977) also identified major differences in editorials in his study of 24 West Coast papers during 1960 and 1975. Some 16 papers had changed from independent to chain during the period; 8 remained independent throughout. In 1960 there were no differences between editorials in the two groups of independent papers. In 1975, however, 7.9% of editorials in the chain papers were argumentative, controversial, and local, contrasted to 17.6% in the independent papers. Thrift concluded: "But clearly, this study demonstrates that chains have had an impact on the editorial quality of the dailies they have purchased on the West Coast. And certainly, the impact is not helpful to readers who seek guidance on local matters when they turn to the editorial pages of their daily newspapers (p. 331). As mentioned earlier, if the local newspaper does not provide guidance on local controversies, who will? Certainly radio and television will not. And neither will magazines or regional newspapers. A local newspaper that timidly avoids commenting on local controversies leaves a vacuum in its community.

Goodman's study of weekly newspapers in Illinois had mixed results. He examined 3 months of editorials in 1980 in 45 Illinois weeklies that were chain owned and 25 that were independent. The study concluded that independent papers published a higher percentage of editorials about local and state subjects (38% to 32% for local topics, 19% to 15% for state). However, the simple percentages are deceptive and miss the critical fact that, because independent papers published fewer editorials, the independents actually published fewer editorials per issue than chain papers about local and state topics (.20 to .29 for local issues, .10 to .13 for state issues). This was true even though the mean circulation of the two groups of papers was about equal (3,668 for chain, 3,206 for independent). Thus, Goodman (1982) found that Illinois chain weeklies published more editorials about local and state subjects, published many more column inches of editorials, and made more political endorsements than independent weeklies. Goodman noted that chain papers within a region frequently share editorials. This practice obviously contributed to the statistically superior performance of the chain papers in the study.

One of the most comprehensive comparisons of chain and independent newspapers is Daugherty's (1983, p. 71) dissertation, which measures front pages and editorial pages of 36 chain and 32 independent dailies. The chain papers in the study came from large organizations with 10 or more papers. The author wanted to "isolate those groups which represent the circumstances most feared by critics—the potential for a few corporate voices . . . to control the newspaper content for a critically large segment of the newspaper reading population." Daugherty analyzed eight issues of each paper from the summer of 1980. Front pages were analyzed for local, state, national, and international stories, features, wire and local photographs. Editorial pages were analyzed for local, state, national, and international editorials, presidential endorsements, letters to the editor, and syndicated columns. In addition to the content analysis, Daugherty surveyed the highest-ranking corporate officers of 167 newspaper chains and 225 independent newspapers concerning the social responsibility of the press.

The content analysis found the two types of front pages to be remarkably similar. A few differences were statistically significant but not of much practical significance. For example, independent papers published more stories on page one—6.4 to 5.8. This may have resulted from the independents devoting less space to mastheads and margins than the chain papers—17% versus 21% of the space. And independents devoted 26% of the front page to national news, compared to 23% for the chain papers. But in all other categories—international news, state news, local news, features, wire photos, and local photos—chain and independent papers were identical. The author concluded: "The most significant finding, based upon the analysis of the front page, is the great similarity between the two newspaper types. Generally speaking, ownership structure does not significantly influence the proportion of attention given to topic categories on the front page" (Daugherty, 1983, p. 154).

Daugherty found greater differences in the editorial pages. Chain papers published 1.9 letters per issue, to 1.4 for independents. And 96% of chain editorial pages had editorials, compared to 82% for independents. Also, more chain editorials discussed local issues than independent ones—26% to 17%. Conversely, fewer group editorials discussed national issues than independents—49% to 58%. However, the two types of newspapers were identical in the number of presidential endorsements and syndicated columns.

Lastly, Daugherty's survey of chain and independent corporate officers found almost no differences. The officers were questioned about 36 tenets concerning social responsibility of the press such as bias of journalists, balance and accuracy in news coverage, and the press as a watchdog of government. On only one of the 36 tenets was there a significant difference, that being government aid for failing media enterprises. Both groups of media officers rejected the concept, but the chain officers were stronger in their opposition. These findings are quite similar to those of Meyer and Wearden that compared privately and publicly owned newspapers.

For the most part, Daugherty found the front pages and editorial pages of chain and independent papers to be more similar than different. He never does report the circulation means for his two samples, and admitted in a phone conversation (June 23, 1986) that the chain papers in his sample may have been larger than the independents. Circulation size may be the hidden variable that explains the greater number of letters and editorials and the greater number of editorials about local and state issues in the chain papers. These differences may have resulted from the greater resources, space, and staff that are devoted to editorial pages in larger papers.

St. Dizier (1986) also examined editorial pages. But he used a survey of editorial page editors and not content analysis of actual pages. In 1984 he surveyed 85 editorial editors at daily newspapers with circulation of over 50,000. The study found statistically significant differences between the political preferences of the editors and publishers at chain and independent papers. At the independents, 55% of editorial editors reported working for Republican publishers, compared to 93% at chain papers. Publishers generally hire like-minded editors. So it is not surprising that 56% of the editors at independent papers called themselves Democrats, compared to 33% at the chain papers.

Despite these differences in party preferences, the two groups of editors were equally satisfied with the way their newspapers handled political endorsements and agreed about the influence of publishers on those endorsements. The two groups of editors also agreed on their presidential vote. Some 57% of chain editors and 58% of independent editors reported voting for the Democratic candidate in 1984, Mondale.

Not surprisingly, the publishers had the last word on the presidential endorsements. Some 65% of chain papers endorsed Reagan, compared to 44% of independents; and only 25% of chain papers endorsed Mondale, to 44% of independents. But did the publishers really have the last word? On candidate endorsements, yes, but not on political issues. St. Dizier also compared the papers' editorials about eight controversial issues that divided the presidential candidates and their party platforms: anti-abortion amendment, school prayer amendment, tuition tax credit, Equal Rights Amendment, tax increase, aid to Nicaraguan Contras, space base defense system, and restrictions of covert operations abroad. On every issue—even Mondale's highly criticized proposal to increase taxes—

the newspapers supported the liberal and Democratic position by wide margins. And this was true of both chain and independent papers. One editorial page editor offered this explanation for the split personality reflected in candidate and issue endorsements: "Thus it happens that so many editorial pages carry a moderate-to-liberal tone on 47 months, and on the 48th month of reckoning turn conservative. Some call the presidential endorsements the publishers' four-year itch, and others, the editorial writers' agony" (p. 3).

In conclusion, one group of researchers agrees with Grotta's 1971 seminal study that found no differences between chain and independent newspapers. These studies—which include Grotta's analysis of 154 papers, Daugherty's statistical study of 68 dailies, and Ghiglione's 10 case studies—found that the similarities between chain and independent papers far outweighed the differences. The differences, when they existed, had little practical effect. However, a growing group of studies found substantial differences betwen chain and independent papers. Thrift found that independent papers published twice as many argumentative editorials about local topics than chain papers. St. Dizier found that 93% of chain newspaper publishers were Republican, compared to 55% of independent publishers. Not surprisingly, 65% of the chain papers in his study endorsed the Republican candidate in 1984, compared to 44% of the independent papers. Perhaps the strongest indictment of chain papers emerged from Donohue's content analysis of 83 newspapers published in Minnesota county seats. During the 15 years of the study, locally owned papers increased their coverage of local conflict by one third, while out-of-state papers decreased such coverage by nearly one-half. The point has been made previously. If newspapers avoid writing editorials about local controversies, they simply go unwritten, because local broadcasters lack the time and resources for controversial and local editorial commentary. And the same can be said about in-depth news coverage of local controversies. If newspapers do not provide such coverage, it simply is unavailable.

A New Study

This study attempted to introduce additional precision and control into the analysis of the editorial pages of chain and independent newspapers. This was accomplished by examining editorial pages of the same newspapers when the papers were independently owned and after they had been purchased by a chain. A greater variety of variables measuring the quality of editorial pages was included in this study, compared to previous ones.

Editorial pages were analyzed because the opinion and commentary section of a newspaper serves as a showcase of how that newspaper satisfies its watchdog obligation to oversee and interpret the actions of government. A survey comparing 1983 and 1975 found that newspaper editorial pages had been strengthened. Some 97% of U.S. dailies devote at least a page a day to opinion and commentary. In recent years the number of staffers and the number of pages committed to editorial sections have increased (Hynds, 1984).

A sample of 28 daily newspapers was created from the list of newspapers sold the previous year that is published in the first issue every January of *Editor & Publisher* magazine. The complete universe of newspapers consisted of 425 dailies that were sold during the 9-year period, January 1976 through December 1984. Papers were selected to represent a maximum number of chains, circulation sizes, and states and geographic regions. Because a purpose of the study was to examine the impact of significant concentration of ownership, the newspaper sample was restricted to chains with six or more papers.

For each sample newspaper, editorial pages were analyzed for the year before the newspaper sold, and for the year after the sale. Editorial pages were examined for the first five weekdays of May the year before the sale, and the first five weekdays in May two years later. Thus, the editorial pages of independent papers were from the time period of 8 to 20 months prior to the ownership change, and editorial pages of chain papers were from the period of 4 to 16 months after the chain acquisition.

Each newspaper was coded for the last year in which the paper was independent, state of publication, specific newspaper chain, chain size, and weekday circulation.

Each editorial page was coded for the following variables: number of editorials about local issues, editorials about regional issues, editorials about national and international issues, number of paragraphs of editorials about local issues, syndicated columns, liberal columns, local guest commentaries, local columns, miscellaneous outside articles, number of pages, letters to the editor, syndicated cartoons, liberal cartoons, local cartoons, local line drawings or photographs, and advertisements.

A list of liberal columnists was created by consulting *Contemporary Authors*; the directory of syndicated services in the July 27, 1985, *Editor & Publisher*; and articles by Hynds (1984, p. 637), *Los Angeles Times* columnist David Shaw (1984, pp. 86–88), and *Boston Globe* columnist David Nyhan (1985, pp. 48–49). The columnists classified as liberal included Jack Anderson, Hodding Carter, Ellen Goodman, Joseph Kraft, Mary McGrory, Richard Reeves, James Reston, and Garry Wills.

The list of liberal political cartoonists was provided by cartoon authority Roy Paul Nelson. Nelson, a journalism professor at the University of Oregon, has published four books on cartooning and comic art. Included on his list were Herbert Block, Pat Oliphant, Bill Mauldin, Paul Conrad, Mike Peters, and Bill Sanders.

Major Findings

The sample of 28 dailies represented 17 chains. Some 11 chains were represented by one paper. Times-Mirror, Capital Cities, and Ottaway were represented by two papers each, Thomson and Cox were represented by three papers each, and Gannett was represented by five papers. The size of the chains that the 28 papers belonged to ranged from 6 to 82, and had a median value of 20.

The newspapers came from 17 states, including four from Pennsylvania; three each from California, Michigan, and Texas; and two each from Indiana and Missouri. Circulation size was well dispersed and ranged from 12,000 to 215,000, with a median of 37,000. There were four papers under 20,000, five papers between 20,000 and 35,000, eight papers between 35,000 and 50,000, five papers between 50,000 and 75,000, and one paper over 75,000. Starting years for the analysis of newspapers ranged from 1975 to 1983, with a mean of 1979.

The mean performance of the 28 dailies for one week (five weekdays) was to publish the following (figures combine the performance under both independent and chain ownership): 2.6 editorials about local issues containing 21.5 paragraphs, 1.3 editorials about state or regional issues, 4.7 editorials about national or international issues, 13.7 syndicated columns, 5.8 liberal columns, .2 local guest commentaries, 1.3 local columns, 2.6 outside miscellaneous articles, 6.3 editorial pages, 12.9 letters to the editor, 9.1 syndicated cartoons, .25 local cartoons, and 2 liberal syndicated cartoons. During an average week a newspaper averaged less than one page with locally produced art and less than one editorial page with advertisements.

For most of the papers the change from independent to chain ownership resulted in only modest change and slight improvement or deterioration. Typical was the *Clarion-Ledger* of Jackson, Mississippi. During one week under independent ownership the paper published five editorials (including four about local issues), 17 syndicated columns (including 11 by liberals), no local columns or local cartoons, 21 letters, 5 cartoons, and 10 pages. Under Gannett ownership 2 years later, the paper published 12 editorials (including four about local issues), 25 syndicated columns (including 16 by liberals), no local columns or local cartoons, 29 letters, 15 political cartoons, and 10 pages. The Jackson paper published thoughtful and provocative editorial pages under both forms of ownership.

An example of a newspaper that improved dramatically was the *Evening Sentinel* of Holland, Michigan. Under independent ownership the small daily had a weak editorial page that consisted largely of advertisements. One week of editorial pages included no editorials about local or regional issues, no letters to the editor, no syndicated cartoons, and seven syndicated columns. Under chain ownership, ads were removed from the editorial page. And in 1 week there were four local or regional editorials, five letters, five political cartoons, and double the number of syndicated columns.

The Holland paper was the exception. The mean performance of the sample of 28 dailies was to remain the same under the two types of ownership. With one rather unimportant exception, there simply were no statistically significant differences between the performance of the 28 dailies under independent and chain ownership. The mean performance of the papers was to publish about the same number of editorial pages, editorials, syndicated columns and cartoons, letters to the editor, local columns and cartoons, local art, and advertisements. On only one of 16 measures was there a difference between independent and chain ownership. That was the category of miscellaneous articles, which dropped from an average of 3.4 per week under independent ownership to 1.9 under chain ownership. This category included a considerable amount of non-editorial-page material, such as feature stories and photographs from wire services and essays from supplementary news services. Thus, the reduction in this category of non-editorial material could be interpreted as a strengthening of the editorial pages under chain ownership.

Correlational data demonstrate that, with the major exception of editorials, individual newspapers published similar amounts of editorial-page materials under both forms of ownership. The strong and positive correlations for cartoons, letters, and columns indicate unchanged performances. If a newspaper published few letters or syndicated columns under independent ownership, it tended to continue to do the same under chain ownership. However, the weak and statistically insignificant correlations for local and national editorials indicate that performance of a paper under independent ownership was not related to performance under chain ownership. There simply was no relationship. This result was puzzling. One explanation is that these small and medium dailies were haphazard about publishing editorials about local and national issues and were not seeking a quota or uniform balance in such content. Such editorials may have been written in response to local and national events and whenever such events merited discussion. And so the patterns and numbers of such editorials varied from week to week.

Discussion

The purpose of this study was to systematically analyze the editorial pages of 28 daily newspapers before and after the papers were purchased by chains. The study differed from previous ones in the use of this before–after design and in the inclusion of a greater variety of variables that measured the quality of editorial pages.

This study supported Hynds's (1984) conclusion that contemporary editorial pages are alive and well. The typical editorial page in this study had a surprising amount of variety and vigor. An average page included three letters, two political cartoons, three syndicated columns, one editorial about national or international issues, half of an editorial or four paragraphs about local issues, and a third of an editorial about regional issues. The quantity of editorials about local and regional issues about equaled the editorials about national and international issues. This certainly was not Afghanistanism, or the practice of editorializing about distant and irrelevant events. Also on the plus side, there were almost no advertisements on these editorial pages. On the negative side, there were very few local columns, local cartoons, local guest commentaries, local drawings, or local photographs. This was not surprising given the staff size of these medium-sized papers with a median circulation of 37,000.

Somewhat surprising was the degree of political balance in the selection of syndicated columnists—42% were liberal. This did not mean that the other 58% were conservative, because some of the columnists were apolitical. It was anticipated that column selection would become more conservative during the 2 years and the change of ownership. The study covered the time period of 1975 through 1985, when moderate and conservative presidents Jimmy Carter and Ronald Reagan dominated national politics. This shift to the right, however, did not materialize. This balance of liberal and conservative columnists mirrored a 1986 Gallup poll that found the public about evenly divided between conservative and liberal columnists. The six best read columnists consisted of three conservatives (William Buckley, James Kilpatrick, and George Will) and three liberals (Art Buckwald, Jack Anderson, and Mike Royko) ("TM Poll Looks," 1986, p. 35). Selection of political cartoons was not as balanced. Only 23% came from Roy Paul Nelson's list of 11 liberal cartoonists. Possible explanations for this apparent imbalance include: the list of liberal cartoonists was incomplete; editors shy away from liberal cartoons, as opposed to liberal syndicated columns, because of the harsh impact of caricature drawings as compared to written messages; or, a significant number of the editorial cartoons may have been moderate or middle-of-the-road in tone and neither liberal nor conservative.

The primary purpose of the study was to search for evidence of diminished commitment to the editorial page by chains that are characterized as greedy and profit-minded. It was anticipated that the chains would devote fewer pages to editorials and commentary, would publish fewer local and regional editorials and letters, and would publish more advertisements and canned editorials. But this did not happen. With one minor exception, there simply were no statistically significant differences for the 16 variables that measured the quality of editorial pages.

Why were there no differences? One explanation is that, in fact, chain newspapers are no different than independent papers, that both are equally concerned about profits and are equally committed to an editorial page. A group of editorial writers in Texas indicated that chain owners are less likely than family owners to dictate day-to-day editorial policy (Starr, 1986, p. 24). It also can be said that independent and chain owners are equally avaricious and greedy and equally unwilling to expand an editorial section and to hire local columnists and local cartoonists. This study demonstrated that editorial pages do not deteriorate under chain ownership. More importantly, it also demonstrated that editorial pages do not improve under chain ownership. Whatever advantages chains enjoy in economic power or expertise is not utilized to improve the editorial page.

Another plausible explanation, and one that was not tested by this study, is that chains do make changes when they purchase independent papers—but not on the editorial page. It would be too noticeable to tamper with the editorial page. Instead, changes are made in other, less-obvious areas such as the size of the reporting staff, the size of the local news hole, salaries of news staff, or amount of coverage of local controversy or conflict.

These "less-obvious" areas, as well as reader or subscriber satisfaction, are logical subjects for future research. Another fruitful approach might be to expand this study by including a larger number of newspapers, adding more sensitive and sophisticated measures of quality, and allowing more than the 4 to 16 months in this study for chain ownership to have an impact. It is not sufficient to measure the number and length of editorials about local issues. The next step is to use Thrift's approach and measure the number of local editorials that advocate a position on a local controversy. It is one thing to write a syrupy editorial praising the Rotary Club for building a new Little League field. It is quite another thing to publish an editorial criticizing the Rotary for not admitting women as members and not seeking minorities as members. An analysis of editorial pages should distinguish between the two types of editorials.

The subject of the quality of chain newspapers obviously deserves additional study. A recent article asked, "Where is the financial support for such a study?"

Private foundations of chains and media conglomerates?
Obviously not.
University journalism programs?
Also unlikely. They have to worry about chain support for buildings, VDTs, scholarships, and the employment of their graduates.
The federal government?
Not if elected members of Congress have anything to do with it. Just one chain, Gannett, publishes in 34 states. Sixty-eight U.S. senators are concerned about Gannett coverage and election endorsements.
State and national press associations?
No chance. They are dominated by chain affiliates that have the time to be active in such organizations (Hale, 1984a, p. 90).

Some argue that newspaper chain ownership is a dead issue, because few independent newspapers remain and business consolidation is a nationwide phenomenon. During deregulation in the 1980s, consolidation is the rule in every industry from hamburgers and steel to advertising and even public relations. (The 20 largest of 825 ad agencies account for 66% of $39.2 billion in annual business; Abrams, 1985–1986, p. 2). It previously has been noted: "The real threat to newspapers does not come from the existing concentration of ownership (with an average of eight papers per chain); it comes from the continued absorption of independents by chains, from the subsequent absorption of small chains by large chains, and by the absorption of newspaper chains by corporate conglomerates" (Hale, 1984b, p. 9). The real concern is not with the existing concentration or leadership in U.S. newspaper chains. Unfortunately, research of current conditions cannot predict the impact of continued expansion of chains on the future quality of news and commentary in American newspapers. Press critic Ben Bagdikian (Holahan, 1986, p. 15) warned that those with power cannot be trusted to always use it wisely: "Power will always be used if the stakes are high enough."

One group worried about chain growth is the Newspaper Guild, which, in June 1985, unanimously approved a resolution urging the federal government to consider placing a ceiling on the total circulation or number of newspapers under the control of a single company. Guild president Charles A. Perlin pointed that the two giants, Gannett and Knight-Ridder, together control 14% of total U.S. circulation: "In an era when chains are acquiring chains, the day of superconcentration may not be as distant as it seems" (Fitzgerald, 1985, p. 14).

The all-time giant, Gannett, makes a difficult target for those who wish to limit the size of chains. For Gannett, with 91 newspapers and numerous other holdings in 1986, is a progressive corporate leader in the promotion of women and minorities and in the protection of the First Amendment. To attack Gannett is to attack a civil liberties crusader. But Gannett's image may be deceptive. One of the company's advertisements, entitled "A salute to the men and women . . . who publish Gannett newspapers," features thumbnail photos of 65 publishers, an impressive 22% of whom are women. Few companies could match that figure. However, the mean circulation of the Gannett dailies headed by women is 25,000, compared to 56,000 for Gannett papers headed by men. With surprising candor, Gannett admitted in 1986 that 60% of the people hired by its newspaper division in 1979 had left the company, and 40% who had been hired in 1982 had since left (Brumm, 1986, p. 27). Despite its liberal image in some areas, employee satisfaction and turnover appear to be problems at Gannett, just as they are at many American newspapers.

PART IV

Issues for Policy Consideration

CHAPTER 12

Antitrust Law and Newspapers

David C. Coulson

Associate Professor and Graduate Director
Reynolds School of Journalism
University of Nevada-Reno

When the forefathers of the United States drafted the First Amendment, newspapers reflected highly partisan viewpoints, but there was widespread and inexpensive access to printing presses. Alexis de Tocqueville (1900, p. 186) observed, when visiting this country in 1831, that the American press has "established no central control over the expression of opinion," remarking that "nothing is easier than to set up a newspaper, and a small number of readers suffices to defray the expenses of the editors." The economics of the newspaper industry has since concentrated in the hands of a few press barons the ability to inform and to influence public opinion.

This chapter examines the threat to freedom of expression posed by newspaper concentration and explores possible application of antitrust law to foster open and competitive newspaper markets. In recognition that newspaper concentration more adversely affects ideas than it does the economic marketplace, primary weight is given to social and political factors in determining anticompetitive market constraints. It is argued that extensive newspaper consolidation inhibits new entry and decreases editorial independence and diversity.

Concentrated newspaper ownership is irreconcilable with a democratic society. A viable marketplace of ideas depends in large measure upon a competitive economic marketplace. In this sense the First Amendment and the antitrust laws do not stand in philosophical opposition to one another.

Government intervention in newspaper markets that results in diversifying market structure or in preventing anticompetitive conduct can foster freedom of expression. But government intervention in the market must be restrained, or it may actually inhibit the public interest in a robust press.

The Supreme Court initially held antitrust law to be consistent with the First Amendment in *Associated Press v. United States* (1945, at 20). Central to the 1945 decision is the concept of a market that is free from constraints which either destroy competition or prohibit newcomers from entering the field. Justice Hugo Black stated in the majority opinion that the First Amendment "rests on the assumption that the widest possible dissemination of information from diverse and antagonistic sources is essential to the welfare of the public, that a free press is a condition of a free society."

The court thus recognized the public's stake in guaranteeing a variety of news and opinions. Justice Oliver Wendell Holmes expressed the notion earlier in *Abrams v. United States* (1919, at 630): "The ultimate good desired is better reached by free trade in ideas—that the best test of truth is the power of the thought to get itself accepted in the competition of the market. . . . That at any rate is the theory of our Constitution."

Economic Characteristics

Understanding the structure and ownership of the newspaper industry in this country is critical to an effective public policy seeking to advance basic First Amendment objectives. The dominant economic characteristics of newspaper ownership today are local monopolies, joint operating agreements, chain ownership, cross-media ownership of a newspaper and television station in the same city, and media conglomerates.

It is paradoxical that an economic system founded on competition has evolved into one which fosters monopoly. Although in recent years the total number of newspapers has remained virtually unchanged, the number of monopoly newspaper cities has grown dramatically. In 1920 there were 700 cities with competing dailies (Bagdikian, 1983, p. 126). By 1987, though the nation's population had more than doubled, there were less than 30 cities with competing dailies (*ASNE Bulletin*, December 1986, p. 5). These statistics do not reflect the number of weeklies and advertising sheets which may operate in the monopoly newspaper's market. While sometimes integral information sources in their communities, they are dissimilar in content and function to the daily newspaper.

Under the Newspaper Preservation Act of 1970 certain dailies are granted special antitrust exemptions (Public Law No. 91-353, 1970). The papers are allowed to merge their advertising, circulation, production, and administrative departments, while keeping their editorial departments separate, in what is termed a joint operating agreement. If the weaker paper in a two-paper market can show that it is "failing" financially, it may combine with its financially healthier competitor to improve its chances for survival. Passed in response to a U.S. Supreme Court ruling against a joint operation in Tucson, Arizona (*Citizen's Publishing Company v. United States*, 1969), the legislation retroactively sanctioned 22 existing joint ventures in danger of antitrust action.[1] But since its enactment, applications have been filed in only five cities—Anchorage, Chattanooga, Cincinnati, Detroit, and Seattle.

Within the last 25 years chain ownership has become the dominant force in newspaper publishing. Of the nation's 1,700 dailies, fewer than 500 have not already been absorbed by the chains,[2] which control 80% of daily newspaper circulation. Six of every seven newspapers sold thus far in the 1980s were bought by chains (Editor & Publisher, April 28, 1984, pp. 76, 88). In addition, chains have begun to merge with each other: four large chains took over six smaller chains in one year alone (Bagdikian, 1977). Gannett, the largest U.S. chain, with 89 dailies, a total circulation of 4.5 million,[3] and 1986 revenues of $2.8 billion (Gannett 1986 Annual Report, p. 56), has absorbed several other chains in recent years.

In Canada, the degree of concentration is much greater. The Southam and Thomson chains account for about 70% of daily English-language circulation. In 1980, in response to simultaneous closings of the Ottawa Journal and the Winnipeg Tribune, which left each of the two chains with a monopoly city, the federal government brought charges under the Anti-Combines Act.

The Canadian government levied eight criminal counts of conspiracy, merger, and monopoly against Thomson and Southam. Following a lengthy trial, they were acquitted of all charges in December 1983. Under the Act, the Crown would have had to prove that the closings were detrimental to the public interest, and that the agreement between the newspaper chains "unduly lessened" competition (Winter, 1985, p. 15).

When television entered the broadcasting field, newspaper owners were among the first to acquire licenses: they had the expertise, resources, and economic incentive to establish stations. In 1982 there were 35 newspaper–television cross-ownerships in the top 100 American markets.[4] This figure contrasts with the 60 stations affiliated with newspapers in their local markets at the beginning of 1973.[5]

---

[1] In addition to Tucson, cities with joint operating agreements included Birmingham; San Francisco; Miami; Honolulu; Evansville; Fort Wayne; Shreveport; St. Louis; Lincoln; Albuquerque; Columbus; Tulsa; Franklin-Oil City; Pittsburgh; Bristol; Knoxville; Nashville; El Paso; Salt Lake City; Charleston; and Madison.

[2] Even fewer independent dailies remain with enough cash flow to attract chain owners; Ben H. Bagdikian, "The Media Monopolies," The Progressive, 42 (June 1978), p. 32.

[3] The figure does not include USA Today, which had a 1.3 million average daily circulation for six months ending March 31, 1987, slightly surpassing the New York Daily News (circulation 1.28 million) but behind schedule with plans to outstrip the Wall Street Journal (circulation 2 million). ABC FAS-FAX, March 31, 1987.

[4] Media outlets in Canada are characterized by a higher degree of cross-ownership. See David Townsend, "Regulation of Newspaper/Broadcasting, Media Cross-Ownership in Canada," University of New Brunswick Law Journal 33 (1984), pp. 261–282.

[5] Herbert H. Howard, "An Update on TV Ownership Patterns," Journalism Quarterly, 60 (Autumn 1983), pp. 395–400. Although the Federal Communications Commission did not require

The current trend is for newspapers and television stations to become cable cross-owners. Citing the growing competition from the new media technologies (such as direct broadcast satellite, video cassettes, low-power VHF), the Federal Communications Commission recently lifted nearly all the rules that have banned television–cable combinations (47 Fed. Reg. 39, 212, 1982, at 39, 217). Now that television broadcasters can enter the local cable market, they likely will generate new capital that will further escalate the value of prime cable franchises—thus prompting newspaper publishers to step up their ownership role in cable (Arlen, 1982, p. 51).

The most expansive form of media concentration is the conglomerate, of which there are two types. The first, vertical ownership, bears a logical relationship to the communications industry. For example, CBS is among the leading companies in television, radio, magazines, and books; Capital Cities, Gannett, and Cox in newspapers and radio; the *Washington Post*, the *New York Times*, and Newhouse in newspapers and magazines; ABC and NBC in television and radio (Bagdikian, 1983, pp. 19–20).

With horizontal ownership, on the other hand, no logical link exists between the media component and the giant corporations' other subsidiaries. Most media conglomerates have elements of both types. There are few American industries that do not own a major media property, or major media that do not own a firm in a major industry. The extent of this trend can best be understood by referring to the annual reports of major corporations whose holdings include media interests.

Literature Review

Studies measuring the effects of media concentration on the information process have generated conflicting results. Substantial evidence suggests that concentration of media corporate influence yields neutral effects. Research focusing on newspaper competition, for example, generally defies the basic tenet of antitrust law that newspaper monopoly diminishes both the quality and diversity of information and opinion. However, recent research indicates monopoly may adversely affect newspapers' financial commitment to the editorial product (Bigman, 1948; Willoughby 1955; Borstel, 1956; Nixon & Jones, 1956; Schweitzer & Goldman, 1975; Hicks & Featherston, 1978; Litman & Bridges, 1986; Lacy, 1987).

Various systematic studies find that community interests are poorly served by concentrated media ownership. An investigation into the effects of cross-ownership of a newspaper and television station in the same city revealed that

---

divestitures in more than a few cases, many owners have sold or exchanged their television holdings to remove any "regulatory cloud" from future operations. **Ibid.**, p. 400.

such combination tends to restrict the variety of news available to the public (Gormley, 1977). A West Coast study showed that after purchase by a chain an independently owned daily's editorials will decline in vigor and be less argumentative (Thrift, 1977; see also Wackman, Gillmor, Graziano, & Dennis, 1975). Papers once competitive that were made monopolies by chains were found to produce "higher prices and lower quality" (Grotta, 1971).

Much discussion of concentration is based on the intuitive reasoning of legal and mass communications scholars. According to law Dean Jerome Barron, the massive changes in the industry suggest media owners' freedom of expression may be constitutionally abridged in order to promote diversity. If the marketplace-of-ideas metaphor is to retain any viability, Barron states, public rights, such as access, must be instituted.[6] This view is less widely held since *Miami Herald Publishing Co. v. Tornillo* (1974), but such concerns were not mitigated by the Supreme Court's repudiation of a constitutional right of access.

Similarly, Professor Bruce Owen's (1975) interpretation of the First Amendment emphasizes its affirmative aspects and downplays its restraints on government intervention. In *Economics and Freedom of Expression*, which typifies one segment of the literature dealing with the structure and conduct of mass communications, he proposes large-scale government intervention, such as transforming newspaper printing and delivery facilities into quasi-public utilities. How views such as Owen's have been formulated into public policies in Western nations and developed into a new theory of state-press relations were explored more recently by Robert Picard (1985).

An exhaustive legal analysis (Lee, 1979, p. 1341) cautions that "the failure of the government to promote open mass communications economic markets would have grave consequences for our society, but equally grave would be the consequences of unrestrained government intervention in those markets." Promoting the dissemination of diverse ideas with a minimum of governmental interference is the goal of the First Amendment, the author points out, and the central problem in applying antitrust laws to the media (p. 1338).

Shortly after *Associated Press*, mass communications legal scholar Zechariah Chafee (1947, p. 537) noted that employing the antitrust laws to prevent media concentration was the most important and difficult problem discussed in his book *Government and Mass Communications*. Throughout his discussion he questions the advisability of combating media concentration with more sweeping enforcement of antitrust laws.

The antitrust laws are inherently negative, prohibiting certain business practices and policing the exercise of economic power. Their negative aspect has evoked suggestions that, coupled with active enforcement against individual

---

[6] Jerome A. Barron, "Access to the Press—A New First Amendment Right," *Harvard Law Review* 80 (1967), p. 1647. See also the recent discussion by David Shelledy, "Access to the Press: A Telelogical Analysis of a Constitutional Double Standard," *George Washington Law Review* 50 (1982), pp. 430–464.

newspaper conduct, an affirmative policy be shaped to promote competition. These suggestions include enlarging the investment tax credit for investors seeking entry into the daily newspaper business ("Newspaper Regulation," 1970–1971).

In 1980 this author wrote that only through government-induced business incentives will the interests of the public receive higher priority from the newspaper industry. The study urged that the focus of antitrust action shift from narrow economic considerations to concern about dissemination of information if antitrust law is to be an effective antidote to media concentration.

Keith Roberts stated in the *Harvard Law Review* (1968) that local newspaper competition would be greatly heightened by vigorous enforcement of antitrust laws and from technological advances, which substantially reduce publishing costs and enhance circulation. Roberts said the scarcity of new entrants into the market can be attributed largely to a variety of artificial restraints. These range from vertical restrictions placed by newspapers on distributors, to the refusal by wire and feature services to accommodate new newspapers, to joint-operating agreements to share physical plants and management departments.

The Newspaper Preservation Act's exemption of joint operating agreements from antitrust enforcement was recently criticized for ignoring the First Amendment interests of other competing newspapers. According to a recent University of Illinois law article (Carlson, 1982; see also Patkus, 1984), the legislation fails adequately to weigh the anticompetitive effects of joint mergers, including the obstacle they raise to new entry. The author recommends that the Act be amended to afford protection to new and independent newspapers.[7]

By shielding newspapers from economic forces, a retrospective analysis suggests, the Act may be creating false conditions under which to maintain separate editorial voices (Barwis, 1980). Questioned also is the granting of a monopoly advantage to two metropolitan newspapers, in preference to independent suburban dailies which would provide alternative media voices.

But findings of a 1984 study lend no support to critics' fears that "joint agreements would result in fewer suburban newspapers and lower circulation for suburban newspapers in affected metropolitan areas." Instead, suburbs in the metropolitan areas examined[8] differed little in the number of newspapers per suburb, and circulation of suburban newspapers in areas with joint agreements

---

[7] For early criticism of the NPA, see Glenn Becker, "Failing Newspaper or Failing Journalism: The Public Versus the Publishers," *University of San Francisco Law Review* 4 (1970) pp. 465–491; John Tebbel, "Failing Newspapers and Antiturst Laws," *Saturday Review* (Dec. 12, 1970), pp. 58–59; John H. Carlson, "Newspaper Preservation Act: A Critique," *Indiana Law Journal* 46 (1971), p. 392–412.

[8] The first in each of the following six pairs is the metropolitan area with a joint agreement: Evansville, IN–Scranton, PA; Tulsa, OK–Austin, TX; Tucson, AZ–Las Vegas, NV; Madison, WI–Sacramento, CA; St. Louis, MO–Denver, CO; Shreveport, LA–Little Rock, AK; Walter E. Niebauer, Jr., "Effects of the Newspaper Preservation Act on the Suburban Press," *Newspaper Research Journal* 5 (Summer 1984), p. 49.

was more than twice that of suburban newspapers in areas with competing dailies.

Limited available research posits that existing antitrust law does not appear capable of halting the trend toward ownership concentration by large newspaper chains. If the trend is to be checked, according to one legal analyst, it will need to result from congressional action. Specifically, he writes, Congress should develop guidelines defining the geographic markets that apply to newspaper chains (Jones, 1976; see also McIntosh, 1977). A corroborative article (Robinson, 1979, p. 851) states, "Absent a national geographic market for readers and advertising with which to measure the competitive effects of chain acquisition or merger, and absent overlap of the two local markets, antitrust laws are not triggered."

In Canada, a similar measure was recommended by the Kent Royal Commission on Newspapers in 1981. A modified version of this recommendation, The Canada Newspaper Act, was drafted by the Federal Liberal Government Cabinet, but was scuttled by the government in 1983. Under that proposed legislation, ownership by any one chain would be restricted to 20% of Canadian daiy circulation, although the Thomson (21%) and Southam (28%) chains' then-current holdings were exempted (Winter, 1985).

A case study concludes that economics and business-management techniques are at the heart of newspaper chain influence. Corporate headquarters sets the economic goals for member newspapers, according to an Iowa journalism researcher, and publishers are evaluated on how well they meet these economic goals. He contends that, too often, the publisher of a chain newspaper serves the interests of the corporation first, and the needs of the community second (Soloski, 1979).

In *The Media Monopoly*, press critic Ben Bagdikian (1983; see also Bagdikian, 1980) provides substantial evidence to prove that, in the last 25 years, some of America's largest corporations have taken control of the country's mass media. The recent book contains listings showing that media subsidiaries owned by the giant companies include seven of the 20 largest newspaper chains and all three dominant television networks. Through interlocking directorates (Drier & Weinberg, 1979), sharing members on boards of directors, Bagdikian (1983, p. 21) observes, the media are now directly influenced by still other powerful industries. When their "most sensitive" economic interests are involved, he writes, the parent corporations normally use their power over public information (p. xix).

Some noted scholars contend that political influence rises as a function of corporate size. According to Harlan Blake (1973, pp. 591–592; see also Pertschuk & Davidson, 1979; Salamon & Siegfried, 1977; Lindblom, 1977), among the most potent economies of scale that giant firms possess is the effective presentation of their case for favorable treatment by government:

(C)onglomerate firms can mobilize special interest support from a much wider range of sources (than a single product firm); they are likely to deal with more unions, more categories of suppliers and customers, and more mass media . . . and they are likely to be, or deal with, important constituents in more states and electoral districts.

Henry Geller (1982) refutes the notion that new technological conditions warrant the elimination of current media ownership rules. The former FCC general counsel points out that people still rely primarily on the newspaper and television for local information—a pattern that will not soon change. Further, he says such new electronic services as discs, subscription television, and direct broadcast satellites are not relevant to local issues. To protect the First Amendment guarantee of diversity, he recommends maintaining the ban on newspaper–television and television–cable cross-ownership.

Discussion

Newspaper Monopoly

The need for antitrust enforcement of competition among daily newspapers is especially urgent because of their crucial role in providing diversity of viewpoints essential to a democratic society. The Supreme Court has consistently held that the newspaper industry should also remain competitive for the traditional antitrust reason, cited in *United States v. Citizen Publishing Co.* (1969), that competition provides the consumer with a better product. In the newspaper industry that product ultimately is an informative publication.

The Court addressed a related concept in *United States v. Times Mirror Co.* (1968):

> the daily newspaper business is a distinct line of commerce and is a product separate and distinct from any other product. It has sufficient peculiar characteristics and uses which make it distinguishable from all other products.

The Court thus rebutted the industry's contention that newspapers cannot be categorized as a market distinct from other media, and that, therefore, no need exists to develop an antitrust policy to promote competition specifically among newspapers.[9]

The argument is made that it is no longer practical to direct antitrust law toward the maintenance of local newspaper competition. Some critics maintain that economic barriers beyond antitrust control are chiefly responsible for the severe decline in local newspaper competition.[10] Economist Bruce Owen (1975, pp. 52–53) views the decline as inevitable:

---

[9] For the American Newspaper Publishers Association position consult Chafee, *Government and Mass Communications*, pp. 621–622.

[10] The courts acknowledged over a quarter century ago that some cities are unable to support two competing newspapers; *Union Leader Corp. v. Newspapers of New England, Inc.*, 180 F. Supp. 125

Head-on competition among newspapers in the same town is a disequilibrium situation, one that will eventually be succeeded by merger, failure of one newspaper, or a joint operating agreement, tantamount to merger. Antitrust action aimed at preserving competition in this sense is simply doomed to failure.

The "bottom line" is that local newspaper competition is not as lucrative to media owners as a monopoly. Eliminating competition allows the surviving publisher to consolidate advertising revenue and to reap the economic benefits of one plant, one staff, and as much news coverage as he or she determines most feasible. His or her troubles are over. The advertisers depend on this forum, and the readers have no other comparable option.

It is a basic principle of economic theory (Scherer, 1980), and an accepted underpinning of antitrust law (see *United States v. Aluminum Corporation of America*, 1945), that monopolies have strong incentives to raise prices and restrict output, thus making their product available to fewer consumers. Where content of a newspaper is concerned, monopoly means that fewer people have access to the ideas contained in the publication, and that fewer advertisers have access to readers. With competition, there is a greater likelihood that a diversity of views will find some outlet to the public. Competition, therefore, should be the goal of antitrust policy in the newspaper industry, as in other industries.

A common defense offered by newspaper monopolists is that they can better withstand advertisers' efforts to manage the news than can a strapped competitor. They also contend that their civic obligation and commercial desire to reach a broad readership prompts them to print diverse news and editorials. Overlooked is the willingness of monopolist publishers to become complacent and to adopt the interests of the community establishment.

Some knowledgeable observers first believed that new technology's ultimate cost savings would prove a panacea for local newspaper competition. However, technological advances may endanger the survival of suburban newspapers. Facsimile transmission and satellite printing plants allow metropolitan dailies easily to create zoned editions for distribution within targeted areas.

By the mid-1980s most major newspapers had invested heavily to expand their suburban markets. Frank McCulloch (*Editor & Publisher*, April 27, 1985, p. 17) of McClatchy Newspapers said in 1985 that while the trend toward zoned editions has just about "crested," metropolitan papers will continue to compete with suburbans to protect their own core circulation. "Zoning costs are unbelievable," he stated. "As often as not, zones don't make a dollar for a newspaper. But they do increase reader loyalty, and that helps protect the core."

(D. Mass., 1959). In markets with a population of less than 650,000, local daily newspaper competition cannot be expected unless the publishers agree to a joint operating arrangement, according to one commentator. Then, the mark can be lowered to approximately 200,000, he says. See Richard J. Barber, "Newspaper Monopoly in New Orleans: The Lessons for Antitrust Policy," *Louisiana Law Review* 24 (1964), p. 543.

Joint Operating Agreements

The Newspaper Preservation Act was designed to maintain two independent editorial voices in a community by allowing separately owned papers to combine all but editorial functions for efficiency and economy. "Regardless of the economic or social wisdom of such a course," a federal judge wrote recently, "it (NPA) does not violate the freedom of the press. Rather it is merely a selective repeal of the antitrust laws. It merely looses the same shady market forces which existed before passage of the Sherman, Clayton and other antitrust laws (Holder, 1982, p. 22).

Those shady forces include combination advertising rates which construct artificial barriers to new entrants. The stronger paper will often raise its advertising rates; then space will be offered in both papers for slightly more than it would cost to advertise in the stronger paper alone.[11] Most advertisers will take advantage of the combination rate, thus discouraging competition by a third paper. The monopoly practices engaged in by joint ventures may also have an adverse effect on other newspapers already competing in the same market and in nearby suburban markets (Carlson, 1982, p. 691).

Despite the Act, there has been a steady decline in the number of metropolitan dailies in recent years: Washington, Philadelphia, Cleveland, Buffalo, Columbus, St. Louis and Baltimore have lost papers since 1980 and have become principally single newspaper-owner towns.[12] The stronger paper in each situation preferred a monopoly to a joint-operating agreement. Newspaper analyst Bruce Thorp (Holder, 1982, p. 22) notes:

> Five or 10 years ago, the stronger paper in Philadelphia or Washington or Cleveland might have jumped at the chance to form a JOA. . . . What's happening now is that papers are losing a lot if they are losing. The *Washington Post* was not interested in a JOA because it would have had to absorb all the losses from the *Star*. The joint revenue would not have been enough to offset the losses.

Joint revenue failed to guarantee solvency for the two newspapers in the St. Louis pact, the *Post-Dispatch* and the *Globe-Democrat*, which lost $11 million from 1978 to 1981 (Massing, 1981). The joint operating agreement was dissolved, and Newhouse Newspapers sold the strapped *Globe* in early 1984 to *Saturday Review* publisher Jeffrey Gluck. Under the audacious owner, the newspaper's circulation "tumbled and its finances became increasingly chaotic."

---

[11] It is argued that this practice may suppress competition and, therefore, not be exempted from antitrust laws by the NPA. See Stephen R. Barnett, "Combination Ad Rates: The Monopoly Stinger," *Columbia Journalism Review* 19 (May/June 1980), p. 44.

[12] Washington has since acquired a second newspaper, the *Times; Editor & Publisher* (May 22, 1982), p. 15. For views on the reasons behind the failures, see "Danger of Being in Second Place," *Time* (Sept. 14, 1981), p. 82; J. E. Vacha, "Death in the Afternoon," *Washington Journalism Review* 3 (October 1981), pp. 41–45.

Despite the last-ditch efforts of new proprietors to revitalize the *Globe*, it folded in late October 1986, after 134 years—and after a troubled recent history that included three owners announcing the paper's death three times in three years (*Editor & Publisher*, November 8, 1986, p. 10).

Professor Dwight Teeter observes that truly failing papers are unlikely to be saved by the NPA and papers saved by the NPA are unlikely to be truly failing (Holder, 1982, p. 22).

The Act may forfeit competition by sanctioning joint agreements when sale to an outside publisher could preserve both editorial and commercial competition. In Seattle, the legislation permitted the *Times* and *Post-Intelligencer* to establish a joint pact in 1983, despite the contention by the Antitrust Division of the Justice Department that the application should be denied because there were potential buyers[13] who would maintain the *Post-Intelligencer* as an independent paper.[14] Communications scholar William E. Ames says of the agreement: "The *P-I* got a wonderful deal and they're doing great. But a lot of people around here don't feel there are really two papers anymore (*Editor & Publisher*, 1984, p. 17). Legislation intended to preserve independent voices may merely increase the profitability of the two newspapers that no longer compete in the normal sense of the term.

Editorial independence in monopoly combinations is seriously inhibited by the close relationship required to make joint business decisions. Jointly operated papers are loath to report on a public issue detrimental to a mutual financial interest.[15] Editors and reporters "curb their tendencies to take to task the businesses or institutions sleeping with the publisher of the other paper," says a former *Post-Intelligencer* investigative reporter (Holder, 1982, p. 24). In addition, a newspaper may not honestly report a dispute involving its joint operating partner. The San Francisco *Examiner*, for example, inadequately covered the *Chronicle*'s failed attempt to renew the broadcast license of its television station (Carlson, 1982, p. 410).

In short, the assumption that the Newspaper Preservation Act will save editorial competition is erroneous. It prohibits new entry into the newspaper mar-

---

[13] It was disclosed during hearings on the application that one prospective buyer was international press magnate Rupert Murdoch, who had approached the Hearst Corporation about the possibility of acquiring the *Post-Intelligencer.* Hearst responded that it was not interested in selling the paper; Lawrence Roberts, "Saving A Newspaper, Seattle Style," *Washington Journalism Review* (January/February 1982), p. 13.

[14] *Committee for an Independent P-I v.* Hearst Corp., 704 F. 2d 467, at 475 (9th Cir. 1983). Although the court of appeals approved the application of the Seattle papers, the opinion raised the possibility that a future application might be refused if there are buyers interested in a "failing" newspaper. See Patkus (1984, p. 446).

[15] Newspaper Preservation Act: Hearings on H.R. 279 Before the Antitrust Subcomm. of the House Comm. on the Judiciary, 91st Cong., 1st Sess. 105, 279 (1969). See S. REP. No. 535 (letter of FTC in opposition).

ket, decreases editorial independence in joint partnerships, and fails to curtail newspaper deaths.

Congress should amend the legislation to lessen its harmful effects. The antitrust exemption, for instance, should apply only to independent newspapers. This would spur chain owners to find buyers or to improve their papers' management. By granting an advantage to independent owners, the NPA would promote antitrust and First Amendment interests. Further, applicants should be required to demonstrate that less-extensive joint operations would not jeopardize continued operation. Finally, the pacts should be prohibited if a legitimate outside buyer can be found.

Newspaper Chains

A chain newspaper enjoys a competitive edge over an independent paper: the chain can achieve the cost savings of large-scale transactions and can withstand temporary losses because of its additional financial reserves. Independently owned newspapers, on the other hand, have difficulty coping with rising costs and the capital investment necessary to buy new computer-oriented technology.

Selling to a chain is often seen by an independent publisher as the best available option. Taxes are the overriding reason. As a rule, independent newspapers are closely held family operations, and when the owner dies his or her heirs must pay estate taxes on the paper's "fair market value." The willingness of chains to pay 60 or more times earnings[16] for some papers has inflated market values to the point where heirs who can resist the lucrative offers are faced with bearing an enormous tax burden.

The taxable value of even small papers runs into the millions. "For example," says estate tax reformist Sen. Steven Symms (R-Idaho) (Good, 1982, p. 35), "if a newspaper were earning $250,000 per year, its value to a chain might be as high as $12 million. The estate tax, at 70 percent,[17] would be over $8.5 million. Should the heir seek to borrow such sums to pay estate taxes, the annual cost of interest on the loan would be more than three times the newspaper's earnings."

Congress should enact legislation that allows independent newspaper owners to establish an estate tax trust fund and to spread payment over a number of years.[18] Most important, the taxes should be assessed at what the newspaper is worth and not at what someone is willing to pay for it. Also, unfair tax breaks should be eliminated that permit chains to offer astronomical prices for indepen-

---

[16] Although chains usually do not report publicly their purchase prices, it is known that in 1979 Gannett paid $54 million for the *Shreveport Times* in Louisiana, or 83 times earnings. The Times Mirror Co. paid $105 million, or only 28 times earnings, for the *Hartford Courant* the same year; Jeffrey Good, "Fugitives from a Chain Gang," *Washington Journalism Review* 4 (May 1982), pp. 36–37.

[17] Limited relief occurred under the Economic Tax Recovery Act which dropped the top rate from 70 to 50% in 1986. Public Law 97-34, U.S. Statutes at Large, 95:172 (1981).

dents (The Internal Revenue Service, for instance, excludes from taxation chain profits earmarked for expansion (*News Media and the Law*, 1977, p. 12).

Legislative action would help independent newspaper owners resist surrender to chains and make unnecessary the elaborate steps taken by Nelson Poynter of the *St. Petersburg Times*. The innovative publisher left his newspaper to The Poynter Institute for Media Studies to insure that the *Times* would remain free from chain control.[19]

The constitutional guarantee of a free press demands a halt to the steady encroachment of newspaper chain ownership before it becomes as centralized as the steel or automobile industries, which it already has in Canada. Existing antitrust law, however, is largely ineffective as a check against chain growth—it does not apply to a collection of individual papers operating in different cities.

But if the chain's line of commerce was measured by total national circulation, the chain would appear vulnerable to antitrust action. Congress, though, as did the Canadian government, ultimately lacks the will to buck the powerful newspaper lobby and extend the typically local geographic market to the national level.

Chain spokesmen make a big point of the idea that each local publisher is wholly independent, but it is difficult to imagine corporate management of the chains as not wielding considerable editorial influence on the newspaper. Although most chains avoid dictating news play or editorial positions,[20] the financial expectations of a centralized administration indirectly affect what is printed. The publisher of a chain newspaper may be forced to sacrifice coverage and editorial diversity for operational profits.

One of the easiest and most obvious ways the chain publisher has to ream costs out of his newspaper is to cut back on the amount of local reporting— editorial employee salaries represent the single largest expenditure in the news-

---

[18] In the late 1970s Representative Morris Udall (D-Ariz.) unsuccessfully introduced such a bill, the Independent Local Newspaper Preservation Act, which stalled in subcommittee hearings. 124 Cong. Rec. H3288 (daily ed. April 26, 1978) (remarks on H.R. 12395).

[19] For discussion of Poynter's legendary aversion to chain ownership, see David C. Coulson, "Nelson Poynter: Study of an Independent Publisher and His Standards of Ownership" (unpublished doctoral dissertation, University of Minnesota, 1982), pp. 65–83.

[20] Noteworthy exceptions do exist. They include Freedom Newspapers, which openly advances its libertarian politics through its local papers; Gary J. Logan, Tom Korosec, and Joanne Jones, "A Libertarian Direction," *The Quill* 68 (July/August 1980), pp. 22–23. Editorial staff members and the publisher of a small Massachusetts chain clashed over instructions to print pro-Republican stories during the 1984 election campaign; *Editor & Publisher* (November 24, 1984), p. 16. In a much publicized 1977 case, Panax Corporation, then publisher of about 50 obscure weeklies and dailies in Michigan, Illinois, and Indiana, told its papers to run two critical and unsubstantiated articles about President Carter on their front pages. When two editors in Michigan balked at the order, Panax President John P. McGoff fired one, while the other resigned; see John L. Hulteng, "The Performance or the Power," *The Quill* 65 (October 1977), pp. 23–29; "What Passes for News at Panax," *Columbia Journalism Review* 16 (September/October 1977), p. 6; "Statement on John P. McGoff and Panax Corporation Policy," *Columbia Journalism Review* 16 (September/October 1977), p. 83.

room budget. There is also the tendency for publishers to depend on the chain's wire features and columnists to reduce costs and thus increase revenues. The result is member papers which include quite similar content, especially on the editorial pages (Soloski, 1979, pp. 19–25).

Elie Abel, head of the Stanford University communication department and a Pulitzer Prize winner, charged recently (*Editor & Publisher*, December 22, 1984, p. 11) that "most chain newspapers will invest not a penny more in editorial excellence than the minimum needed to meet their daily deadlines." But whether chains publish distinguished newspapers or not is almost beside the point. The loss of competition and the gathering of the nation's press into a few massive chains all invite loss of public confidence.

Cross-Media Ownership

Since the public relies primarily upon newspapers and television for its news coverage, any concern over media concentration must seriously consider news-paper–television combination. Such jointly owned media may be separately operated and may be competitive on occasion, but it is unrealistic to expect true diversity (see Johnson & Hoak, 1970). Even where there is a conscious effort to maintain separate voices, jointly owned media are more likely to be protective rather than antagonistic toward each other.[21] The danger that an issue will not get covered is lessened when local newspaper and television reporters work for different owners.

In the instance of newspaper-owned television stations, certain benefits are offered as defense against a doctrinaire approach to the cross-ownership issue (see Toohey, 1966, pp. 54–55). Because their owners come from a journalistic tradition, it is often argued that newspaper-owned television stations are more news and public service oriented than non-newspaper-run stations. Whether or not this is a correct assumption, the desired public policy solution would appear to be for the FCC to hold all television operators to a higher standard of public service, rather than to trade a loss in diversity in media ownership for a gain in the quality of public service programming (see Phillips, 1975, pp. 1152–1153).

Antitrust's effect on newspaper–television combination at the local level has never been tested. The Justice Department is reluctant to file antitrust suits against renewal of a television license held by a local newspaper. Such efforts might fail and would have to be waged through long trials on a city-by-city basis.

The FCC, however, does have authority to refuse to license television stations to the owners of daily newspapers in the same community. Not only has the commission forbidden such newspaper–television mergers in the future,[22] but it

---

[21] Second Report and Order, Docket No. 18110, 40 Fed. Reg. 6449 (1975), at 6454 (Appendix A).

also has prohibited television licenses from being sold or transferred to the same town's newspaper (*FCC v. National Citizens Committee for Broadcasting*, 1978). The FCC takes the position, though, that separation of existing combinations is not required unless evidence exists that such a joint ownership is clearly detrimental to the public interest.

The cross-ownership rules are intended to increase diversity; yet, by sparing existing newspaper–television combinations, the rules diminish diversity by creating artificial barriers to entry. Since most such joint ownerships involve monopoly newspapers, divestiture to allow another voice to be heard in the community is consistent with the public interest and outweighs entrepreneural concerns. By its public interest mandate, the commission should be required to promote economic competition as a means of increasing diversity. Although it is well established that the FCC cannot enforce the antitrust laws directly (see *United States v. Radio Corp. of America* (1959); *National Broadcasting Co. v. United States*, 1943), the principles of antitrust law should be applied to newspaper–television combinations.

Media Conglomerates

Conflict of interest emerges as the foremost concern in discussing media conglomerates. When a newspaper or television station is but one of a giant corporation's many properties, "the danger is that information of vital importance to the public relating to another of the conglomerate's financial interests will be given minimum coverage or be suppressed altogether (Roach, 1979, p. 265). Because news is merely a by-product of many corporate activities, it may be subordinated or manipulated as necessary to promote or safeguard the profit-making potential of other subsidiaries. Furthermore, there is the fear that the news media's guise of integrity may mislead a public unaware that the content of a newspaper article or television broadcast may be shaped by economic incentives created by corporate interests unassociated with the job of informing the public (Roach, 1979, p. 265).

Large media concerns are often defended as strong enough to withstand improper pressure from non-media corporations seeking preferential treatment. But through interlocking directorates—sharing members on boards of directors—giant media companies are directly and indirectly influenced by other powerful industries (see Chapter 6). "Almost every major industry whose activities dominate the news of the 1980s—the leading defense contractors and oil companies—sit on controlling boards of the leading media of the country," says Ben Bagdikian (1983, pp. 265–266).

---

[22] Multiple Ownership of Standard, FM and Television Broadcast Stations, 50 FCC 2d 1046 (1975) (Second Report and Order).

Interlocks develop links with other institutions important to the media firm's corporate growth and relations with government. The Gannett newspaper chain shares directors with Allegheny Airlines, Phillips Petroleum, Merrill Lynch, McDonnell Douglas Aircraft, Standard Oil of Ohio, McGraw-Hill, Kerr-McGee (oil gas, nuclear power, aero-space), 20th Century Fox, Kellogg, and New York Telephone, among others (Dreier & Weinberg, 1979, p. 55). The interlocks extend beyond the corporate sector. Newspaper companies have more than 100 direct ties with universities, and most of these firms have directors on the boards of the local United Way or Chamber of Commerce (Dreier & Weinberg, 1979, p. 52).

The adverse journalistic effects of interlocks may be subtle—such as self-censorship—or the effects may be apparent—reporters pressured, stories not covered or spiked when written. "Because of the tremendous shared interests at the top," a *Chicago Tribune* business reporter said several years ago (Dreier & Weinberg, 1979, p. 68), "coverage is limited and certain questions never get asked."

An all too typical example is illustrated by the former relationship between Cleveland's daily newspaper and Ohio's largest bank.

> Through a trust, the bank shared control of the *Cleveland Plain Dealer . . .* for more than half a century. The bank's chairman was also the paper's chairman, and one minority shareholder recalls discovering that the paper "had $7 million in a checking account at the bank drawing no interest. Yet they had no liabilities except normal ones." The Newhouse chain[23] bought the paper in 1967. . . . After the sale, the *Plain Dealer's* columns began criticizing the bank. "How much the bank (had) managed the news I'm not sure," says a former staff member, "but I do know we never printed the story that (the late bank chairman George) Gund was the biggest slumlord in town." ("Why the Big Traders," 1970, p. 54; see also Freilich, 1979)

Most newspaper companies have no plans to limit interlocks despite a long series of inquiries into the practice, including a 1978 report by the Senate Committee on Governmental Affairs (U.S. Congress, 1978, p. 280) which called for congressional action against such ties and concluded: "These patterns of director interrelationships imply an overwhelming potential for antitrust abuse and possible conflicts of interest which could . . . control the shape and direction of the nation's economy."

Concern over conglomerate practices, however, extends beyond traditional worries about antitrust. It focuses on "the flow of information and the vitality of journalism as something absolutely disinterested and relentlessly independent (Dreier & Weinberg, 1979, p. 53). Bagdikian (1978, p. 32) states:

---

[23] No information is available on the interlocks of Newhouse, one of the most closed private corporations and the only U.S. newspaper company that refuses to divulge the names of its directors.

There is a qualitative difference in the social impact of media conglomerates as against companies that make plastics or musical instruments. If an ordinary conglomerate uses one of its companies to further the interests of another of its companies, it may be unfair competition but it is largely an economic matter. If a conglomerate uses its newspaper company to further the interests of another of its subsidiaries, that is dishonest news.

Media conglomerates create special problems for the government's antitrust division, which must prove anticompetitive effects. The Justice Department's success under existing legislation depends on imaginative application of antitrust law and on the courts' willingness to expand the range of factors germane to the illegality of media conglomerates.

A carefully crafted legislative approach might be devised which limits large media-enterprise transactions that pose the greatest potential threat to the unfettered exchange of information. Coupled with a broader judicial interpretation of First Amendment policy, such action would help antitrust enforcers to combat conglomerate economic domination of the press.

Conclusion

Newspaper concentration leads to loss of diversity and conflict of interest. The public is ill-served by a press preoccupied with its profit margins. The gathering of newspaper ownership into larger and more centralized units justifies government economic intervention to promote diversity of expression. But because a chief press function is to scrutinize the actions of government, the press should remain as free as possible from government regulation. Antitrust law allows the competitive forces to fulfill the "regulatory" role—avoiding the need for government intrusion into First Amendment processes.

As long as the scope of antitrust law is confined to narrow economic concerns, however, antitrust seldom will pose an effective deterrent to newspaper concentration. Successful antitrust enforcement will depend on the Supreme Court's willingness to view newspapers' restrictive business practices as substantially lessening competition in the marketplace of ideas. If the government were to weigh societal interests when considering the desirability of newspaper concentration, antitrust law and First Amendment principles would coalesce to protect freedom of expression from the newspaper industry's powerful economic influence.

CHAPTER 13

Policy Implications

A major concern of those taking part in the Press Concentration and Monopoly Research Project is the implications of developments in the field to public policies affecting the press. This chapter reports policies proposed by the participating researchers on the various issues dealt with in the research project. Participants in the project brought with them a range of personal political/economic philosophies and attitudes toward state intervention, leading to significant internal debate on some policy proposals. General agreement was reached by the participants on most policy proposals.

This chapter presents a synthesis of the views of participants in the project, including majority and minority views wherever they existed. The chapter divides the issue of concentration and monopoly into seven major topical areas, with specific questions being addressed in each area. Participants were asked to comment on the questions in light of the results of the project's studies, previous research, and their own views of the role of the state in such issues. The positions do not necessarily represent the views of any single member of the project, or of the Association for Education in Journalism and Mass Communication.

Intercity Competition Issues

What types of pricing policies by large metropolitan newspapers violate, or should be viewed as violating, antitrust laws?

Majority View

Predatory and must-buy pricing should be seen as violations of antitrust law. New interpretation of existing law, amendment of existing law, and new statutes should be sought to halt such pricing policies.

Predatory pricing is that which offers advertising space or subscriptions below cost. Such pricing policies, especially for zoned or outstate editions, should be forbidden and halted because of the damage they inflict and can inflict on smaller suburban daily papers and weekly publications that are necessary to promote economic competition and diversity.

Predatory pricing should be determined by standardizing a relevant measure so that any prices below that would be predatory per se. Potential measures include short-run marginal cost, long-run marginal cost, average variable cost, or average cost per unit (if such a cost includes all costs of production, including capital) measures.

Intent to commit predatory pricing, evidenced even in action alone, should also be shown to maintain a claim of predatory pricing.

Must-buy pricing policies that require advertisers to purchase advertising in more than one publication, either through direct requirements or inducements made by quantity or other discounts that result in below-cost pricing, should also be forbidden. This especially applies to joint operating agreement and joint monopoly papers where such combination prices are common and detrimental to competition. The prohibition should also extend to "shoppers" and other nonweekly publications produced by daily metropolitan and suburban newspapers.

Such pricing policies should apply to all areas in which the paper markets circulation or advertising. Prohibitions against predatory or must-buy pricing should apply equally in both the areas of advertising and circulation.

Minority Positions

(1) Predatory pricing policies should only violate antitrust laws when there is a reasonable probability that a smaller paper might be driven out of business by a larger paper's activities.

When claims of predatory pricing are made against a metropolitan paper by a suburban daily paper, pricing policies relevant to the discussion should only be those involving pricing by the metropolitan paper for its zoned editions circulating within the retail trading zone of the suburban paper.

(2) Prices of monopoly, joint monopoly, and joint operating agreement papers should be regulated to ensure that the loss of competition benefits to the public does not disadvantage circulation or advertising consumers. Without such competition, publishers have shown a willingness to set prices that are unregulated by the market and most advantageous to publishers. Authorization to regulate pricing should be sought especially for joint operating agreement papers, which already constitute a government-licensed monopoly and are already subject to some economic regulation.

Should the concept of the marketplace of ideas play a role in antitrust action in this area, or should the Justice Department or Ministry of Justice be limited to dealing with economic issues alone?

Majority Position

Because the press plays a pivotal role in political and social life, and is a primary institution in political participation, it is important to separate the newspaper industry from manufacturing and other service industries in terms of public policy. Therefore, those agencies charged with overseeing the economic activities of the news industry need to consider more than mere economic definitions of antitrust when dealing with developments in the industry and protecting public welfare.

Monopolies in, and concentrated ownership of, newspapers are irreconcilable with democratic society. A viable marketplace of ideas depends in large measure upon a competitive economic marketplace. Government intervention in newspaper markets that results in diversifying market structure, promoting competition, and preventing anticompetitive conduct improves the marketplace of ideas and fosters freedom of expression. This intervention must be restrained, however, so it does not inhibit a robust and diverse press. Use of antitrust law in a regulatory role over economic aspects of the newspaper industry to promote diversity can be used to avoid the danger of government intruding into editorial matters to pursue such purposes and conflict with First Amendment values.

The importance of newspapers in the democratic process, technology developments, and the economic realities of the newspaper industry make it necessary for justice officials to consider the marketplace of ideas and to set standards of economic behavior for the newspaper industry that are higher than for any other industry.

The government has a positive responsibility for ensuring the private sector does not destroy the marketplace of ideas. Such a position permitted government action against the Associated Press and joint operating newspapers, regulation of broadcasting, and regulation of cross and multiple ownership. This intervention can be broadened to cover intercity newspaper competition issues.

Minority Position

The marketplace cannot play a role given the way antitrust laws are construed. In *The Antitrust Paradox*, Robert Bork states, "Antitrust is concerned with the effects of market behavior and structure upon consumer welfare. Other matters, if they raise problems, must be taken care of by other laws" (1978, p. 248). Thus it would require change in the First Amendment to permit the government to intervene and police the marketplace of ideas. No thank you. It is safer if justice officials deal only with economic considerations. The marketplace of ideas is pretty difficult to operationalize, and thus it would be difficult to deal with it in statutes and regulations.

Large metropolitan newspapers have an advantage from economies of scale. Is there any subsidy or change in tax laws that could help smaller newspapers in the face of this advantage?

Majority Position

It is desirable to encourage smaller newspapers because of the diversity and the potential for diversity they provide. As alternative voices, these papers carry local views and stories not often found in metropolitan dailies, and some nonweeklies provide even more local coverage than found in suburban dailies. These smaller papers also have the potential to grow into larger papers that can compete directly with current monopoly papers.

The tax code has been used in many different ways to create incentives for various industries to survive and prosper. Some incentives could be earmarked to help newly entering daily newspaper firms or certain-sized papers. These incentives could come in the forms of investment tax credits or accelerated depreciation. They should be short-term in nature to prevent their exploitation by existing firms or those who would not normally qualify unless they changed their economic situations.

An additional tax advantage could come by permitting the competing smaller papers or new papers to pay no or less taxes on capital investment to lower barriers to entry.

Excise tax and sales tax exemptions should be removed for the largest newspaper in a market.

Serious consideration should be given to providing loans to small papers, just as loans are provided to other small businesses, to encourage their development and success.

Minority Positions

(1) Significant news competition exists for big-city dailies because of television, radio, cable, magazine, and suburban newspaper competitors, so there is no need to increase competition through subsidies and tax policies in these markets. Selective assistance to newspapers would violate the First Amendment; it is not acceptable. Nothing should be done to promote survival of alternative papers. The natural competitive forces should be allowed to work without government interference.

(2) In addition to tax breaks, subsidies should be provided to help start up new daily newspapers in monopoly markets. This could be done with revenue raised by a tax on newsprint or from general fund expenditures. A variety of such plans exist in Western nations and should be explored.

Should weekly shoppers or advertising publications without or with little news content be given the same protection and consideration as newspapers with news content?

Advertising is an important source of information for individuals in society and should not be disadvantaged merely because of its commercial nature.

Shoppers and other nonnews sheets should be as protected from damaging price practices of other publishers as any other paper. News content, or the lack of it, should be irrelevant to the provision of protection.

Such papers, however, should not be the beneficiary of tax breaks or other fiscal advantages designed to promote editorial diversity and the establishment of newspapers. Only papers carrying editorial content should benefit from such special provisions.

Direct Intracity Competition Issues

Should or can government policy promote this type of competition?

Majority Position

Yes. But the question is how. The major difficulties in intracity competition are the dependence on advertising for the majority of revenue and the disadvantages to the smaller papers because of the economics of scale generally enjoyed by larger papers.

Competition should be fostered, however, by rigid antitrust enforcement in the declining number of cities where direct competition exists and by the provision of tax advantages to the secondary papers or the removal of existing advantages from the leading papers.

Low-interest loans and investment incentives, such as tax credits, should be provided secondary papers to help them improve their situations, so they may more effectively compete for advertising and circulation, or expand their markets to help improve their ability to survive.

Minority Positions

(1) Such competition should be promoted even if it means creating quasi-public newspapers, akin to public broadcasting operations. These could be funded through a tax on commercial publications or general funds, as well as through advertising and contributions.

(2) Ample intermedia competition exists in many cities, and there is no need to provide assistance to or otherwise encourage new competition.

Should the government attempt to separate the news gathering of newspapers from production functions?

Majority Position

The government can encourage competing papers to share printing facilities so that joint production efficiencies would ensue, without creating joint operating newspapers. This could also be done with distribution facilities. The result would be a neutralization of the printing and distribution stages, while keeping the news gathering and marketing aspects separate.

Such a printing facility could be promoted through the provision of low-interest loans or tax advantages. It would be necessary to provide the opportunity for smaller publications to use such a facility as well, or to assist them in setting up their own cooperative printing and distribution system. Suburban dailies and weeklies would be harmed if they were not permitted to use the service.

Minority Position

Tax laws should not be used to promote such competition. People should not be *forced* to pay money for newspapers they do not want.

Joint Operating Agreements

Should the Newspaper Preservation Act be scrapped?

Majority Position

Yes. It provides only the illusion of competition and precludes real competition. It should be replaced with measures suggested above to promote competition.

The act is applicable to only a few situations, and it appears that the number of JOAs will decline rather than increase as dominant papers in agreements find that repudiating their agreement when it runs out will lead to the demise of the weaker member.

Under its current formulation and interpretation, the act is so broad that it permits the wealthiest companies in the newspaper business to gain larger profits through JOAs and permits an ominous concentration of market power.

At the very least, no new JOAs should be permitted, and inducements to break up existing JOAs provided.

Minority Positions

(1) We do not have sufficient information to answer this question. No consensus has been reached on what constitutes good performance of newspapers, and so we may not accurately address the question of whether monopoly, competitive, or some hybrid situation such as joint operating agreements is the superior market structure.

(2) JOAs should not be scrapped, because they afford the opportunity to share costs and increase technical efficiency in the market. And, considering the economies of scale from current technology and the joint product nature of newspapers, JOA cities may be the only competitive markets left in 20 years.

Although the NPA should not be legislated out of existence, ways must be found to eliminate price fixing and profit pooling, which were authorized by the act.

If it is not scrapped, should the NPA be amended to give the public more control over JOA newspapers?

Majority Position

Yes. Several changes need to be instituted in the act. First, the definition of *failing* newspaper needs to be refined and strengthened to eliminate artificially induced situations. For instance, a concerted effort to sell the paper should be required before any JOA is allowed. The market would then be used to separate out a hopeless situation from one of merely bad management.

Second, existing JOAs should be reviewed regularly by justice officials to ensure they are not misusing the significant market power that accompanies such an operation.

Third, the joint agency should be separate from the papers. The boards of the agencies should not be made up solely of representatives of the two papers and should not be dominated by one paper. The public should be represented by a substantial number of citizens to guarantee that this local exception to antitrust laws is not abusive or predatory.

Fourth, the agency portion of the agreement should be operated as a public utility and required to print any local paper desiring services.

Sixth, the distribution of profits should not be negotiated between the two papers in a JOA but distributed, based on the proporation of circulation within the retail trading zone, or a comparable measure, held by each paper. This would encourage competition and make the papers more responsive to their readers and advertisers.

Minority Positions

(1) Agreements should be for 50 or 100 years, so the operations will not break up when one paper gets the upper hand.

(2) The length of the agreement should be stipulated in each JOA and only be permitted for as long as it takes to recoup previous losses.

(3) The NPA should be amended to apply only to independently owned newspapers. This would spur chain owners to improve their management or find buyers for the paper who might keep it from becoming a joint operating paper.

(4) The NPA should not be amended, but scrapped entirely. It serves no useful public interest, only the interests of publishers.

(5) Amending the NPA to give the public more control over JOA papers could lead to government control of the editorial process. It should not be altered.

Chain Ownership

At what point do groups become a threat to the free flow of information to the public?

Majority Position

Groups become a threat when they achieve such a level of concentration that it becomes expensive, in terms of time or actual costs, for the consumer to search for a balanced diet of daily information. When a 20% to 25% share of total national circulation is in the hands of any one group, a dangerous situation is developing, and antitrust law should limit further growth. Similarly, where around 50% or more of a regional or state market is accounted for by a single group, a dangerous situation exists and antitrust mechanisms should be applied.

It must be noted that groups do not necessarily mean a problem for local autonomy, but the potential problem is always there, and there is significant evidence that problems exist in many chain ownership situations.

The desire for a free press demands a halt to the steady encroachment of newspaper ownership before it becomes as centralized as some other industries.

Minority Positions

(1) No chains should be permitted to grow any larger in total circulation, number of newspapers, or number of other media properties than the Gannett Co. is currently. Now is the time for caps on such numbers.

(2) This is not a relevant question in the area of media economics and economic policy, but a political issue.

What actions can the government take to limit the growth of groups?

Majority Position

Legislate and stick to limits on size. If they require divestment by some firms, allow time for selling of papers and provide tax advantages to independent purchasers. Another mechanism would be the removal of tax advantages for chains that permit them to reinvest their profits in acquisitions. By removing the incentive to buy media properties, and thus lowering the cost of newspapers at sale, more independent ownership or small-chain ownership would be promoted.

Legislation should be enacted to allow independent newspaper owners to establish an estate-tax trust fund and to spread out payment over a number of years, so they may avoid being forced to sell to chains to pay taxes. This situation could be avoided entirely if estate taxes were assessed at the rate based on the return of the paper, rather than on what chains are willing to pay, if it is sold.

Should government take action to stop group growth that may affect intercity umbrella competition?

Yes. It should use antitrust laws as in the Times Mirror case, where a large metropolitan paper sought to purchase a smaller competitor within its market.

This area requires significantly more study to determine what damage is done if group papers acquire satellite city papers outside of their retail trading zones. In some less-populous states, acquisition of even a single paper, even well outside its primary marketing area, may have harmful effects on economics and diversity.

Cross-Ownership and Interlocking Directorships

Should cross-ownership of various media continue to be discouraged?

Majority Position

Yes. Cross-ownership is damaging to diversity when the cross-ownership is in the same market. Since most cross-ownership situations involve monopoly newspapers as well as cross-ownership of other media, it is imperative that no new cross-ownership situations be permitted, and desirable that divestment be required in existing situations.

Cross-ownership not only creates situations where hegemony is evident in information, but also those where pricing behavior of the firms can seriously disadvantage consumers.

At the very least, statutes should prohibit owning more than two media in one market, and cross-ownership of a local television station or cable system by a newspaper should be banned. This will prevent the most egregious forms of price gouging and ensure diverse ownership of the major forms of information and advertising delivery.

Minority Position

(1) There is no economic reason to prevent cross-ownership, if the cross-ownership is below a local market concentration threshold. The rationale for cross-ownership prohibitions consists mainly of noneconomic criteria such as diversity.

Should corporations outside the media industry be allowed to purchase newspaper firms?

Majority Position

Ownership by such firms should be limited. Because of their unique role in political social processes, newspapers and other media should serve their audiences directly and not economic interests unconcerned about the breadth and depth of information but the bottom line. At the very least, a company's non-media holdings should not be permitted to exceed its media holdings.

News is not merely a commercial product, and placing corporate control over content in an already heavily monopolized industry hardly can be expected to serve the public interest.

Some mechanism of control should be established, although it would be difficult in the United States, given the Constitution and economic system.

Minority Position

(1) No firm outside the media industries should be allowed to own or hold an interest in a media company, because of the dangers of conflict of interests and controls of information.

(2) Who may own newspapers and other media should not be limited. Anyone and any company should have the right to own.

Should media firms be allowed to purchase firms outside media industries?

Majority Position

It is preferable if they do not, but if they do, their holdings should be limited so they do not exceed media holdings. This should be done to avoid conflicts of interest. Legislation should be carefully drafted to devise limits to large media enterprise transactions that pose the greatest potential threat to the unfettered exchange of information.

Minority Positions

(1) Media companies should not be allowed to own any other types of companies, because the potential for conflict of interest is too great, and many examples of media operating for the benefit of their other companies rather than the public interest have been documented.

(2) Media companies' ability to own other types of companies should not be limited in any way.

Should government follow a policy of requiring media firms, and their parent firms if any, to make public their directors' names and affiliations with other firms, and to make public any affiliations the media firms themselves have with nonmedia firms?

In the absence of forbidding interlocking directorships, media ownership by nonmedia firms, and media ownership of other firms, disclosure of all such links should be made. A condensed form of such information could be required in SEC 10-K reports, annual reports, etc., with a detailed version including all interlocks created by company directors, names and addresses of controlling investors in the media company, disclosure of ownership of other companies by the media firm, etc., available on request.

Should government prohibit interlocking directorships between media firms and media firms and nonmedia firms?

Majority Position

Yes. Large media concerns are often defended as strong enough to withstand pressure from nonmedia corporations seeking preferential treatment. But, through interlocking directorates, giant media companies have been, and are being, influenced by other powerful industries and investors.

In addition, prohibitions against executives or legal counsels for various firms serving other firms, or serving as board members of other firms, should be enacted.

Minority Position

No. If the media want to be biased and represent their own interests, economic policy should play no role to prevent this. The Constitution guarantees a free press, not an unbiased one.

Antitrust Law

Are antitrust laws sufficient for protecting the public against financial interests that may interfere with the public information function of newspapers? If not, how should they be altered?

Majority Position

Newspapers are not comparable to other industry products and services and must be treated as a special case. Legislation is needed specifically for newspapers. Interpretations placed on current antitrust statutes and existing antitrust regulation are not enough to protect the public interest.

Consideration needs to be paid to the interaction of the advertising and information markets and to determining how antitrust laws can be applied. New legislation needs to stipulate what will be considered predatory pricing in the newspaper industry and to define clearly what relevant markets are to be considered. Clear and separate guidelines should be stipulated for behavior of papers in umbrella competition and for group-owned papers. Determinations need to be made as to what substitutes are relevant for newspapers within markets.

Specific changes in existing antitrust law, or replacement with new legislation, would be complicated. Such changes should be suggested by a study committee not directly connected to any administration or newspaper industry group. The committee should be charged with finding ways to alter antitrust and other laws to deal with the problems of concentration and monopoly, mergers and takeovers, and chain ownership, while protecting editorial independence.

Minority Position

(1) Current laws are sufficient if antitrust regulators paid attention to the broader social interests and did not focus merely on narrow economic considerations. (2) The public functions of newspapers should not be the focus of antitrust laws.

Market Issues

What are the relevant geographic markets for newspapers?

Majority Position

For retail and classified advertising and circulation, it should be the retail trading zone in nearly every situation. In some unique situations, such as those in which a paper dominates a state or several states or a large portion of a state, a case should be made for expanding the relevant market into a regional market.

In some cases a national market is relevant. This should be applied to national advertising and to newspapers which market circulation nationally and have the majority of their circulation outside of the city of main publication.

Bibliography

Books

Anderson, Charles H. *The Political Economy of Social Class.* Englewood Cliffs, NJ: Prentice-Hall, 1974.

Baer, Walter, Henry Geller, Joseph Grundfest, and Karen Possner. *Concentration of Mass Media Ownership: Assessing the Current State of Knowledge* (Rand Reports, R-1584-NSF). Santa Monica, CA: Rand Corporation, 1974.

Bagdikian, Ben H. *The Media Monopoly.* Boston: Beacon Press, 1983.

Bain, Joe S. *Industrial Organization.* New York: John Wiley & Sons, 1968.

Bliss, M. *A Living Profit.* Toronto: McClelland and Stewart, 1974.

Bork, Robert H. *The Antitrust Paradox: A Policy At War With Itself.* New York: Basic Books, 1978.

Bradden, R. *Roy Thomson of Fleet Street.* New York: Walker, 1965.

Caves, Richard. *American Industry: Structure, Conduct, Performance.* Fifth Edition. Englewood Cliffs, NJ: Prentice-Hall, 1982.

Chafee, Zechariah. *Government and Mass Communications.* Chicago: University of Chicago Press, 1947.

Chamberlin, Edward H. *The Theory of Monopolistic Competition.* Sixth Edition. Cambridge, MA: Harvard University Press, 1950.

Clement, Wallace. *The Canadian Corporate Elite.* Toronto: McClelland and Stewart, 1975.

Compaine, Benjamin M. *The Newspaper Industry in the 1980s: An Assessment of Economics and Technology.* White Plains, NY: Knowledge Industry, 1982a.

Compaine, Benjamin M., Christopher H. Sterling, Thomas Guback, and J. Kendrick Noble, Jr. *Who Owns the Media? Concentration of Ownership in the Mass Com-*

munications Industry. Second Edition. White Plains, NY: Knowledge Industry, 1982b.

Curran, James, Michael Gurevitch, and Janet Woolacott. *Mass Communication and Society.* Beverly Hills, CA: Sage, 1977.

Cyert, R.M., and J.G. March. *A Behavioral Theory of the Firm.* Englewood Cliffs, NJ: Prentice-Hall, 1965.

Domhoff, G. William. *The Powers That Be: Processes of Ruling Class Domination in America.* New York: Random House, 1979.

De Tocqueville, Alexis. *Democracy in America.* New York: Colonial Press, 1900.

Editor & Publisher International Yearbook. New York: Editor & Publisher, 1980.

Editor & Publisher International Yearbook. New York: Editor & Publisher, 1985.

Epstein, Edward J. *News From Nowhere: A Study of CBS Evening News, NBC Nightly News, Newsweek, and Time.* New York: Vintage Books, 1979.

Ferguson, James M. *The Advertising Rate Structure in the Daily Newspaper Industry.* Englewood Cliffs, NJ: Prentice-Hall, 1963.

Gans, Herbert. *Deciding What's News.* New York: Pantheon Books, 1978.

Ghiglione, Loren. *The Buying and Selling of America's Newspapers.* Indianapolis, IN: R.J. Berg, 1984.

Gitlin, Todd. *The Whole World is Watching: Mass Media and the Making and Unmaking of the New Left.* Berkeley, CA: University of California Press, 1980.

Gollin, A., and T. Anderson. *America's Children and the Mass Media.* New York: Newspaper Advertising Bureau, 1980.

Innis, Harold. *The Fur Trade in Canada.* Toronto: University of Toronto Press, 1970.

Janowitz, Morris. *The Community Press in an Urban Setting.* New York: Free Press, 1952.

Johnstone, John, Edward Slawski, and William Bowman. *The News People.* Urbana, IL: University of Illinois Press, 1976.

Kesterson, Wilfred H. *A History of Journalism in Canada.* Toronto: McClelland and Stewart, 1967.

Kotler, Philip. *Marketing Management.* Fourth Edition. Englewood Cliffs, NJ: Prentice-Hall, 1980.

Langdon, Steven. *The Emergence of the Canadian Working Class Movement, 1845–1875.* Toronto: New Hogtown Press, 1975.

Lindblom, Charles Edward. *Politics and Markets.* New York: Basic Books, 1977.

Mansfield, Edwin. *Principles of Microeconomies.* Fourth Edition. Toronto: W.W. Norton, 1983.

McClure, Leslie. *Newspaper Advertising and Promotion.* New York: Macmillan, 1950.

McKinney, John. *How to Start Your Own Community Newspaper.* Port Jefferson, NY: Meadow Press, 1977.

Mills, C. Wright. *The Power Elite.* New York: Oxford University Press, 1956.

Nader, Ralph, Mark Green, and Joel Seligman. *Taming the Giant Corporation.* New York: W.W. Norton & Co., 1976.

Nafziger, Ralph O., and Thomas F. Barnhart. "Red Wing and Its Daily Newspaper," No. 9 in *The Community Basis for Postwar Planning.* Minneapolis, MN: University of Minnesota Press, 1946.

Neufeld, E. P. *The Financial System of Canada.* Toronto: Macmillan, 1972.

Oppenheim, S. Chesterfield, and Carrington Shields. *Newspaper and Antitrust Laws.* Charlottesville, VA: Michie Co., 1981.

Owen, Bruce M. *Economics and Freedom of Expression: Media Structure and the First Amendment.* Cambridge, MA: Ballinger, 1975.

Patterson, Thomas. *The Mass Media Election.* New York: Praeger, 1980.

Peterson, Susan, and Morris Heath. *Canadian Directorship Practices: A Critical Self-Examination.* Ottawa: The Conference Board of Canada, 1977.

Pfeffer, J., and G. Salanick. *The External Control of Organizations.* New York: Harper & Row, 1978.

Picard, Robert G. *The Press and the Decline of Democracy: The Democratic Socialist Response in Public Policy.* Westport, CT: Greenwood, 1985.

Porter, John. *The Vertical Mosaic.* Toronto: University of Toronto Press, 1965.

Reynolds, L.G. *The Control of Competition in Canada.* Cambridge, MA: Harvard University Press, 1940.

Roscho, Bernard. *Newsmaking.* Chicago: University of Chicago Press, 1975.

Rucker, Frank W., and Herbert L. Williams. *Newspaper Organization and Management.* Fourth Edition. Ames, IA: Iowa State University Press, 1974.

Rutherford, Paul. *The Making of the Canadian Media.* Toronto: McGraw-Hill, 1978.

Ryerson, S. B. *Unequal Union.* Toronto: Progress Books, 1968.

Scherer, F. M. *Industrial Market Structure and Economic Performance.* Second Edition. Chicago: Rand McNally, 1980.

Schramm, Wilbur. "Channels and audiences." In Ithiel deSola Pool and Wilbur Schramm (Eds.), *Handbook of Communication.* Chicago: Rand McNally, 1973.

Schudson, Michael. *Discovering the News: A Social History of American Newspapers.* New York: Basic Books, 1978.

Schumpeter, Joseph A. *Capitalism, Socialism and Democracy.* Third Edition. New York: Harper and Brothers, 1950.

Shepherd, William G. *The Economics of Industrial Organization.* Englewood Cliffs, NJ: Prentice-Hall, 1979.

Siebert, Fred S., Theodore Peterson, and Wilbur Schramm. *Four Theories of the Press.* Urbana, IL: University of Illinois Press, 1956.

Sigal, Leon V. *Reporters and Officials: The Organization and Politics of Newsmaking.* Lexington, MA: D.C. Heath, 1973.

Smythe, Dallas W. *Dependency Road: Communications, Capitalism, Consciousness and Canada.* Norwood, NJ: Ablex, 1981.

Spencer, Milton H. *Contemporary Microeconomies.* Fourth Edition. New York: Worth, 1980.

Tichenor, Phillip, George Donohue, and Clarice Olien. *Community Conflict and the Press.* Beverly Hills, CA: Sage, 1980.

Trigger, Bruce. *Natives and Newcomers.* Montreal: McGill-Queens University Press, 1985.

Tuchman, Gaye. *Making News.* New York: Free Press, 1978.

Udell, John G. *The Economics of the American Newspaper.* New York: Hastings House, 1978.

Urquart, M.C. *Historical Statistics of Canada.* Toronto: Macmillan, 1965.

Weaver, David, Doris Graber, Maxwell McCombs, and Eyal Chaim. *Media Agenda-Setting in a Presidential Election.* New York: Praeger, 1981.

Wicker, Tom. *On Press.* New York: Viking Press, 1978.

Articles, Monographs, and Pamphlets

Abrams, Bill. "Pair of Ad Executives Pampered but Restless, Set Out on Their Own," *Wall Street Journal* (1985–86 Educational Edition), p. 2.

Allen, Vernon and David Wilder. "Social Comparison, Self-Evaluation, and Conformity to the Group." In Jerry Suls and Richard Miller (Eds), *Social Comparison Processes*. Washington, DC: Hemisphere Publishing, 1977.

American Newspaper Publishers Association. *Facts About Newspapers*. Washington, DC: American Newspaper Publishers Association, 1986.

Ardoin, Birthney. "A Comparison of Newspapers Under Joint Printing Contracts," *Journalism Quarterly* 50:340–347 (1973).

Arlen, Gary. "Cable Cross-Ownership," *Washington Journalism Review* (January/February 1982), p. 51.

Asch, Salomon. "Effects of Group Pressure upon the Modification and Distortion of Judgement." In Harold Guetckow (Ed.), *Groups, Leadership, and Men*. Pittsburgh, PA: Carnegie, 1951.

Audit Bureau of Circulations. *Audit Report-Newspapers: Los Angeles Herald-Examiner*. Chicago: Audit Bureau of Circulations, 1985.

Bagdikian, Ben H. "The Media Monopolies," *The Progressive* (June 1978), pp. 31–34.

Bagdikian, Ben H. "Newspaper Mergers—The Final Phase," *Columbia Journalism Review* (March/April 1977), pp. 10–19.

Bagdikian, Ben H. "Conglomeration Concentration and the Media," *Journal of Communication* 30(2):59–64 (1980).

Bagdikian, Ben H. "The U.S. Media: Supermarket or Assembly Line?" *Journal of Communication* 35(3):97–109 (1985).

Baldridge, Paul D. "Group- and Non-Group Owner Programming: A Comparative Analysis," *Journal of Broadcasting* 11:125–130 (1967).

Barber, Richard J. "Newspaper Monopoly in New Orleans: The Lessons for Antitrust Policy," *Louisiana Law Review* 24:504–554 (1964).

Barnett, Stephen R. "Combination Ad Rates: The Monopoly Stinger," *Columbia Journalism Review* (May/June 1980), p. 44.

Barnett, Stephen R. "Monopoly Games—Where Failures Win Big," *Columbia Journalism Review* (May/June 1980), p. 41.

Barron, Jerome A. "Access to the Press—A New First Amendment Right," *Harvard Law Review* 80:1641–1678 (1967).

Barwis, Gail Lund. "The Newspaper Preservation Act: A Retrospective Analysis," *Newspaper Research Journal* 1:27–38 (1980).

Becker, Glenn. "Failing Newspaper or Failing Journalism: The Public Versus the Publishers," *University of San Francisco Law Review* 4:465–491 (1970).

Becker, Lee B., Randy Beam, and John Russial. "Correlates of Daily Newspaper Performance in New England," *Journalism Quarterly* 55:100–108 (1978).

Becker, Lee, Idowu Sobowale, and Robin Cobbey. "Reporters and Their Professional and Organizational Commitment," *Journalism Quarterly* 56:753–763 (1979).

Bigman, Stanley. "Rivals in Conformity: A Study of Two Competing Dailies," *Journalism Quarterly* 25:127–131 (1948).

Bishop, R. "The Rush to Chain Ownership," *Columbia Journalism Review* (November/December 1972), pp. 10–19.

Blake, Harlan M. "Conglomerate Mergers and the Antitrust Laws," *Columbia Journalism Review* 73:591–592 (1973).

Blankenburg, William B. "Determinants of Pricing of Advertising in Weeklies," *Journalism Quarterly* 57:663–666 (1980).

Blankenburg, William B. "Newspaper Ownership and Control of Circulation to Increase Profits," *Journalism Quarterly* 59:390–398 (1982).

Blankenburg, William B. "A Newspaper Chain's Pricing Behavior," *Journalism Quarterly* 60:275–280 (1983).

Blankenburg, William B. "Consolidation in Two-Newspaper Firms," *Journalism Quarterly* 62:474–481 (1973).

Block, Paul, Jr. "Facing Up to the 'Monopoly' Charge," *Nieman Reports* 9:3–7 (1955).

Bogart, Leo, and F.E. Orenstein. "Mass Media and the Community Indentity in An Interurban Setting," *Journalism Quarterly* 42:179–188 (1965).

Borstel, Gerald. "Ownership, Competition and Comment in 20 Small Dailies," *Journalism Quarterly* 33:220–222 (1956).

Breed, Warren. "Social Control in the Newsroom," *Social Forces* 37:178–194 (May 1958a).

Breed, Warren. "Mass Communication and Socio-Cultural Structure," *Social Forces* 37:109–116 (December 1958b).

Broom, Glen, and George Smith. "Testing the Practitioner's Impact on Clients," *Public Relations Review* 5:47–59 (Fall 1979).

Brumm, Barbara. "Gannett Opportunity and Pay Seen as Keys to Retaining Good People," *Gannetteer* (January 1986), p. 27.

Busterna, John C. "Ownership, CATV and Expenditures for Local Television News," *Journalism Quarterly* 53:223–230 (1976).

California Newspaper Publishers Association. "Canadian Sports/Media Magnate Buys L.A. Daily News," *Confidential Bulletin* (December 1985), pp. 71–72.

Carlson, Anita M. "The Newspaper Preservation Act: The Seattle Application," *University of Illinois Law Review* 3:669–699 (1982).

Carlson, John H. "Newspaper Preservation Act: A Critique," *Indiana Law Journal* 46:392–412 (1971).

Carroll, W.K., John Fox, and Michael Ornstein. "The Network of Directorate Links Among the Largest Canadian Firms," *Canadian Review of Sociology and Anthropology* 19:46–69 (February 1982).

Chaffee, Steven, Scott Ward, and Leonard Tipton. "Mass Communication and Political Socialization," *Journalism Quarterly* 47:647–659 (1970).

Chaney, Jerry. "Thomson: The Giant Chain Puts Its Brand on a Formerly Independent Daily . . ." *Publishers' Auxiliary* (September 6, 1982a).

Chaney, Jerry. "Kokomo Editor Ousted by Thomson Publisher," *Publishers' Auxiliary* (October 4, 1982b), p. 3.

Compaine, Benjamin M. "Newspapers." In Christopher H. Sterling, Thomas Guback, and J. Kendrick Noble, Jr. (Eds.), *Who Owns the Media? Concentration of Ownership in the Mass Communications Industry*, Second Edition. White Plains, NY: Knowledge Industry Publications, 1982a, Chapter 2.

Conglomerates and Press Freedom: A Canadian View," *Columbia Journalism Review* (November/December 1981), p. 57.

Corden, W.M. "The Maximisation of Profit by a Newspaper," *Review of Economic Studies* 20:181–190 (1952–53).

Coulson, David C. "Antitrust Law and the Media: Making the Newspapers Safe for Democracy," *Journalism Quarterly* 57:79–85 (1980).

"Daily Newspaper Sales Were Up During 1985," *Editor & Publisher* (January 4, 1986), p. 44.

"Danger of Being in Second Place," *Time* (September 14, 1981), p. 82.

Deutschman, Paul, and Wayne Danielson. "Diffusion of Knowledge of a Major News Story," *Journalism Quarterly* 37:345–355 (1960).

Donohue, George A., Clarice N. Olien, and Phillip J. Tichenor. "Reporting Conflict by Pluralism, Newspaper Type and Ownership," *Journalism Quarterly* 62:489–499, 507 (1985).

Donohue, Thomas, and Theodore Glasser. "Homogeneity in Coverage of Connecticut Newspapers," *Journalism Quarterly* 55:592–596 (1978).

Dooley, P.C. "The Interlocking Directorate," *American Economic Review* 59:314–323 (1969).

Dreier, Peter, and Steven Weinberg. "Interlocking Directorates," *Columbia Journalism Review* (November/December 1979), pp. 51–68.

Dunn, S. Watson. "Advertising Rate Policy: A Neglected Area of Study," *Journalism Quarterly* 33:488–492, 512 (1956).

Elliott, Philip. "Media Organizations and Occupations: An Overview." In James Curran, Michael Gurevich, and Janet Woolacott (Eds.), *Mass Communication and Society*. Beverly Hills, CA: Sage, 1977.

Endicott, R.C. "100 Leading Media Companies: 1986 Edition," *Advertising Age* (June 30, 1986).

Engwall, Lars. "Newspaper Competition: A Case for Theories of Oligopoly," *Scandinavian Economic History Review* 29:145–154 (1981).

Entman, Robert M. "Newspaper Competition and First Amendment Ideals: Does Monopoly Matter?" *Journal of Communication* 35(3):147–165 (1985).

Ferguson, James M. "Daily Newspaper Advertising Rates, Local Media Cross-Ownership, Newspaper Chains, and Media Competition," *Journal of Law and Economics* 28:635–654 (1983).

Fitzgerald, Mark. "Newspaper Guild Talks Tough," *Editor & Publisher* (July 6, 1985), p. 14.

"Foreign Publishers Top U.S. Sales," *Editor & Publisher* (January 7, 1984), pp. 40–42.

Freilich, Ellen S. "Cleveland 'Plain Dealer,' Pressured by Reporters, Prints a Story It Stifled," *Columbia Journalism Review* (May/June 1979), pp. 49–57.

Furhoff, Lars. "Some Reflections on Newspaper Concentration," *Scandinavian Economic History Review* 21:1–27 (1973).

Galbraith, John Kenneth, Walter Adams, and Williard F. Mueller. "How Much Competition Is There in the 'New Industrial State'?" In Kenneth G. Elzinga (Ed.), *Economics: A Reader*, Second Edition. New York: Harper & Row, 1975, Chapter 20.

Geller, Henry. "FCC Media Ownership Rules: The Case for Regulation," *Journal of Communication* 32(4): 148–156 (1982).

Gerbner, George. "Cultural Indicators: The Third Voice." In George Gerbner, Larry Gross, and William H. Melody (Eds.), *Communications Technology and Social Policy*. New York: John Wiley and Sons, 1973.

Good, Jeffrey. "Fugitives From A Chain Gang," *Washington Journalism Review* (May 1982), pp. 36–37.

Gordon, Richard L. "Ad Starvation Sinks 'Star'," *Advertising Age* (July 27, 1981), p. 1.

Gormley, William. "How Cross-Ownership Affects News-Gathering," *Columbia Journalism Review* (May/June 1977), pp. 38–43.

Gottlieb, B. "The Decline of the *Herald-Examiner*," *Columbia Journalism Review* (July/August 1977), pp. 23–40.

Grotta, Gerald L. "Consolidation of Newspapers: What Happens to the Consumer," *Journalism Quarterly* 48:245–250 (1971).

"Group Owned Dailies: 1,186; Independents: 489," *Presstime* (March 1986), p. 68.

"Group Ownership Trend Continues—32 Out of 36," *Editor & Publisher* (January 1, 1983), p. 34.

"Groups Still Own Most U.S. Dailies," *Editor & Publisher* (April 28, 1984).

Grush, Joseph, Kevin McKeough, and Robert Ahlering. "Extrapolating Laboratory Exposure Research to Actual Political Elections," *Journal of Personality and Social Psychology* 36:257 (1968).

Gustafsson, Karl Erik. "The Circulation Spiral and the Principle of Household Coverage," *Scandinavian Economic History Review* 26:1–14 (1978).

Haerle, D. "Clash of the Titans," *feed/back* (Spring 1984), p. 8–10.

Hale, F. Dennis. "An In-Depth Look at Chain Ownership," *Editor and Publisher* (April 28, 1984a), p. 30.

Henry, William A., III. "'McPaper' Stakes Its Claim," *Time* (July 9, 1984), p. 69.

Henry, William A., III. "Learning to Love the Chains," *Washington Journalism Review* (September 1986), p. 16.

Hicks, Ronald, and James S. Featherston. "Duplication of Newspaper Content in Contrasting Ownership Situations," *Journalism Quarterly* 55:549–553 (1978).

"Hoiles Leaves Freedom Group in Feud over Philosophy," *Editor & Publisher* (April 14, 1984), p. 4.

Holahan, Chuck. "Chains Are Not Going to Be Good for Journalism," *Publishers' Auxiliary* (April 21, 1986), p. 15.

Holder, Dennis. "MMI—Nelson Poynter's Anti-Chain Reaction," *Washington Journalism Review* (October 1981), p. 19.

Holder, Dennis. "Joint Operating Agreements: If You Can't Beat 'Em, Join 'Em," *Washington Journalism Review* (November 1982), pp. 20–24.

Howard, Herbert H. "An Update on TV Ownership Patterns," *Journalism Quarterly* 60:395–400 (1983).

Hulteng, John L. "The Performance or the Power," *The Quill* (October 1977), pp. 23–29.

Humphrey, T.E. "The Newspaper Preservation Act: An Ineffective Step in the Right Direction," *Boston College Industrial and Commercial Law Review* 12:937–954 (1970–71).

Hynds, Ernest C. "Editorials, Opinion Pages Still Have Vital Roles at Most Newspapers," *Journalism Quarterly* 61:634–639 (1984).

John Morton Newspaper Research Newsletter (April 2, 1982).

Johnson, Nicholas, and James M. Hoak, Jr. "Media Concentration: Some Observations on the United States Experience," *Iowa Law Review* 56:267–291 (1970).

Johnstone, John. "Organizational Constraints on Newswork," *Journalism Quarterly* 53:5–13 (1976).

Jones, Gregory Neill. "Antitrust Malaise in the Newspaper Industry: The Chains Continue to Grow," *St. Mary's Law Journal* 8:160–174 (1976).

Keep, Paul M. "Newspaper Preservation Act Update," Freedom of Information Center Report No. 456, University of Missouri (1982).

Kerbo, Harold R., and L. Richard Della Fave. "Corporate Linkage and Control of the Corporate Economy: New Evidence and a Reinterpretation," Sociological Quarterly (Spring 1983), p. 201.

Kerton, Robert R. "Price Effects of Market Power in the Canadian Newspaper Industry," Canadian Journal of Economics 6:602–606 (November 1973).

Kessel, John. "Cognitive Dimensions and Political Activity," Public Opinion Quarterly 29:377–389 (1965).

Lacy, Paul. "Gannett Is Shopping for More Newspapers, Stations This Year," Gannetteer (January/February 1985), p. 20.

Lacy, Stephen. "Competition Among Metropolitan Daily, Small Daily, and Weekly Newspapers," Journalism Quarterly 61:640–644 (1984).

Lacy, Stephen. "Monopoly Metropolitan Dailies and Inter-City Competition," Journalism Quarterly 62:640–644 (1985).

Lago, Armando. "The Price Effects of Joint Mass Communication Ownership," Antitrust Bulletin 16:789–813 (1971).

Lang, Kurt, and Gladys Lang. "The Mass Media and Voting." In Bernard Berelson and Morris Janowitz (Eds.), Public Opinion and Communication. New York: Free Press, 1966.

Leadbeater, David. "An Outline of Capitalist Development in Alberta." In David Leadbeater (Ed.), Essays on the Political Economy of Alberta. Toronto: New Hogtown Press, 1984, pp. 1–76.

Lee, William E. "Antitrust Enforcement, Freedom of the Press, and the 'Open Market': The Supreme Court on the Structure and Conduct of Mass Media," Vanderbilt Law Review 32:1249–1341 (1979).

Litman, Barry, and Janet Bridges. "An Economic Analysis of Daily Newspaper Performance," Newspaper Research Journal 7:9–26 (1986).

Logan, Gary J., Tom Korosec, and Joanne Jones. "A Libertarian Direction," The Quill (July/August 1980), pp. 22–23.

Louis, Arthur M. "Growth Gets Harder at Gannett," Fortune (April 20, 1981), p. 120.

Malan, R. "Paper Giant," California Magazine (October 1982), pp. 88–95.

Malone, John R. "Comments." In Federal Trade Commission, Proceedings of the Symposium on Media Concentration, Volume 2, pp. 536–538. Washington, DC: Government Printing Office, 1979.

Martel, J.S., and V.J. Haydel. "Judicial Application of the Newspaper Preservation Act: Will Congressional Intent Be Relegated to the Back Pages?" Brigham Young University Law Review 123–168 (1984).

Massing, Michael. "The Missouri Compromise," Columbia Journalism Review (November/December 1981), pp. 35–41.

Mathewson, G. F. "A Note on the Price Effects of Market Power in the Canadian Newspaper Industry," Canadian Journal of Economics 5:298–301 (1972).

McCombs, Maxwell. "Editorial Endorsements: A Study of Influence," Journalism Quarterly 44:545–548 (1967).

McIntosh, Toby. "Why the Government Can't Stop Press Mergers," Columbia Journalism Review (May/June 1977), pp. 48–50.

McLeod, Jack, Carrol Glynn, and Daniel McDonald. "Issues and Images: The Influence of Media Reliance in Voting Decisions," *Communication Research* 10:37–58 (1983).

McNeil, Robert. "The Mass Media and Public Trust," *Occasional Papers* No. 1. New York: Gannett Center for Media Studies, 1985.

Meyer, P., and Wearden, S. T. "The Effects of Public Ownership on Newspaper Companies: A Preliminary Inquiry," *Public Opinion Quarterly* 48:564–577 (1984).

Neuharth, Al. "Gannett Marks Growth across the Board—With More To Come," *Gannetteer* (January 1986), p. 2.

"Newspaper Regulation and the Public Interest: The Unmasking of a Myth," *University of Pittsburgh Law Review* 32:595–606 (1971).

Niebauer, Walter E., Jr. "Effects of Newspaper Preservation Act on the Suburban Press," *Newspaper Research Journal* 5:41–49 (1984).

Nixon, Raymond B., and Robert L. Jones. "The Content of Non-Competitive vs. Competitive Newspapers," *Journalism Quarterly* 33:299–314 (1956).

Noelle-Neumann, Elizabeth. "The Spiral of Silence: A Theory of Public Opinion," *Journal of Communication* 24(2), 43–51 (1974).

Noelle-Neumann, Elizabeth. "Mass Media and Social Change in Developed Societies." *Mass Communication Review Yearbook* 1:657–678 (1980).

Nyhan, David. "Left in the Lurch," *Washington Journalism Review* (December 1985), pp. 48–49.

Olien, Clarice, George Donohue, and Phillip Tichenor. "The Community Editor's Power and the Reporting of Conflict," *Journalism Quarterly* 45:243–252 (1968).

Ornstein, Michael. "Interlocking Directorates in Canada: Intercorporate or Class Alliance?" *Administrative Science Quarterly* 29:210–231 (1984).

Owen, Bruce M. "Empirical Results of the Price Effects of Joint Ownership in the Mass Media," *Research Memorandum* No. 93, Research Center in Economic Growth, Stanford University, (1969).

Palmgreen, Philip. "Mass Media Use and Political Knowledge," *Journalism Monographs* 61 (1979).

Park, Robert E. "The Natural History of Newspapers." Reprinted in *Mass Communication*, Wilbur-Schramm (Ed.). Champaign-Urbana, IL: University of Illinois Press, 1980.

Patkus, J.P. "The Newspaper Preservation Act: Why It Fails to Preserve Newspapers," *Akron Law Review* 17:435–452 (1984).

Pentland, H.C. "The Development of a Capitalistic Labour Market in Canada," *The Canadian Journal of Economics and Political Science* 25:450–461 (1959).

Pertschuk, Michael, and Kenneth M. Davidson. "What's Wrong With Conglomerate Mergers?" *Fordham Law Review* 48:1–24 (1979).

Picard, Robert G. "Pricing Behavior in Monopoly Newspapers: Ad and Circulation Differences in Joint Operating and Single Newspaper Monopolies, 1972–1982," *LSU School of Journalism Research Bulletin* (1985).

Picard, Robert G. "Pricing in Competing and Monopoly Newspapers, 1972–1982," *LSU School of Journalism Research Bulletin* (1986).

Picard, Robert G., and Gary D. Fackler, "Price Changes in Competing and Joint Operating Newspapers: Advertising and Circulation Differences, 1972 and 1982," *LSU School of Journalism Research Bulletin* (May 1985).

"Privately Held Groups Did Most of the Buying," *Editor & Publisher* (January 5, 1985), p. 46.

Radolf, Andrew. "Readjustments in Detroit," *Editor & Publisher* (March 15, 1986), p. 20.

Rarick, Galen, and Barrie Hartman. "The Effects of Competition on One Daily News-paper's Content," *Journalism Quarterly* 43:459–462 (1966).

Reddaway, W.B. "The Economics of Newspapers," *Economic Journal* 73:201–218 (1963).

Reinhardt, R. "Not the Los Angeles Times," *Columbia Journalism Review* (May/June 1986), pp. 42–48.

Roberts, Keith. "Antitrust Problems in the Newspaper Industry," *Harvard Law Review* 82:319–366 (1968).

Roberts, Lawrence. "Saving A Newspaper, Seattle Style," *Washington Journalism Review* (January/February 1982), p. 13.

Robinson, John. "The Press as King Maker: What Surveys from the Last Five Campaigns Show," *Journalism Quarterly* 51:587–594 (1974).

Robinson, Steven V. "Individual and Chain Newspaper Conduct Versus the Antitrust Laws: What Boundaries Do the Traditional Means of Checking Economic Con-centration Establish for the Newspaper Industry?" *Gonzaga Law Review* 14:819–853 (1979).

Rockmore, Milton. "What are Acquisitions and Mergers Doing to Journalistic Careers?" *Editor & Publisher* (April 19, 1986), p. 130.

"Roger Simon to Depart Sun-Times," *Editor & Publisher* (September 15, 1984), p. 38.

Rosse, James N. "Daily Newspapers, Monopolistic Competition, and Economies of Scale," *American Economic Review* 57:522–533 (1967).

Rosse, James N. "The Decline of Direct Newspaper Competition," *Journal of Commu-nication* 30(2):65–71 (1980).

Rosse, James N. "Economic Limits of Press Responsibility," *Studies in Industry Econom-ics* No. 56, Department of Economics, Stanford University (1975).

Rosse, James N., and James N. Dertouzos. "The Evolution of One Newspaper Cities." In Federal Trade Commission, *Proceedings of the Symposium on Media Con-centration*, Volume 2, pp. 429–471. Washington, DC: Government Printing Office, 1979.

Salamon, Lester M., and John J. Siegfried. "Economic Power and Political Influence: The Impact of Industry Structure and Public Policy," *American Political Science Review* 71:1026–1043 (1977).

Sanoff, Alvin P. "Behind the Demise of Family Newspapers," *U.S. News & World Report* (February 11, 1985), p. 60.

Sargent, Ben. Letter to the Editor, *Texas Observer* (June 9, 1978), p. 24.

"Schonfeld Tracks Ad Spending," *Advertising Age* (July 15, 1985), p. 39.

Schweitzer, John, and Elaine Goldman. "Does Newspaper Competition Make a Dif-ference to Readers?" *Journalism Quarterly* 52:706–710 (1975).

Shaw, David. "Conservative Political Columnists Gain," *Editor & Publisher* (June 9, 1984), pp. 86–88.

Shaw, Donald L. "Technology and Conformity: A Study of Newsgathering in the Ameri-can Press, 1820–1860." *Journalism Monographs* (1972).

Shelledy, David. "Access to the Press: A Teleological Analysis of a Constitutional Double Standard," *The George Washington Law Review* 50:430–464 (1982).

Sigelman, Leo. "Reporting the News: An Organizational Analysis." *American Journal of Sociology* 79:132–151 (1973).

Smith, Kim. "Perceived Influence of Media on What Goes on in a Community," *Journalism Quarterly* 61:260–264 (1984).

Society of Professional Journalists/Sigma Delta Chi. *Code of Ethics.* Chicago, IL: Society of Professional Journalists, 1973.

Soloski, John. "Economics and Management: The Real Influence of Newspaper Groups," *Newspaper Research Journal* 1:19–24 (November 1979).

"St. Louis Daily Shifts Support," *Editor & Publisher* (March 24, 1984), p. 26.

Stark, Rodney. "Policy and the Pros: An Organizational Analysis of a Metropolitan Newspaper," *Berkeley Journal of Sociology* 7:11–31 (Spring 1962).

Starr, Douglas. "Chains Said Less Likely to Dictate Editorial Policy," *Publishers' Auxiliary* (April 7, 1986), p. 24.

"Statement on John P. McGoff and Pantax Corporation Policy," *Columbia Journalism Review* (September/October 1977), p. 83.

Steeper, Frederick T. "Public Response to Gerald Ford's Statements on Eastern Europe in the Second Debate." In George F. Bishop, Robert G. Meadow, and Marilyn Jackson-Beeck (Eds.), *The Presidential Debates.* New York: Praeger, 1978.

Stempel, Guido, III. "Effects on Performance of a Cross-Media Monopoly," *Journalism Monographs* 29 (1973).

Taylor, A. "The Fortune 500 Special Report: Thin Profits in a Lean, Mean Year," *Fortune* (April 1986), pp. 174–232.

Tebbel, John. "Failing Newspapers and Antitrust Laws," *Saturday Review* (December 12, 1970), p. 58.

Thrift, Ralph, Jr. "How Chain Ownership Affects Editorial Vigor of Newspapers," *Journalism Quarterly* 54:327–331 (1977).

Times Mirror. *Factbook.* Los Angeles: Times Mirror Co., 1979.

"TM Poll Looks at Top Features," *Editor & Publisher* (February 8, 1986), p. 35.

Toohey, Daniel W. "Newspaper Ownership of Broadcast Facilities," *Federal Communications Bar Journal* 20:54–55 (1966).

Townsend, David. "Regulation of Newspaper/Broadcasting, Media Cross-Ownership in Canada," *University of New Brunswick Law Journal* 33:261–282 (1984).

Traves, T. "Security without Regulation." In M.S. Cross and G.S. Kealey (Eds.), *The Consolidation of Capitalism, 1896-1929.* Toronto: McClelland and Stewart, 1983, pp. 19–44.

Trim, Katherine, Gary Pizante, and James Yaraskavitch. "The Effect of Monopoly on the News: A Before and After Study of Two Canadian One Newspaper Towns," *Canadian Journal of Communication* 9(3):33–56 (1983).

Tuchman, Gaye. "Myth and the Consciousness Industry." In Elihu Katz & Tamos Szecsko (Eds.), *Mass Media and Social Change* (pp. 83–100). Beverly Hills, CA: Sage, 1981.

Union-Tribune Publishing Company. *Major Daily Newspaper Penetration in Southern California.* San Diego: Marketing Department, Union-Tribune Publishing Co., 1986.

Union-Tribune Publishing Company. *San Diego 1986: Staying Ahead of the Times.* San Diego: Marketing Department, Union-Tribune Publishing Co., 1986.

Vacha, J.E. "Death in the Afternoon," *Washington Journalism Review* (October 1981), pp. 41–45.

Wackman, Daniel B., Donald M. Gillmor, Cecilie Graziano, and Everette E. Dennis.

"Chain Newspaper Autonomy As Reflected in Presidential Campaign Endorsements," *Journalism Quarterly* 52:411–420 (1975).

Wagenburg, Ronald, and Walter Soderland. "The Influence of Chain Ownership on Editorial Comment In Canada," *Journalism Quarterly* 52:93–98 (1975).

Weaver, David H., and L.E. Mullins. "Content and Format Characteristics of Competing Daily Newspapers," *Journalism Quarterly* 52:257–264 (1975).

Weintraub, D.M., and N. Ray. "Big Changes on the Way for North San Diego County," *Los Angeles Times* (San Diego County Edition) (October 9, 1983), pp. 4–6.

Westell, Dan. "Newspaper Profits Expected to Rise," *The Globe and Mail* (January 1984).

"What Passes For News at Pentax," *Columbia Journalism Review* (September/October 1977), p. 6.

"Why the Big Traders Worry Industry," *Business Week* (July 25, 1970), p. 54.

Wilder, David. "Perception of Groups, Size of Opposition, and Social Influence," *Journal of Experimental Social Psychology* 13:253–268 (1977).

Willoughby, Wesley F. "Are Two Competing Dailies Necessarily Better Than One?" *Journalism Quarterly* 32:197–204 (1955).

Winski, Joseph M. "How Gannett Took Oregon," *Advertising Age* (July 8, 1981), p. 155.

Wirth, Michael O., and James A. Wollert. "Public Interest Program Performance of Multimedia-owned TV Stations," *Journalism Quarterly* 53:223–230 (1976).

Wirth, Michael O., and James A. Wollert. "Market Structure on Television News Pricing," *Journal of Broadcasting* 28:215–224 (1984).

Zukin, Cliff, and Robin Snyder. "Passive Learning: When the Media Environment is the Message," *Public Opinion Quarterly* 48:629–638 (1984).

Legal Cases

Abrams v. United States 250 U.S. 616 (1919).

Associated Press v. United States, 326 U.S. 1 (1945).

Brown Shoe Co. v. United States, 370 U.S. 294 (1962).

Citizens Publishing Company v. United States, 394 U.S. 131 (1969).

Committee for an Independent P-I v. Hearst Corp., 704 F.2d 467 (9th cir. 1983).

FCC v. National Citizens Committee for Broadcasting, S.Ct. 2096 (1978).

Greenville Publishing Co. v. Daily Reflector, Inc., 496 F.2d 391 (4th cir. 1974).

Huron Valley Publishing Co. v. Booth Newspapers, Inc., 336 F. Supp. 659 (E.D. Mich. 1972).

Kansas City Star Co. v. United States, 240 F.2d 643 (8th cir. 1957).

Munn v. Illinois, 94 U.S. 113,132 (1877).

National Broadcasting Company v. United States, 319 U.S. 190 (1943).

Syracuse Broadcasting Corp. v. Newhouse, 236 F.2d 522 (2d cir. 1956).

Times-Picayune Publishing Co. v. United States, 345 U.S. 594 (1953).

Union Leader Corp. v. Newspapers of New England, Inc., 180 F. Supp. 125 (D. Mass., 1959).

United States v. Aluminum Company of America, 148 F. 2d 416 (1945).

United States v. Citizen Publishing Co., 280 F. Supp. 978 (D. Ariz. 1968), aff'd, 394 U.S. 131 (1969).

United States v. E.I. duPont de Nemours & Co., 351 U.S. 377 (1956).
United States v. Paramount Pictures, Inc., 334 U.S. 131 (1948).
United States v. Radio Corp. of America, 355 U.S. 334 (1959).
United States v. Times Mirror Co., 274 F. Supp. 606 (C.D. Cal. 1967), aff'd per curiam, 390 U.S. 712 (1968).
United States v. United States Steel Corp., 251 U.S. 417 (1920).

Unpublished Materials

American Society of Newspaper Editors Ethics Committee. "News and Editorial Independence: A Survey of Group and Independent Editors." Unpublished report, April 1980.

Barnett, Stephen R. "Statement of Stephen R. Barnett," U.S. Congress. House. Committee on the Judiciary. Newspaper Preservation Act. Hearings before the Antitrust Subcommittee on H.R. 279 and Related Bills, 91st Congress, 1st Session, 247–267 (1969).

Benham, William, John Finnegan, Jr., and Patrick Parsons, "The Chain-Independent Debate Reassessed: Some New Evidence and an Interpretation," paper presented at the annual convention of the Association for Education in Journalism, Athens, Ohio, 1982.

Bloomfield, Edward. "Media Cross-Ownership, Newspaper Chains, Competition, and Daily Newspaper Advertising Rates," (Ph.D. dissertation, University of Rochester, 1978).

Bowers, Ian. "An Analysis of the Influence of the Competitive Structure upon Daily Newspapers' Advertising Rates and Lineage," (M.S. thesis, University of Illinois, 1969).

Brown, Richard D. "Market Behavior of Daily Newspapers" (Ph.D. dissertation, University of Illinois, 1967).

Bruce, Jean. "A Content Analysis of Thirty Canadian Daily Newspapers Published During the Period January 1–March 31, 1965, With a Comparative Study of Newspapers Published in 1960 and 1955." Report presented to the Royal Commission on Bilingualism and Biculturalism, 1966.

Busterna, John C. "The Effects of Multiple Ownership and Newspaper Ownership of Television Stations on Economic and Programming Performance," (M.A. Thesis, University of Wisconsin, 1976).

Charette, Michael F., C. Lloyd Brown-John, Walter I. Romanow, and Walter C. Soderland. "Effects of Chain Acquisitions and Terminations on Advertising Rates of Canadian Newspapers," paper presented to the annual meeting of the Canadian Communication Association, University of British Columbia, June 1983.

Coulson, David C. "Nelson Poynter: Study of an Independent Publisher and His Standards of Ownership," (Ph.D. dissertation, University of Minnesota, 1982).

Daugherty, David Bruce. "Group-Owned Newspapers vs. Independently-Owned Newspapers: An Analysis of the Differences and Similarities," (Ph.D. dissertation, University of Texas, 1983).

Dimmick, John. "Levels of Analysis in Mass Media Decision-Making: A Taxonomy and Research Strategy," paper presented at the annual convention of the Association for Education in Journalism, 1978.

Dozier, David, and Michael Gottesman. "Subjective Dimensions of Organizational

Roles Among Public Relations Practitioners," paper presented at the annual convention of the Association for Education in Journalism, Athens, Ohio, 1982.

Ghiglione, Loren. Presentation in the "Media Management and Economics" series at the University of Minnesota, February 2, 1984.

Goodman, Mark Lee. "Newspaper Ownership and the Weekly Editorial in Illinois," (M.A. thesis, South Dakota State University, 1982).

Hale, F. Dennis "Chains Versus Independent Newspaper and Market Characteristics," paper presented at the annual convention of the Association for Education in Journalism and Mass Communication, Gainesville, Florida, August, 1984b.

Lacy, Stephen. "The Effects of Intra-City Newspaper Competition on News and Editorial Content," paper presented at the annual convention of the Association for Education in Journalism and Mass Communication, Norman, Oklahoma, August 3–6, 1986.

Lacy, Stephen. "The Effects of Ownership and Competition on Daily Newspaper Content," (Ph.D. dissertation, University of Texas, 1986).

Lau, T. Y. "Survival of the Fittest: Competition Among Chinese Newspapers in the U.S.," (unpublished manuscript, Michigan State University, 1985).

Lauriston, Toni. "A Marxist Analysis of Monopoly Capitalism and its Nature in the Canadian Press," (M.A. thesis, University of Windsor, 1986).

Levine, Joel L., and William S. Roy. "A Study of Interlocking Directorates: Vital Concepts in Organizations," (unpublished paper, 1975; cited in Carroll, Fox, and Ornstein, 1982.)

Malone, John R. "Statement of John R. Malone," U.S. Congress. House. Committee on the Judiciary. Newspaper Preservation Act. Hearings before the Antitrust Subcommittee on H.R. 279 and Related Bills, 91st Congress, 1st Session, 337–344 (1969).

Matsunaga, S.M. "Statement in Support of the Newspaper Preservation Act," U.S. Congress. House. Committee on the Judiciary. Newspaper Preservation Act. Hearings before the Antitrust Subcommittee on H.R. 279 and Related Bills, 91st Congress, 1st Session, 8–15 (1969).

McCulloch, William M. "Statement of William M. McCulloch," U.S. Congress. House. Committee on the Judiciary. Newspaper Preservation Act. Hearings before the Antitrust Subcommittee on H.R. and Related Bills, 91st Congress, 1st Session, 6 (1969).

Nixon, Raymond B. "Statement of Raymond B. Nixon," U.S. Congress. House. Committee on the Judiciary. Newspaper Preservation Act. Hearings before the Antitrust Subcommittee on H.R. 279 and Related Bills, 91st Congress, 1st Session, 118–135 (1969).

St. Dizier, Byron. "Republican Endorsements, Democratic Positions: An Editorial Page Contradiction," (unpublished manuscript, 1986).

Winter, James P. "National and Binational Ramifications of the 'Free Press' Marketplace: A Canadian Perspective," paper presented to the annual conference of the International Communication Association, Honolulu, May, 1985.

Government Reports and Documents

Canada, Royal Commission on Corporate Concentration. *Report.* Ottawa: Minister of Supply and Services, 1978.

Canada. Royal Commission on Newspapers (Kent Commission). *Report.* Hull, Quebec: Canadian Government Printing Centre, 1981.

Canada. Special Senate Committee on Mass Media (Davey Committee). *Report: The Uncertain Mirror*. Ottawa: Supply and Services, 1970, Volume 1. (Also published Ottawa: Crown, 1972.)

U.S. Congress. House. Committee on the Judiciary. "Newspaper Preservation Act." Hearings before the Antitrust Subcommittee on H.R. 279 and Related Bills, 91st Congress, 1st Session, 1969.

U.S. Congress. Senate. Committee on Governmental Affairs. "Interlocking Directorates Among Major U.S. Corporations." June 1978.

Author Index

A

Abrams, B., 175, *211*
Adams, W., 7, *213*
Ahlerling, R., 122, *214*
Allen, V., 123, *211*
Anderson, C.H., 109, *208*
Anderson, T., 120, *209*
Ardoin, B., 152, *211*
Arlen, G., 182, *211*
Asch, S., 123, *211*

B

Baer, W., 91, *208*
Bagdikian, B.H., 71, 108, 162, 164, 180,
    181, 182, 185, 193, 194, *208*, *211*
Bain, J.S., 37, 50, *208*
Baldridge, P.D., 166, *211*
Barber, R.J., 187, *211*
Barnett, S.R., 149, 188, *211*, *220*
Barnhart, T.F., 130, *209*
Barron, J.A., 183, *211*
Barwis, G.L., 184, *211*
Beam, R., 15, *211*
Becker, G., 184, *211*
Becker, L., 15, 92, 94, 95, 97, *211*
Benham, W., 92, *220*
Bigman, S., 118, 130, 182, *211*
Bishop, R., 71, *211*
Blake, H.M., 185, *212*
Blankenburg, W.B., 62, 66, 67, 152, *212*
Bliss, M.A., 105, *208*
Block, P., Jr., 151, *212*
Bloomfield, E., 66, *220*
Bogart, L., 83, *212*
Bork, R.H., 199, *208*
Borstel, G., 117, 166, 182, *212*
Bowers, I., 64, 65, *220*
Bowman, W., 94, 97, *209*
Bradden, R., 111, *208*

C

Breed, W., 93, 119, *212*
Bridges, J., 33, 182, *215*
Broom, G., 92, *212*
Brown, R.D., 58, *220*
Brown-John, C.L., 65, 66, *220*
Bruce, J., 132, *220*
Brumm, B., 176, *212*
Busterna, J.C., 68, *212*, *220*

C

Carlson, A.M., 184, 188, 189, *212*
Carlson, J.H., 148, 151, 184, *212*
Carroll, W.K., 106, 110, 113, *212*
Caves, R., 7, *208*
Chafee, Z., 183, *208*
Chaffee, S., 120, *212*
Chaim, E., 121, *210*
Chamberlin, E.H., 155, *208*
Chaney, J., 162, 163, *212*
Charette, M.F., 65, 66, *220*
Clement, W., 108, 110, 141, *208*
Cobbey, R., 92, 94, 95, 97, *211*
Compaine, B.M., 25, 30, 43, 49, 163, 165,
    208, *212*
Corden, W.M., 155, *212*
Coulson, D.C., *213*, *220*
Curran, J., *208*
Cyert, R.M., 109, *209*

D

Danielson, W., 120, *213*
Daugherty, D.B., 168, 169, *220*
Davidson, K.M., 185, *216*
Della Fave, L.R., 108, 109, *215*
Dennis, E.E., 91, 119, 183, *218*
Dertouzos, J.N., 25, 32, *217*
de Tocqueville, A., 179, *209*
Deutschman, P., 120, *213*
Dimmick, J., 93, *220*

Domhoff, G.W., 109, 209
Donohue, G., 83, 94, 165, 210, 213, 216
Donohue, T., 118, 130, 213
Dooley, P. C., 109, 213
Dozier, D., 92, 220
Dreier, P., 108, 110, 185, 194, 213
Dunn, W., 56, 58, 213

E
Elliott, P., 92, 213
Endicott, R.C., 73, 213
Engwall, L., 59, 213
Entman, R.M., 140, 213
Epstein, E.J., 130, 209

F
Fackler, G.D., 63, 67, 216
Featherston, J.S., 144, 153, 182, 214
Ferguson, J.M., 58, 63, 66, 68, 209, 213
Finnegan, J., Jr., 92, 220
Fitzgerald, M., 176, 213
Fox, J., 106, 110, 113, 212
Freilich, E.S., 194, 213
Furhoff, L., 59, 213

G
Galbraith, J.K., 7, 213
Gans, H., 119, 130, 209
Geller, H., 91, 186, 208, 213
Gerbuer, G., 125, 213
Ghiglione, L., 45, 161, 162, 164, 166, 209,
    220
Gillmor, D.M., 91, 119, 167, 183, 218
Gitlin, T., 130, 209
Glasser, T., 118, 130, 213
Glynn, C., 121, 215
Goldman, E., 118, 182, 217
Gollin, A., 120, 209
Good, J., 190, 213
Goodman, M.L., 167–168, 220
Gordon, R.L., 61, 213
Gormley, W., 119, 183, 214
Gottesman, M., 92, 220
Gottlieb, B., 74–75, 214
Graber, D., 121, 210
Graziano, C., 91, 119, 183, 218
Green, M., 109, 209
Grotta, G.L., 64, 65, 66, 151, 165, 183, 214
Grundfest, J., 91, 208
Grush, J., 122, 214
Guback, T., 43, 49, 163, 208

Gurevitch, M., 208
Gustafsson, K.E., 16, 59, 150, 214

H
Haerle, D., 77, 214
Hale, D.F., 67, 175, 176, 214, 220
Hartman, B., 117, 217
Haydel, V.J., 147, 148, 150, 215
Heath, M., 109, 210
Henry, W.A., III., 163, 214
Hicks, R., 144, 153, 182, 214
Hoak, J.M., Jr., 192, 214
Holahan, C., 176, 214
Holder, D., 151, 188, 189, 214
Howard, H.H., 181, 214
Hulteng, J.L., 191, 214
Humphrey, T.E., 150, 160, 214
Hynds, E.C., 171, 173, 214

I
Innis, H., 105, 209

J
Janowitz, M., 92, 94, 209
Johnson, N., 192, 214
Johnstone, J., 94, 97, 209, 214
Jones, G.N., 185, 214
Jones, J., 191, 215
Jones, R.L., 15, 117, 130, 136, 182, 216

K
Keep, P.M., 148, 149, 150, 215
Kenneth, J., 213
Kerbo, H.R., 108, 215
Kerton, R.H., 64, 66, 151, 215
Kessel, J., 121, 215
Kesterson, W.H., 107, 209
Korosec, T., 191, 215
Kotler, P., 56, 209

L
Lacy, P., 164, 215
Lacy, S., 27, 72, 153, 182, 215, 220, 221
Lago, A., 66, 215
Lang, G., 119, 215
Lang, K., 119, 215
Langdon, S., 105, 209
Lau, T.Y., 17, 221
Lauriston, T., 105, 106, 107, 221
Leadbeater, D., 106, 215
Lee, W.E., 183, 215

Levine, J.L., 110, 221
Lindblom, C.E., 185, 209
Litman, B., 33, 182, 215
Logan, G.J., 191, 215
Louis, A.M., 215

M
Malan, R., 77, 215
Malone, J.R., 30, 149, 215, 221
Mansfield, E., 4, 209
March, J.G., 109, 209
Martel, J.S., 147, 148, 150, 215
Massing, M., 188, 215
Mathewson, G.F., 64, 66, 68, 151, 215
Matsunaga, S.M., 148, 150, 152, 221
McClure, L., 56, 58, 60, 209
McCombs, M., 121, 122, 210, 215
McCulloch, W.M., 150, 221
McDonald, D., 121, 215
McIntosh, T., 185, 215
McKeough, K., 122, 214
McKinney, J., 57, 209
McLeod, J., 121, 215
McNeil, R., 125, 216
Meyer, P., 216
Mills, C.W., 109, 209
Mueller, W.F., 7, 213
Mullins, L.E., 15, 130, 218

N
Nader, R., 109, 209
Nafziger, R.O., 130, 209
Neufeld, E.P., 106, 209
Neuharth, A., 164, 216
Niebauer, W.E., Jr., 152, 184, 216
Nixon, R.B., 15, 117, 130, 136, 149, 150,
    182, 216, 221
Noble, J.K., Jr., 43, 49, 163, 208
Noelle-Neumann, E., 123, 124, 216
Nyhan, D., 171, 216

O
Olien, C., 83, 94, 95, 165, 210, 213, 216
Oppenheim, S.C., 41, 209
Orenstein, F.E., 83, 212
Ornstein, M., 106, 110, 113, 212, 216
Owen, B.M., 44, 45, 49, 151, 160, 183, 186,
    209, 216

P
Palmgreen, P., 121, 216
Park, R.E., 92, 94, 216

Parsons, P., 92, 220
Patkus, J.P., 148, 151, 152, 184, 189, 216
Patterson, T., 120, 210
Pentland, H.C., 105, 216
Pertschuk, M., 185, 216
Peterson, S., 109, 210
Peterson, T., 140, 210
Pfeffers, J., 109, 210
Picard, R.G., 63, 65, 67, 183, 210, 216
Pizante, G., 118, 144, 218
Porter, J., 108, 110, 210
Possner, K., 91, 208

R
Radolf, A., 163, 217
Rarick, G., 117, 217
Ray, N., 75, 219
Reddaway, W.B., 155, 217
Reinhardt, R., 73, 217
Reynolds, L.G., 106, 210
Roberts, K., 72, 184, 217
Roberts, L., 189, 217
Robinson, J., 122, 217
Robinson, S.V., 185, 217
Rockmore, M., 163, 217
Romanow, W.I., 65, 66, 220
Roscho, B., 130, 210
Rosse, J.N., 25, 32, 42, 71, 79, 82, 83, 150,
    155, 156, 217
Roy, W.S., 110, 221
Rucker, F.W., 57, 210
Russial, J., 15, 211
Rutherford, P., 111, 210
Ryerson, S.B., 105, 210

S
Salamon, L.M., 185, 217
Salanick, G., 109, 210
Sanoff, A.P., 164, 217
Sargent, B., 163, 217
Scherer, F.M., 12, 23, 37, 38, 187, 210
Schramm, W., 140, 210
Schudson, M., 129, 210
Schumpeter, J.A., 7, 210
Schweitzer, J., 118, 182, 217
Seligman, J., 109, 209
Shaw, D., 171, 217
Shaw, D.L., 129, 217
Shelledy, D., 217
Shepherd, W.G., 23, 210
Shields, C., 41, 209

Siebert, F.S., 140, *210*
Siegfried, J. J., 185, *217*
Sigal, L.V., 130, *210*
Slawski, E., 94, 97, *209*
Smith, G., 92, *212*
Smith, K., 122, *217*
Smythe, D.W., 141, *210*
Snyder, R., 119, *219*
Sobowale, I., 92, 94, 95, 97, *211*
Soderland, W.C., 65, 66, 91, 166, *218*, *220*
Soloski, J., 66, 91, 99, 100, 185, 192, *218*
Spencer, M.H., 4, *210*
St. Dizier, B., 169, 170, *221*
Stark, R., 93, 95, *218*
Starr, D., 174, *218*
Steeper, F.T., 122, *218*
Stempel, G., III., 119, 144, *218*
Sterling, C.H., 43, 49, 163, *208*

T
Taylor, A., 73, *218*
Tebbel, J., 184, *218*
Thrift, R., Jr., 91, 119, 167, 183, *218*
Tichenor, P., 83, 94, 95, 165, *210*, *213*
Tipton, L., 120, *212*
Toohey, D.W., 192, *218*
Townsend, D., *218*
Traves, T., 106, *218*
Trigger, B., 105, *210*
Trim, K., 118, 144, *218*
Tuchman, G., 119, *210*

U
Udell, J.G., 57, 60, *210*
Urquart, M.C., 106, *210*

V
Vacha, J.E., 188, *218*

W
Wackman, D.B., 91, 119, 167, 183, *218*
Wagenburg, R., 91, 166, *218*
Ward, S., 120, *212*
Wearden, S.T., *216*
Weaver, D., 15, 121, 130, *210*, *218*
Weinberg, S., 108, 110, 185, 194, *213*
Weintraub, D.M., 75, *219*
Westell, D., 112, *219*
Wicker, T., *210*
Wilder, D., 123, *211*, *219*
Williams, H.L., 57, *210*
Willoughby, W.F., 130, 182, *219*
Winski, J.M., 60, *219*
Winter, J.P., 181, 185, *221*
Wirth, M.O., 68, *219*
Wollert, J.A., 68, *219*
Woolacott, J., *208*

Y
Yaraskavitch, J., 118, 144, *218*

Z
Zukin, C., 119, *219*

Subject Index

A

Abrams v. United States, 180
Advertising, 39, 40
 demand, 55–56
 for product differentiation, 9
 impact on circulation, 16, 55–56, 60–61
 market of newspapers, 16, 25, 43, 55–56
 pricing, see Pricing—advertising
Albuquerque Journal, 147, 157
Albuquerque Tribune, 147, 157
Alton Telegraph, 161
American Newspaper Publishers Association,
 57
American Society of Newspaper Editors, 101
Anaheim Bulletin, 79
Anchorage Daily News, 149
Anchorage Times, 149
Anti-Combines Act, 108, 139
Antitrust, 53, 130, 136, 159, 179–195, 198–
 199, 207
Atchison Daily Globe, 166
Associated Press v. United States, 180
Austin Statesman-Journal, 163
Average total cost (AC), see Cost
Average variable cost (AVC), see Cost

B

Barriers to entry, see Entry—conditions of
Brown Shoe Co. v. United States, 36
Burbank Daily Review, 79
Business cycle, 58
Buying and Selling of America's Newspapers,
 The, 166

C

Canada, 105–115, 130–137, 166–167, 181,
 185, 191
Capacity, excess, 9
Chain ownership, see Ownership—chains

Charleston Gazette, 158
Charleston Daily Mail, 158
Chicago Daily News, 149
Chicago Sun-Times, 149, 162
Circulation, newspaper
 expenses of, 26–27
 impact on advertising, 16, 57, 59, 60–61
 market structure and, 154–155
Circulation spiral, 16, 150
Citizen Publishing Co. v. United States, 40–
 41, 148, 180, 186
Competition
 intermedia, 41–42, 55, 59, 139–140
 intramedia, 55, 129–137, 197–202
 irrational, 17
 monopolistic, 3, 8–9, 155–156
 perfect or pure, 3, 7
 perfect, theory of, 3–6
 umbrella, 42, 62, 71–87
Concentration, 37, 105–106
 in newspaper markets, 35, 42, 44, 48, 71
Concentration of ownership, 42–43, 66–67,
 71, 105, 117, 179
Conditions of entry, see Entry—conditions of
Content, newspaper, 91, 117–119
 budgets for, 154–159
 editorials, 117, 159, 165–170, 183
 endorsements, 119, 167, 169–176
 geographical dispersion of, 134–135
 homogenity of, 117, 120–125, 136–137
  effects on political cognitions, 120–121
  in shaping attitudes, 121–123
  and conformity, 123–124
 local news, 117–118
 market structure and, 153–155, 165–170,
  191–192
 space allocation, 153–154, 155–159
 sources of, 135–136
Copley Newspapers, 73, 81

Cost(s)
  average Total (AC), 17, 150
  first copy, 25–26, 44, 150
  fixed, 17, 25, 44, 52
  historical, 23
  long-run average, 17–25
  long-run marginal (MC), 25–29
  variable, 17
Cost curves
  long-run average, 18–25, 64–65
    measurement of, 22–25
    movements on, 22
    shapes of, 21–22, 64–65
Cost efficiencies, 3, 45
Cost structure, 38–39

D
Daily Advance, 166
Daily Californian, 73
Demand
  cross-elasticity of, 43, 155–56
  elasticity of, 9
  inelasticity of, 10
Demand curve
  downward-sloping, 8
  horizontal, 4–5
  industry, 6
  kinked, 11
Density, economies of, 19
Des Moines *Register*, 161
Detroit *Free Press*, 43
Detroit *News*, 161, 163
Differentiation, *see* Product differentiation
Diseconomies
  external, 22
  of scale, *see* Scale—diseconomies
Donrey Media, 73, 161, 166
Duopoly, 15

E
Economics and Freedom of Expression, 183
Economics of the American Newspaper, 57
Economy
  market, *see* Market economy
  mixed, *see* Mixed economy
Economies of density, *see* Density—economies
  of
Economies of scale, *see* Scale—economies of
Economies of scope, *see* Scope—economies of
Efficiency
  allocative, 40, 48–50

  pecuniary, 19
  technical, 40, 48–50
Elasticity of demand, 9
Employment, full, 40
Engineering estimates, 23
Entry
  barriers to, 7, 10, 45, 151
  conditions of, 3, 38
Equilibrium
  long-run, 5
  short-run, 9
  standards, 5–6
Equity, 40
Escondido *Times-Advocate*, 73
Evening Sentinel, 172–173

F
FP Publications, 107
First copy costs, *see* Costs—first copy
Fixed costs, *see* Costs—fixed
Freedom Newspapers, 73, 81

G
Gannett Co., 66, 67, 141, 161, 162, 164,
    165, 172, 176, 181
Geographic market, *see* Market—geographic
Globe and Mail, 106
*Greenville Publishing Co. v. Daily Reflector,
  Inc.*, 41

H
Hamilton *Spectator*, 111
Hearst Corporation, 73
*Huron Valley Publishing Co. v. Booth News-
  papers*, 41

I
Independent Newspaper Group, 161
Industrial organization model, 3, 35–40
Inelastisity, 6
  of demand, 10
Information market
  impact on advertising, 55
  of newspapers, 16, 25, 43, 55
Ingersoll Publications, 73, 161, 166
Integration, vertical, 39, 45, 52
Interfirm distance, 113
Interlocking directorships, 107–111, 194
  direct, 112
  first-order, 112
  in newspaper firms, 108, 111, 205–207

J

Jackson *Clarion-Ledger*, 172
Joint monopolies, *see* Monopolies—joint
Joint product, 34
Joint Operating Agreements (JOAs), 67–68,
    147–160, 180, 184–185, 188–190
    content of, 152–160

K

Kansas City Star v. United States, 46
Kent Report, *see* Royal Commission on
    Newspapers
Knight-Ridder Co., 43, 73, 76, 81, 176
Knoxville *Journal*, 157–158
Knoxville *News-Sentinel*, 157–158
Kokomo *Tribune*, 161

L

Labor costs, 26
La Opinion, 79
Long Beach *Press-Telegram*, 76–87
Long-run average cost, *see* Costs—long-run
    average
Los Angeles *Daily News*, 72, 73–87
Los Angeles *Herald Examiner*, 73–87
Los Angeles *Times*, 42, 73–87

M

Macroeconomics theory, 3
Management
    separation of ownership from, 7
Managerial control theory, 109
Marginal cost (MC), *see* Cost
Marginal product, *see* Product—marginal
Marginal rate of substitution, *see* Substitution
Market
    capital, 7
    geographic, 43, 185, 208
    of newspapers, *see* Advertising—market for
        newspapers and information market of
        newspapers
Market conduct, 36, 39–40
    of newspapers, 45–48
Market performance, 36, 40
    of newspapers, 48–50
Market power, 3–4, 6–7
Market structure, 3–14, 35, 37–39
    of newspapers, 14–17
Media Monopoly, The, 185
Midland *Reporter-Telegram*, 161

Monopoly, 3, 6–8, 105
    in newspaper markets, 47, 117–118, 124–
        125, 129, 130, 139–145, 180, 186–
        187
Monopolies, joint, 14
Montreal *Gazette*, 130–137
Montreal *Star*, 130–137
Munn v. Illinois, 6

N

National Newspaper Publishers Association, 57
New York *Daily News*, 156
New York *Post*, 44, 156
New York *Times*, 16, 32, 44, 156
New York Times Co., 161
Newspaper Advertising and Promotion, 56
Newspaper Advertising Bureau, 57
Newspaper Guild, the, 149, 176
Newspaper Organization and Management, 57
Newspaper Preservation Act, 46, 69, 140,
    147–151, 159–160, 180, 184, 188,
    202–203
Norman *Transcript*, 161

O

Oceanside *Blade-Tribune*, 73
Oligopoly, 3, 10–14, 105
    in newspaper markets, 14–17, 47, 130
Orange Coast Daily Pilot, 73
Oregon Statesman and Capitol Journal, 60
Organizational commitment, 96–100
Output, restriction of, 6, 187
Ottawa *Citizen*, 107, 111
Ottawa *Journal*, 107
Ownership
    chain, 17, 42–43, 66–67, 69, 71, 73–74,
        91, 119, 161–176, 180–181, 190–192,
        203–205
    cross, 68, 118–119, 180, 182, 192–195,
        205–207
    privately held, 49
    publicly held, 49–50
    separation from management, 7

P

Power, market, *see* Market power
Predatory practices, 7, 46, 48
Price
    discrimination, 46–47
    leadership, 12
    markup, 12
    standardized, 12–13

Price maker, 6
Price taker, 4
Prices
    newspaper advertising, 15, 55–69
    newspaper circulation, 15, 55–69
Pricing
    behavior, 39
    competition-oriented, 58
    demand-oriented, 58
    in cross-ownership situations, 68
    in joint operating agreements, 67–68
    in monopoly situations, 6, 63–65, 183, 187
    in monopolistic competition, 9
    in oligopoly, 10–13
    in competitive situations, 4, 62–63, 197–198
    target return, 48
Pricing strategy, 39
    for advertising, 56–58, 62–69
    for circulation, 62–69
Product differentiation, 8–9, 37, 44
    newspaper strategies, 32–34
Product market, see Market—product
Product performance, 50
Profits
    excess, 5, 6–7
    marginal, 150
    monopoly, 151
    normal, 5, 9
    short term excess, 5, 9
Profit maximization
    in monopoly, 6
    in monopolistic competition, 9
    output, 4, 18
Progress, 40

R
Rates
    advertising, 56–69
    differential, 58
Redlands Daily Facts, 166
The Register, 73–87
Research and development/innovation, 39
Retail trading zone (RTZ), 41–42, 48, 53
Role theory, 92–96, 98, 103
Royal Commission of Newspapers, 107, 139, 164, 185

S
San Bernardino Sun, 42
San Diego Tribune, 73–87

San Diego Union, 73–87
San Francisco Chronicle, 148, 156–157
San Francisco Examiner, 148, 189
Sante Fe New Mexican, 166
Scale
    diseconomies of, 18
    economies of, 7, 17
        in newspapers, 25–34, 150
        minimum efficient, 18
        returns to, 19
Scope, economies of, 19
Scripps-Howard Newspapers, 73
Seattle Post-Intelligencer, 148, 189
Seattle Times, 148, 189
Sherman Antitrust Act, 11, 147
Socialization
    in organizations, 98–100
Southam, 107, 111–113, 130, 139, 141, 181
Southeast News Signal, 79
St. Louis Globe-Democrat, 161, 188–189
St. Louis Post-Dispatch, 188
St. Paul Pioneer Press and Dispatch, 43
St. Petersburg Times, 191
Substitutes, 156
Supply and demand, 5
Syracuse Broadcasting Corp. v. Newhouse, 46

T
Taxes, 190, 199–200, 202
Television
    cable, 14
Theory of the firm, 3
Thomson Newspapers, 73, 97, 107, 111–112, 113–114, 130, 139, 141, 162–163, 166, 181
Times Mirror Co., 73
Times-Picayune Publishing Co. v. United States, 46
Timmins Press, 111
Toronto Star, 107, 111
Torstar Corporation, 107, 112
The Transcript, 166
Tribune Co., 73
Triopolies, 15
Tuscaloosa News, 161

U
United States v. Aluminum Corporation of America, 187
United States v. Citizen Publishing Co., see Citizen Publishing Co. v. United States

United States v. E.I. duPont de Memours &
   Co., 36
United States v. Paramount Pictures Inc., 39
United States v. Times Mirror Co., 41, 186
USA Today, 16, 32, 44, 47

V

Vertical integration, *see* Integration—vertical

W

Wall Street Journal, 16, 34, 44
Washington *Post*, 60–61
Washington *Star*, 60–61, 149
West Warwick Pawtuxet Valley Times, 161
Winnipeg *Free Press*, 107, 130–137, 141–145
Winnipeg *Tribune*, 130–131, 141–145